Cram101 Textbook Outlines to accompany:

International Marketing

Cateora and Graham, 12th Edition

An Academic Internet Publishers (AIPI) publication (c) 2007.

You have a discounted membership at www.Cram101.com with this book.

Get all of the practice tests for the chapters of this textbook, and access in-depth reference material for writing essays and papers. Here is an example from a Cram101 Biology text:

When you need problem solving help with math, stats, and other disciplines, www.Cram101.com will walk through the formulas and solutions step by step.

With Cram101.com online, you also have access to extensive reference material.

You will nail those essays and papers. Here is an example from a Cram101 Biology text:

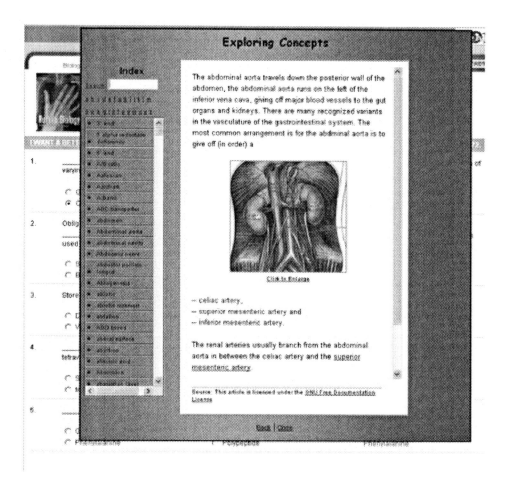

Learning System

Cram101 Textbook Outlines is a learning system. The notes in this book are the highlights of your textbook, you will never have to highlight a book again.

How to use this book. Take this book to class, it is your notebook for the lecture. The notes and highlights on the left hand side of the pages follow the outline and order of the textbook. All you have to do is follow along while your intructor presents the lecture. Circle the items emphasized in class and add other important information on the right side. With Cram101 Textbook Outlines you'll spend less time writing and more time listening. Learning becomes more efficient.

Cram101.com Online

Increase your studying efficiency by using Cram101.com's practice tests and online reference material. It is the perfect complement to Cram101 Textbook Outlines. Use self-teaching matching tests or simulate in-class testing with comprehensive multiple choice tests, or simply use Cram's true and false tests for quick review. Cram101.com even allows you to enter your in-class notes for an integrated studying format combining the textbook notes with your class notes.

Visit **www.Cram101.com**, click Sign Up at the top of the screen, and enter **DK73DW2099** in the promo code box on the registration screen. Access to www.Cram101.com is normally $9.95, but because you have purchased this book, your access fee is only $4.95. Sign up and stop highlighting textbooks forever.

International Marketing
Cateora and Graham, 12th

CONTENTS

Exporter	A firm that sells its product in another country is an exporter.
Boeing	Boeing is the world's largest aircraft manufacturer by revenue. Headquartered in Chicago, Illinois, Boeing is the second-largest defense contractor in the world. In 2005, the company was the world's largest civil aircraft manufacturer in terms of value.
Technology	The body of knowledge and techniques that can be used to combine economic resources to produce goods and services is called technology.
Revenue	Revenue is a U.S. business term for the amount of money that a company receives from its activities, mostly from sales of products and/or services to customers.
Service	Service refers to a "non tangible product" that is not embodied in a physical good and that typically effects some change in another product, person, or institution. Contrasts with good.
Production	The creation of finished goods and services using the factors of production: land, labor, capital, entrepreneurship, and knowledge.
Marketing	Promoting and selling products or services to customers, or prospective customers, is referred to as marketing.
Commerce	Commerce is the exchange of something of value between two entities. It is the central mechanism from which capitalism is derived.
Yield	The interest rate that equates a future value or an annuity to a given present value is a yield.
Gain	In finance, gain is a profit or an increase in value of an investment such as a stock or bond. Gain is calculated by fair market value or the proceeds from the sale of the investment minus the sum of the purchase price and all costs associated with it.
Foundation	A Foundation is a type of philanthropic organization set up by either individuals or institutions as a legal entity (either as a corporation or trust) with the purpose of distributing grants to support causes in line with the goals of the foundation.
Joint venture	Joint venture refers to an undertaking by two parties for a specific purpose and duration, taking any of several legal forms.
Appreciation	Appreciation refers to a rise in the value of a country's currency on the exchange market, relative either to a particular other currency or to a weighted average of other currencies. The currency is said to appreciate. Opposite of 'depreciation.' Appreciation can also refer to the increase in value of any asset.
International trade	The export of goods and services from a country and the import of goods and services into a country is referred to as the international trade.
Remainder	A remainder in property law is a future interest created in a transferee that is capable of becoming possessory upon the natural termination of a prior estate created by the same instrument.
International Business	International business refers to any firm that engages in international trade or investment.
Productivity	Productivity refers to the total output of goods and services in a given period of time divided by work hours.
Market	A market is, as defined in economics, a social arrangement that allows buyers and sellers to discover information and carry out a voluntary exchange of goods or services.
Market system	All the product and resource markets of a market economy and the relationships among them are called a market system.
Demographic	A demographic is a term used in marketing and broadcasting, to describe a demographic grouping or a market segment.

Go to **Cram101.com** for the Practice Tests for this Chapter.

Information technology	Information technology refers to technology that helps companies change business by allowing them to use new methods.
WorldCom	WorldCom was the United States' second largest long distance phone company (AT&T was the largest). WorldCom grew largely by acquiring other telecommunications companies, most notably MCI Communications. It also owned the Tier 1 ISP UUNET, a major part of the Internet backbone.
Enron	Enron Corportaion's global reputation was undermined by persistent rumours of bribery and political pressure to secure contracts in Central America, South America, Africa, and the Philippines. Especially controversial was its $3 billion contract with the Maharashtra State Electricity Board in India, where it is alleged that Enron officials used political connections within the Clinton and Bush administrations to exert pressure on the board.
Economy	The income, expenditures, and resources that affect the cost of running a business and household are called an economy.
United airlines	United Airlines is a major airline of the United States headquartered in unincorporated Elk Grove Township, Illinois, near Chicago's O'Hare International Airport, the airline's largest traffic hub, with 650 daily departures. On February 1, 2006, it emerged from Chapter 11 bankruptcy protection under which it had operated since December 9, 2002, the largest and longest airline bankruptcy case in history.
Layoff	A layoff is the termination of an employee or (more commonly) a group of employees for business reasons, such as the decision that certain positions are no longer necessary.
Trial	An examination before a competent tribunal, according to the law of the land, of the facts or law put in issue in a cause, for the purpose of determining such issue is a trial. When the court hears and determines any issue of fact or law for the purpose of determining the rights of the parties, it may be considered a trial.
Antiglobaliz-tion	Antiglobalization is a term most commonly ascribed to the political stance of people and groups who oppose certain aspects of globalization in its current form, often including the domination of current global trade agreements and trade-governing bodies such as the World Trade Organization by powerful corporations.
Globalization	The increasing world-wide integration of markets for goods, services and capital that attracted special attention in the late 1990s is called globalization.
Reclamation	The right of a seller or lessor to demand the return of goods from the buyer or lessee under specified situations is called reclamation. The right of the person with title to a property to recover it from the debtor in the event of a bankruptcy.
Disney	Disney is one of the largest media and entertainment corporations in the world. Founded on October 16, 1923 by brothers Walt and Roy Disney as a small animation studio, today it is one of the largest Hollywood studios and also owns nine theme parks and several television networks, including the American Broadcasting Company (ABC).
Stock	In financial terminology, stock is the capital raized by a corporation, through the issuance and sale of shares.
Capital	Capital generally refers to financial wealth, especially that used to start or maintain a business. In classical economics, capital is one of four factors of production, the others being land and labor and entrepreneurship.
Subculture	A subgroups within the larger, or national, culture with unique values, ideas, and attitudes is a subculture.
Specialist	A specialist is a trader who makes a market in one or several stocks and holds the limit order book for those stocks.

Go to **Cram101.com** for the Practice Tests for this Chapter.

Communism	Communism refers to an economic system in which capital is owned by private government. Contrasts with capitalism.
Black market	Black market refers to an illegal market, in which something is bought and sold outside of official government-sanctioned channels. Black markets tend to arise when a government tries to fix a price without providing an alternative allocation method
Wall Street Journal	Dow Jones & Company was founded in 1882 by reporters Charles Dow, Edward Jones and Charles Bergstresser. Jones converted the small Customers' Afternoon Letter into The Wall Street Journal, first published in 1889, and began delivery of the Dow Jones News Service via telegraph. The Journal featured the Jones 'Average', the first of several indexes of stock and bond prices on the New York Stock Exchange.
Portfolio	In finance, a portfolio is a collection of investments held by an institution or a private individual. Holding but not always a portfolio is part of an investment and risk-limiting strategy called diversification. By owning several assets, certain types of risk (in particular specific risk) can be reduced.
Journal	Book of original entry, in which transactions are recorded in a general ledger system, is referred to as a journal.
Manufacturing	Production of goods primarily by the application of labor and capital to raw materials and other intermediate inputs, in contrast to agriculture, mining, forestry, fishing, and services a manufacturing.
Exporting	Selling products to another country is called exporting.
Firm	An organization that employs resources to produce a good or service for profit and owns and operates one or more plants is referred to as a firm.
Competitor	Other organizations in the same industry or type of business that provide a good or service to the same set of customers is referred to as a competitor.
Developing country	Developing country refers to a country whose per capita income is low by world standards. Same as LDC. As usually used, it does not necessarily connote that the country's income is rising.
Free trade area	Free trade area refers to a group of countries that adopt free trade on trade among group members, while not necessarily changing the barriers that each member country has on trade with the countries outside the group.
Free market	A free market is a market where price is determined by the unregulated interchange of supply and demand rather than set by artificial means.
Dissolution	Dissolution is the process of admitting or removing a partner in a partnership.
Free trade	Free trade refers to a situation in which there are no artificial barriers to trade, such as tariffs and quotas. Usually used, often only implicitly, with frictionless trade, so that it implies that there are no barriers to trade of any kind.
Trend	Trend refers to the long-term movement of an economic variable, such as its average rate of increase or decrease over enough years to encompass several business cycles.
Union	A worker association that bargains with employers over wages and working conditions is called a union.
Scope	Scope of a project is the sum total of all projects products and their requirements or features.
Distribution	Distribution in economics, the manner in which total output and income is distributed among individuals or factors.
Investment	Investment refers to spending for the production and accumulation of capital and additions to inventories. In a financial sense, buying an asset with the expectation of making a return.

Go to **Cram101.com** for the Practice Tests for this Chapter.
And, **NEVER** highlight a book again!

Conglomerate	A conglomerate is a large company that consists of divisions of often seemingly unrelated businesses.
Domestic	From or in one's own country. A domestic producer is one that produces inside the home country. A domestic price is the price inside the home country. Opposite of 'foreign' or 'world.'.
Export	In economics, an export is any good or commodity, shipped or otherwise transported out of a country, province, town to another part of the world in a legitimate fashion, typically for use in trade or sale.
Internationa-ization	Internationalization refers to another term for fragmentation. Used by Grossman and Helpman.
Emerging markets	The term emerging markets is commonly used to describe business and market activity in industrializing or emerging regions of the world. It is sometimes loosely used as a replacement for emerging economies, but really signifies a business phenomenon that is not fully described by or constrained to geography or economic strength; such countries are considered to be in a transitional phase between developing and developed status.
Emerging market	The term emerging market is commonly used to describe business and market activity in industrializing or emerging regions of the world.
Strategic plan	The formal document that presents the ways and means by which a strategic goal will be achieved is a strategic plan. A long-term flexible plan that does not regulate activities but rather outlines the means to achieve certain results, and provides the means to alter the course of action should the desired ends change.
Globalization of markets	Moving away from an economic system in which national markets are distinct entities, isolated by trade barriers and barriers of distance, time, and culture, and toward a system in which national markets are merging into one global market is globalization of markets.
Industry	A group of firms that produce identical or similar products is an industry. It is also used specifically to refer to an area of economic production focused on manufacturing which involves large amounts of capital investment before any profit can be realized, also called "heavy industry".
Toyota	Toyota is a Japanese multinational corporation that manufactures automobiles, trucks and buses. Toyota is the world's second largest automaker by sales. Toyota also provides financial services through its subsidiary, Toyota Financial Services, and participates in other lines of business.
Brand	A name, symbol, or design that identifies the goods or services of one seller or group of sellers and distinguishes them from the goods and services of competitors is a brand.
Sony	Sony is a multinational corporation and one of the world's largest media conglomerates founded in Tokyo, Japan. One of its divisions Sony Electronics is one of the leading manufacturers of electronics, video, communications, and information technology products for the consumer and professional markets.
Firestone Tire	The Firestone Tire and Rubber Company was founded to supply pneumatic tires for wagons, buggies, and other forms of wheeled transportation common in the era. They soon saw the huge potential for marketing tires for automobiles and befriended Henry Ford, the first industrialist to produce them using the techniques of mass production. This relationship was used to become the original equipment supplier of Ford Motor Company automobiles, and was also active in the replacement market.
Chrysler	The Chrysler Corporation was an American automobile manufacturer that existed independently from 1925–1998. The company was formed by Walter Percy Chrysler on June 6, 1925, with the remaining assets of Maxwell Motor Company.
Zenith	Zenith is an American manufacturer of televisions headquartered in Lincolnshire, Illinois. It was the inventor of the modern remote control, and it introduced HDTV in North America.
Acquisition	A company's purchase of the property and obligations of another company is an acquisition.
Dealer	People who link buyers with sellers by buying and selling securities at stated prices are referred to

Go to **Cram101.com** for the Practice Tests for this Chapter.

Go to **Cram101.com** for the Practice Tests for this Chapter.
And, **NEVER** highlight a book again!

	as a dealer.
Weber	Weber was a German political economist and sociologist who is considered one of the founders of the modern study of sociology and public administration. His major works deal with rationalization in sociology of religion and government, but he also wrote much in the field of economics. His most popular work is his essay The Protestant Ethic and the Spirit of Capitalism.
Disparagement	Disparagement, in United States trademark law, is a cause of action that permits a party to petition the Trademark Trial and Appeal Board to cancel a trademark registration that "may disparage or falsely suggest a connection with persons, living or dead, institutions, beliefs, or national symbols, or bring them into contempt or disrepute."
Market share	That fraction of an industry's output accounted for by an individual firm or group of firms is called market share.
Honda	With more than 14 million internal combustion engines built each year, Honda is the largest engine-maker in the world. In 2004, the company began to produce diesel motors, which were both very quiet whilst not requiring particulate filters to pass pollution standards. It is arguable, however, that the foundation of their success is the motorcycle division.
BMW	BMW is an independent German company and manufacturer of automobiles and motorcycles. BMW is the world's largest premium carmaker and is the parent company of the BMW MINI and Rolls-Royce car brands, and, formerly, Rover.
Ford	Ford is an American company that manufactures and sells automobiles worldwide. Ford introduced methods for large-scale manufacturing of cars, and large-scale management of an industrial workforce, especially elaborately engineered manufacturing sequences typified by the moving assembly lines.
Channel	Channel, in communications (sometimes called communications channel), refers to the medium used to convey information from a sender (or transmitter) to a receiver.
Contribution	In business organization law, the cash or property contributed to a business by its owners is referred to as contribution.
Operation	A standardized method or technique that is performed repetitively, often on different materials resulting in different finished goods is called an operation.
Profit	Profit refers to the return to the resource entrepreneurial ability; total revenue minus total cost.
Conference Board	The Conference Board is the world's preeminent business membership and research organization, best known for the Consumer Confidence Index and the index of leading indicators. For 90 years, The Conference Board has equipped the world's leading corporations with practical knowledge through issues-oriented research and senior executive peer-to-peer meetings.
Asset	An item of property, such as land, capital, money, a share in ownership, or a claim on others for future payment, such as a bond or a bank deposit is an asset.
Users	Users refer to people in the organization who actually use the product or service purchased by the buying center.
Marketing Plan	Marketing plan refers to a road map for the marketing activities of an organization for a specified future period of time, such as one year or five years.
Consumer behavior	Consumer behavior refers to the actions a person takes in purchasing and using products and services, including the mental and social processes that precede and follow these actions.
Promotion	Promotion refers to all the techniques sellers use to motivate people to buy products or services. An attempt by marketers to inform people about products and to persuade them to participate in an exchange.
Short run	Short run refers to a period of time that permits an increase or decrease in current production volume

Go to **Cram101.com** for the Practice Tests for this Chapter.

	with existing capacity, but one that is too short to permit enlargement of that capacity itself (eg, the building of new plants, training of additional workers, etc.).
Long run	In economic models, the long run time frame assumes no fixed factors of production. Firms can enter or leave the marketplace, and the cost (and availability) of land, labor, raw materials, and capital goods can be assumed to vary.
Marketing mix	The marketing mix approach to marketing is a model of crafting and implementing marketing strategies. It stresses the "mixing" or blending of various factors in such a way that both organizational and consumer (target markets) objectives are attained.
Evaluation	The consumer's appraisal of the product or brand on important attributes is called evaluation.
Policy	Similar to a script in that a policy can be a less than completely rational decision-making method. Involves the use of a pre-existing set of decision steps for any problem that presents itself.
Exxon	Exxon formally replaced the Esso, Enco, and Humble brands on January 1, 1973, in the USA. The name Esso, pronounced S-O, attracted protests from other Standard Oil spinoffs because of its similarity to the name of the parent company, Standard Oil.
Security	Security refers to a claim on the borrower future income that is sold by the borrower to the lender. A security is a type of transferable interest representing financial value.
Variable	A variable is something measured by a number; it is used to analyze what happens to other things when the size of that number changes.
Product strategy	Decisions on the management of products or services based on the conditions of a given market is product strategy. Two general strategies that are well known in the marketing discipline are marketing mix and relational marketing.
Optimum	Optimum refers to the best. Usually refers to a most preferred choice by consumers subject to a budget constraint or a profit maximizing choice by firms or industry subject to a technological constraint.
Eastman Kodak	Eastman Kodak Company is an American multinational public company producing photographic materials and equipment. Long known for its wide range of photographic film products, it has focused in recent years on three main businesses: digital photography, health imaging, and printing. This company remains the largest supplier of films in the world, both for the amateur and professional markets.
Management	Management characterizes the process of leading and directing all or part of an organization, often a business, through the deployment and manipulation of resources. Early twentieth-century management writer Mary Parker Follett defined management as "the art of getting things done through people."
Devise	In a will, a gift of real property is called a devise.
Legal system	Legal system refers to system of rules that regulate behavior and the processes by which the laws of a country are enforced and through which redress of grievances is obtained.
Negotiation	Negotiation is the process whereby interested parties resolve disputes, agree upon courses of action, bargain for individual or collective advantage, and/or attempt to craft outcomes which serve their mutual interests.
Samsung	On November 30, 2005 Samsung pleaded guilty to a charge it participated in a worldwide DRAM price fixing conspiracy during 1999-2002 that damaged competition and raized PC prices.
Host country	The country in which the parent-country organization seeks to locate or has already located a facility is a host country.
Authority	Authority in agency law, refers to an agent's ability to affect his principal's legal relations with third parties. Also used to refer to an actor's legal power or ability to do something. In addition, sometimes used to refer to a statute, case, or other legal source that justifies a particular result.
Corruption	The unauthorized use of public office for private gain. The most common forms of corruption are

Go to **Cram101.com** for the Practice Tests for this Chapter.

Go to **Cram101.com** for the Practice Tests for this Chapter.
And, **NEVER** highlight a book again!

	bribery, extortion, and the misuse of inside information.
Socialization	Socialization is the process by which human beings or animals learn to adopt the behavior patterns of the community in which they live. For both humans and animals, this is typically thought to occur during the early stages of life, during which individuals develop the skills and knowledge necessary to function within their culture and environment.
Holding	The holding is a court's determination of a matter of law based on the issue presented in the particular case. In other words: under this law, with these facts, this result.
Ethnocentrism	Ironically, ethnocentrism may be something that all cultures have in common. People often feel this occurring during what some call culture shock. Ethnocentrism often entails the belief that one's own race or ethnic group is the most important and/or that some or all aspects of its culture are superior to those of other groups.
Cultural values	The values that employees need to have and act on for the organization to act on the strategic values are called cultural values.
Common mistake	A common mistake is where both parties hold the same mistaken belief of the facts.
Mistake	In contract law a mistake is incorrect understanding by one or more parties to a contract and may be used as grounds to invalidate the agreement. Common law has identified three different types of mistake in contract: unilateral mistake, mutual mistake, and common mistake.
Napster	Napster is an online music service which was originally a file sharing service created by Shawn Fanning. Napster was the first widely-used peer-to-peer (or P2P) music sharing service, and it made a major impact on how people, especially university students, used the Internet.
Intellectual property protection	Intellectual property protection refers to laws that establish and maintain ownership rights to intellectual property. The principal forms of this protection are patents, trademarks, and copyrights.
Intellectual property	In law, intellectual property is an umbrella term for various legal entitlements which attach to certain types of information, ideas, or other intangibles in their expressed form. The holder of this legal entitlement is generally entitled to exercise various exclusive rights in relation to its subject matter.
Property	Assets defined in the broadest legal sense. Property includes the unrealized receivables of a cash basis taxpayer, but not services rendered.
Intellectual property rights	Intellectual property rights, such as patents, copyrights, trademarks, trade secrets, trade names, and domain names are very valuable business assets. Federal and state laws protect intellectual property rights from misappropriation and infringement.
Intellectual property right	Intellectual property right refers to the right to control and derive the benefits from something one has invented, discovered, or created.
Social responsibility	Social responsibility is a doctrine that claims that an entity whether it is state, government, corporation, organization or individual has a responsibility to society.
Property rights	Bundle of legal rights over the use to which a resource is put and over the use made of any income that may be derived from that resource are referred to as property rights.
Shareholder	A shareholder is an individual or company (including a corporation) that legally owns one or more shares of stock in a joined stock company.
Bertelsmann	Bertelsmann is a transnational media corporation founded in 1835, based in Gütersloh, Germany. Bertelsmann made headlines on May 17, 2002, when it announced it would acquire the assets of Napster for $8 million.
Equity	Equity is the name given to the set of legal principles, in countries following the English common law

Go to **Cram101.com** for the Practice Tests for this Chapter.

	tradition, which supplement strict rules of law where their application would operate harshly, so as to achieve what is sometimes referred to as "natural justice."
Aid	Assistance provided by countries and by international institutions such as the World Bank to developing countries in the form of monetary grants, loans at low interest rates, in kind, or a combination of these is called aid. Aid can also refer to assistance of any type rendered to benefit some group or individual.
Market potential	Market potential refers to maximum total sales of a product by all firms to a segment during a specified time period under specified environmental conditions and marketing efforts of the firms.
Agent	A person who makes economic decisions for another economic actor. A hired manager operates as an agent for a firm's owner.
Tactic	A short-term immediate decision that, in its totality, leads to the achievement of strategic goals is called a tactic.
Interest	In finance and economics, interest is the price paid by a borrower for the use of a lender's money. In other words, interest is the amount of paid to "rent" money for a period of time.
Buyer	A buyer refers to a role in the buying center with formal authority and responsibility to select the supplier and negotiate the terms of the contract.
Subsidiary	A company that is controlled by another company or corporation is a subsidiary.
Strategic management	A philosophy of management that links strategic planning with dayto-day decision making. Strategic management seeks a fit between an organization's external and internal environments.
Enterprise	Enterprise refers to another name for a business organization. Other similar terms are business firm, sometimes simply business, sometimes simply firm, as well as company, and entity.
Multinational enterprise	Multinational enterprise refers to a firm, usually a corporation, that operates in two or more countries.
Middle class	Colloquially, the term is often applied to people who have a degree of economic independence, but not a great deal of social influence or power in their society. The term often encompasses merchants and professionals, bureaucrats, and some farmers and skilled workers[citation needed]. While most Americans identify themselves as middle class, only 20% live the lifestyle indicative of the American middle class.
Fixed cost	The cost that a firm bears if it does not produce at all and that is independent of its output. The presence of a fixed cost tends to imply increasing returns to scale. Contrasts with variable cost.
Global marketing	A strategy of using a common marketing plan and program for all countries in which a company operates, thus selling the product or services the same way everywhere in the world is called global marketing.
Market segmentation	The process of dividing the total market into several groups whose members have similar characteristics is market segmentation.
Marketing research	Marketing research refers to the analysis of markets to determine opportunities and challenges, and to find the information needed to make good decisions.
Business strategy	Business strategy, which refers to the aggregated operational strategies of single business firm or that of an SBU in a diversified corporation refers to the way in which a firm competes in its chosen arenas.
International division	Division responsible for a firm's international activities is an international division.
Business unit	The lowest level of the company which contains the set of functions that carry a product through its life span from concept through manufacture, distribution, sales and service is a business unit.

Interdependence	The extent to which departments depend on each other for resources or materials to accomplish their tasks is referred to as interdependence.
Competitiveness	Competitiveness usually refers to characteristics that permit a firm to compete effectively with other firms due to low cost or superior technology, perhaps internationally.
Marketing management	Marketing management refers to the process of planning and executing the conception, pricing, promotion, and distribution of ideas, goods, and services to create mutually beneficial exchanges.
Complexity	The technical sophistication of the product and hence the amount of understanding required to use it is referred to as complexity. It is the opposite of simplicity.
Extension	Extension refers to an out-of-court settlement in which creditors agree to allow the firm more time to meet its financial obligations. A new repayment schedule will be developed, subject to the acceptance of creditors.
Marketing strategy	Marketing strategy refers to the means by which a marketing goal is to be achieved, usually characterized by a specified target market and a marketing program to reach it.
Advertising campaign	A comprehensive advertising plan that consists of a series of messages in a variety of media that center on a single theme or idea is referred to as an advertising campaign.
Advertising	Advertising refers to paid, nonpersonal communication through various media by organizations and individuals who are in some way identified in the advertising message.
Standardization	Standardization, in the context related to technologies and industries, is the process of establishing a technical standard among competing entities in a market, where this will bring benefits without hurting competition.
Marketing orientation	When an organization focuses its efforts on continuously collecting information about customers' needs and competitors' capabilities, sharing this information across departments, and using the information to create customer value, we have marketing orientation.
Global marketing strategy	The practice of standardizing marketing activities when there are cultural similarities and adapting them when cultures differ is referred to as global marketing strategy.
Intel	Intel Corporation, founded in 1968 and based in Santa Clara, California, USA, is the world's largest semiconductor company. Intel is best known for its PC microprocessors, where it maintains roughly 80% market share.
Ford Motor Company	Ford Motor Company introduced methods for large-scale manufacturing of cars, and large-scale management of an industrial workforce, especially elaborately engineered manufacturing sequences typified by the moving assembly lines. Henry Ford's combination of highly efficient factories, highly paid workers, and low prices revolutionized manufacturing and came to be known around the world as Fordism by 1914.
Customs	Customs is an authority or agency in a country responsible for collecting customs duties and for controlling the flow of people, animals and goods (including personal effects and hazardous items) in and out of the country.
Ancillary	An ancillary receiver is a receiver who has been appointed in aid of, and in subordination to, the primary receiver.

Go to **Cram101.com** for the Practice Tests for this Chapter.
And, **NEVER** highlight a book again!

Tariff	A tax imposed by a nation on an imported good is called a tariff.
Trade barrier	An artificial disincentive to export and/or import, such as a tariff, quota, or other NTB is called a trade barrier.
Market	A market is, as defined in economics, a social arrangement that allows buyers and sellers to discover information and carry out a voluntary exchange of goods or services.
Industry	A group of firms that produce identical or similar products is an industry. It is also used specifically to refer to an area of economic production focused on manufacturing which involves large amounts of capital investment before any profit can be realized, also called "heavy industry".
Economy	The income, expenditures, and resources that affect the cost of running a business and household are called an economy.
Business opportunity	A business opportunity involves the sale or lease of any product, service, equipment, etc. that will enable the purchaser-licensee to begin a business
Protectionism	Protectionism refers to advocacy of protection. The word has a negative connotation, and few advocates of protection in particular situations will acknowledge being protectionists.
Gain	In finance, gain is a profit or an increase in value of an investment such as a stock or bond. Gain is calculated by fair market value or the proceeds from the sale of the investment minus the sum of the purchase price and all costs associated with it.
Free trade	Free trade refers to a situation in which there are no artificial barriers to trade, such as tariffs and quotas. Usually used, often only implicitly, with frictionless trade, so that it implies that there are no barriers to trade of any kind.
World Trade Organization	The World Trade Organization is an international, multilateral organization, which sets the rules for the global trading system and resolves disputes between its member states, all of whom are signatories to its approximately 30 agreements.
General Agreement on Tariffs and Trade	The General Agreement on Tariffs and Trade was originally created by the Bretton Woods Conference as part of a larger plan for economic recovery after World War II. It included a reduction in tariffs and other international trade barriers and is generally considered the precursor to the World Trade Organization.
Economic development	Increase in the economic standard of living of a country's population, normally accomplished by increasing its stocks of physical and human capital and improving its technology is an economic development.
Capitalism	Capitalism refers to an economic system in which capital is mostly owned by private individuals and corporations. Contrasts with communism.
Communism	Communism refers to an economic system in which capital is owned by private government. Contrasts with capitalism.
Dissolution	Dissolution is the process of admitting or removing a partner in a partnership.
Marketing	Promoting and selling products or services to customers, or prospective customers, is referred to as marketing.
Brief	Brief refers to a statement of a party's case or legal arguments, usually prepared by an attorney. Also used to make legal arguments before appellate courts.
Manufacturing	Production of goods primarily by the application of labor and capital to raw materials and other intermediate inputs, in contrast to agriculture, mining, forestry, fishing, and services a manufacturing.
Labor supply	The number of workers available to an economy. The principal determinants of labor supply are

	population, real wages, and social traditions.
Production	The creation of finished goods and services using the factors of production: land, labor, capital, entrepreneurship, and knowledge.
Personnel	A collective term for all of the employees of an organization. Personnel is also commonly used to refer to the personnel management function or the organizational unit responsible for administering personnel programs.
Inflation	An increase in the overall price level of an economy, usually as measured by the CPI or by the implicit price deflator is called inflation.
Domestic	From or in one's own country. A domestic producer is one that produces inside the home country. A domestic price is the price inside the home country. Opposite of 'foreign' or 'world.'.
Merchant	Under the Uniform Commercial Code, one who regularly deals in goods of the kind sold in the contract at issue, or holds himself out as having special knowledge or skill relevant to such goods, or who makes the sale through an agent who regularly deals in such goods or claims such knowledge or skill is referred to as merchant.
Supply	Supply is the aggregate amount of any material good that can be called into being at a certain price point; it comprises one half of the equation of supply and demand. In classical economic theory, a curve representing supply is one of the factors that produce price.
Labor	People's physical and mental talents and efforts that are used to help produce goods and services are called labor.
Wage	The payment for the service of a unit of labor, per unit time. In trade theory, it is the only payment to labor, usually unskilled labor. In empirical work, wage data may exclude other compenzation, which must be added to get the total cost of employment.
Standard of living	Standard of living refers to the level of consumption that people enjoy, on the average, and is measured by average income per person.
Retaliation	The use of an increased trade barrier in response to another country increasing its trade barrier, either as a way of undoing the adverse effects of the latter's action or of punishing it is retaliation.
Great Depression	The period of severe economic contraction and high unemployment that began in 1929 and continued throughout the 1930s is referred to as the Great Depression.
Depression	Depression refers to a prolonged period characterized by high unemployment, low output and investment, depressed business confidence, falling prices, and widespread business failures. A milder form of business downturn is a recession.
Recession	A significant decline in economic activity. In the U.S., recession is approximately defined as two successive quarters of falling GDP, as judged by NBER.
Uruguay round	The eighth and most recent round of trade negotiations under GATT is referred to as Uruguay round.
Global marketing	A strategy of using a common marketing plan and program for all countries in which a company operates, thus selling the product or services the same way everywhere in the world is called global marketing.
Investment	Investment refers to spending for the production and accumulation of capital and additions to inventories. In a financial sense, buying an asset with the expectation of making a return.
Export	In economics, an export is any good or commodity, shipped or otherwise transported out of a country, province, town to another part of the world in a legitimate fashion, typically for

	use in trade or sale.
Multinational corporations	Firms that own production facilities in two or more countries and produce and sell their products globally are referred to as multinational corporations.
Multinational corporation	An organization that manufactures and markets products in many different countries and has multinational stock ownership and multinational management is referred to as multinational corporation.
Direct investment	Direct investment refers to a domestic firm actually investing in and owning a foreign subsidiary or division.
Corporation	A legal entity chartered by a state or the Federal government that is distinct and separate from the individuals who own it is a corporation. This separation gives the corporation unique powers which other legal entities lack.
Controlling interest	A firm has a controlling interest in another business entity when it owns more than 50 percent of that entity's voting stock.
Controlling	A management function that involves determining whether or not an organization is progressing toward its goals and objectives, and taking corrective action if it is not is called controlling.
Interest	In finance and economics, interest is the price paid by a borrower for the use of a lender's money. In other words, interest is the amount of paid to "rent" money for a period of time.
Retailing	All activities involved in selling, renting, and providing goods and services to ultimate consumers for personal, family, or household use is referred to as retailing.
Trademark	A distinctive word, name, symbol, device, or combination thereof, which enables consumers to identify favored products or services and which may find protection under state or federal law is a trademark.
Exchange	The trade of things of value between buyer and seller so that each is better off after the trade is called the exchange.
Service	Service refers to a "non tangible product" that is not embodied in a physical good and that typically effects some change in another product, person, or institution. Contrasts with good.
Joint venture	Joint venture refers to an undertaking by two parties for a specific purpose and duration, taking any of several legal forms.
Policy	Similar to a script in that a policy can be a less than completely rational decision-making method. Involves the use of a pre-existing set of decision steps for any problem that presents itself.
Acquisition	A company's purchase of the property and obligations of another company is an acquisition.
Regulation	Regulation refers to restrictions state and federal laws place on business with regard to the conduct of its activities.
Firm	An organization that employs resources to produce a good or service for profit and owns and operates one or more plants is referred to as a firm.
Common market	Common market refers to a group of countries that eliminate all barriers to movement of both goods and factors among themselves, and that also, on each product, agree to levy the same tariff on imports from outside the group.
Economic growth	Economic growth refers to the increase over time in the capacity of an economy to produce goods and services and to improve the well-being of its citizens.

Developing country	Developing country refers to a country whose per capita income is low by world standards. Same as LDC. As usually used, it does not necessarily connote that the country's income is rising.
Competitor	Other organizations in the same industry or type of business that provide a good or service to the same set of customers is referred to as a competitor.
Enterprise	Enterprise refers to another name for a business organization. Other similar terms are business firm, sometimes simply business, sometimes simply firm, as well as company, and entity.
Subsidiary	A company that is controlled by another company or corporation is a subsidiary.
Exporter	A firm that sells its product in another country is an exporter.
Commerce	Commerce is the exchange of something of value between two entities. It is the central mechanism from which capitalism is derived.
Capital	Capital generally refers to financial wealth, especially that used to start or maintain a business. In classical economics, capital is one of four factors of production, the others being land and labor and entrepreneurship.
Stock	In financial terminology, stock is the capital raized by a corporation, through the issuance and sale of shares.
Balance of merchandise trade	The value of a country's merchandise exports minus the value of its merchandise imports is a balance of merchandise trade.
Balance	In banking and accountancy, the outstanding balance is the amount of money owned, (or due), that remains in a deposit account (or a loan account) at a given date, after all past remittances, payments and withdrawal have been accounted for. It can be positive (then, in the balance sheet of a firm, it is an asset) or negative (a liability).
Balance of trade	Balance of trade refers to the sum of the money gained by a given economy by selling exports, minus the cost of buying imports. They form part of the balance of payments, which also includes other transactions such as the international investment position.
Trade deficit	The amount by which imports exceed exports of goods and services is referred to as trade deficit.
Deficit	The deficit is the amount by which expenditure exceed revenue.
Holding	The holding is a court's determination of a matter of law based on the issue presented in the particular case. In other words: under this law, with these facts, this result.
International trade	The export of goods and services from a country and the import of goods and services into a country is referred to as the international trade.
Driving force	The key external pressure that will shape the future for an organization is a driving force. The driving force in an industry are the main underlying causes of changing industry and competitive conditions.
North American Free Trade Agreement	A 1993 agreement establishing, over a 15-year period, a free trade zone composed of Canada, Mexico, and the United States is referred to as the North American Free Trade Agreement.
Free trade area	Free trade area refers to a group of countries that adopt free trade on trade among group members, while not necessarily changing the barriers that each member country has on trade with the countries outside the group.
Trade pattern	What goods a country trades, with whom, and in what direction. Explaining the trade pattern

is one of the major purposes of trade theory, especially which goods a country will export and which it will import.

Integration	Economic integration refers to reducing barriers among countries to transactions and to movements of goods, capital, and labor, including harmonization of laws, regulations, and standards. Integrated markets theoretically function as a unified market.
Union	A worker association that bargains with employers over wages and working conditions is called a union.
Organization for economic cooperation and development	Organization for economic cooperation and development refers to Paris-based intergovernmental organization of 'wealthy' nations whose purpose is to provide its 29 member states with a forum in which governments can compare their experiences, discuss the problems they share, and seek solutions that can then be applied within their own national contexts.
World Bank	The World Bank is a group of five international organizations responsible for providing finance and advice to countries for the purposes of economic development and poverty reduction, and for encouraging and safeguarding international investment.
A share	In finance the term A share has two distinct meanings, both relating to securities. The first is a designation for a 'class' of common or preferred stock. A share of common or preferred stock typically has enhanced voting rights or other benefits compared to the other forms of shares that may have been created. The equity structure, or how many types of shares are offered, is determined by the corporate charter.
Consumer market	All the individuals or households that want goods and services for personal consumption or use are a consumer market.
Nestle	Nestle is the world's biggest food and beverage company. In the 1860s, a pharmacist, developed a food for babies who were unable to be breastfed. His first success was a premature infant who could not tolerate his own mother's milk nor any of the usual substitutes. The value of the new product was quickly recognized when his new formula saved the child's life.
Brand	A name, symbol, or design that identifies the goods or services of one seller or group of sellers and distinguishes them from the goods and services of competitors is a brand.
Samsung	On November 30, 2005 Samsung pleaded guilty to a charge it participated in a worldwide DRAM price fixing conspiracy during 1999-2002 that damaged competition and raized PC prices.
Restructuring	Restructuring is the corporate management term for the act of partially dismantling and reorganizing a company for the purpose of making it more efficient and therefore more profitable.
Market opportunities	Market opportunities refer to areas where a company believes there are favorable demand trends, needs, and/or wants that are not being satisfied, and where it can compete effectively.
Exporting	Selling products to another country is called exporting.
Operation	A standardized method or technique that is performed repetitively, often on different materials resulting in different finished goods is called an operation.
Internationa-ization	Internationalization refers to another term for fragmentation. Used by Grossman and Helpman.
Stock market	An organized marketplace in which common stocks are traded. In the United States, the largest stock market is the New York Stock Exchange, on which are traded the stocks of the largest U.S. companies.
Technology	The body of knowledge and techniques that can be used to combine economic resources to

Go to **Cram101.com** for the Practice Tests for this Chapter.

	produce goods and services is called technology.
Financial transaction	A financial transaction involves a change in the status of the finances of two or more businesses or individuals.
Emerging markets	The term emerging markets is commonly used to describe business and market activity in industrializing or emerging regions of the world. It is sometimes loosely used as a replacement for emerging economies, but really signifies a business phenomenon that is not fully described by or constrained to geography or economic strength; such countries are considered to be in a transitional phase between developing and developed status.
Financial crisis	A loss of confidence in a country's currency or other financial assets causing international investors to withdraw their funds from the country is referred to as a financial crisis.
Emerging market	The term emerging market is commonly used to describe business and market activity in industrializing or emerging regions of the world.
Balance of payments	Balance of payments refers to a list, or accounting, of all of a country's international transactions for a given time period, usually one year.
Financial statement	Financial statement refers to a summary of all the transactions that have occurred over a particular period.
Liability	A liability is a present obligation of the enterprise arizing from past events, the settlement of which is expected to result in an outflow from the enterprise of resources embodying economic benefits.
Credit	Credit refers to a recording as positive in the balance of payments, any transaction that gives rise to a payment into the country, such as an export, the sale of an asset, or borrowing from abroad.
Debit	Debit refers to recording as negative in the balance of payments, any transaction that gives rise to a payment out of the country, such as an import, the purchase of an asset, or lending to foreigners. Opposite of credit.
Asset	An item of property, such as land, capital, money, a share in ownership, or a claim on others for future payment, such as a bond or a bank deposit is an asset.
Central Bank	Central bank refers to the institution in a country that is normally responsible for managing the supply of the country's money and the value of its currency on the foreign exchange market.
Insurance	Insurance refers to a system by which individuals can reduce their exposure to risk of large losses by spreading the risks among a large number of persons.
Dividend	Amount of corporate profits paid out for each share of stock is referred to as dividend.
Aid	Assistance provided by countries and by international institutions such as the World Bank to developing countries in the form of monetary grants, loans at low interest rates, in kind, or a combination of these is called aid. Aid can also refer to assistance of any type rendered to benefit some group or individual.
Portfolio investment	Portfolio investment refers to the acquisition of portfolio capital. Usually refers to such transactions across national borders and/or across currencies.
Unilateral transfer	A transfer payment is a unilateral transfer. An item in the current account of a country's accounting books that corresponds to gifts from foreigners, or pension payments to foreign residents who once worked in the host country
Official reserves	The reserves of foreign-currency-denominated assets that a central bank holds, sometimes as backing for its own currency, but usually only for the purpose of possible future exchange

	market intervention are official reserves.
Capital movement	Capital inflow and/or outflow is referred to as capital movement.
Foreign exchange	In finance, foreign exchange means currencies, such as U.S. Dollars and Euros. These are traded on foreign exchange markets.
Current account	Current account refers to a country's international transactions arising from current flows, as opposed to changes in stocks which are part of the capital account. Includes trade in goods and services plus inflows and outflows of transfers. A current account is a deposit account in the UK and countries with a UK banking heritage.
Capital account	The capital account is one of two primary components of the balance of payments. It tracks the movement of funds for investments and loans into and out of a country.
Portfolio	In finance, a portfolio is a collection of investments held by an institution or a private individual. Holding but not always a portfolio is part of an investment and risk-limiting strategy called diversification. By owning several assets, certain types of risk (in particular specific risk) can be reduced.
Fund	Independent accounting entity with a self-balancing set of accounts segregated for the purposes of carrying on specific activities is referred to as a fund.
International Business	International business refers to any firm that engages in international trade or investment.
Exchange rate	Exchange rate refers to the price at which one country's currency trades for another, typically on the exchange market.
Purchasing power	The amount of goods that money will buy, usually measured by the CPI is referred to as purchasing power.
Rate of exchange	Rate of exchange refers to the price paid in one's own money to acquire 1 unit of a foreign currency; the rate at which the money of one nation is exchanged for the money of another nation.
Exchange market	Exchange market refers to the market on which national currencies are bought and sold.
Purchasing	Purchasing refers to the function in a firm that searches for quality material resources, finds the best suppliers, and negotiates the best price for goods and services.
Foreign exchange market	A market for converting the currency of one country into that of another country is called foreign exchange market. It is by far the largest market in the world, in terms of cash value traded, and includes trading between large banks, central banks, currency speculators, multinational corporations, governments, and other financial markets and institutions.
Business Week	Business Week is a business magazine published by McGraw-Hill. It was first published in 1929 under the direction of Malcolm Muir, who was serving as president of the McGraw-Hill Publishing company at the time. It is considered to be the standard both in industry and among students.
Quota	A government-imposed restriction on quantity, or sometimes on total value, used to restrict the import of something to a specific quantity is called a quota.
Market structure	Market structure refers to the way that suppliers and demanders in an industry interact to determine price and quantity. Market structures range from perfect competition to monopoly.
Distribution	Distribution in economics, the manner in which total output and income is distributed among individuals or factors.
Capital accumulation	The growth of capital resources is referred to as capital accumulation. In economics, accounting and Marxian economics, capital accumulation is often equated with investment,

	especially in real capital goods.
Infant industry	Infant industry refers to a young industry that may need temporary protection from competition from the established industries of other countries to develop an acquired comparative advantage.
Accumulation	The acquisition of an increasing quantity of something. The accumulation of factors, especially capital, is a primary mechanism for economic growth.
Real wage	The wage of labor -- or more generally the price of any factor -- relative to an appropriate price index for the goods and services that the worker consumes is referred to as real wage.
Argument	The discussion by counsel for the respective parties of their contentions on the law and the facts of the case being tried in order to aid the jury in arriving at a correct and just conclusion is called argument.
Raw material	Raw material refers to a good that has not been transformed by production; a primary product.
Commodity	Could refer to any good, but in trade a commodity is usually a raw material or primary product that enters into international trade, such as metals or basic agricultural products.
Wall Street Journal	Dow Jones & Company was founded in 1882 by reporters Charles Dow, Edward Jones and Charles Bergstresser. Jones converted the small Customers' Afternoon Letter into The Wall Street Journal, first published in 1889, and began delivery of the Dow Jones News Service via telegraph. The Journal featured the Jones 'Average', the first of several indexes of stock and bond prices on the New York Stock Exchange.
Journal	Book of original entry, in which transactions are recorded in a general ledger system, is referred to as a journal.
Vendor	A person who sells property to a vendee is a vendor. The words vendor and vendee are more commonly applied to the seller and purchaser of real estate, and the words seller and buyer are more commonly applied to the seller and purchaser of personal property.
Comparative advantage	The ability to produce a good at lower cost, relative to other goods, compared to another country is a comparative advantage.
Absolute advantage	A country has an absolute advantage economically over another when it can produce something more cheaply. This term is often used to differentiate between comparative advantage.
Political economy	Early name for the discipline of economics. A field within economics encompassing several alternatives to neoclassical economics, including Marxist economics. Also called radical political economy.
Gold standard	The gold standard is a monetary system in which the standard economic unit of account is a fixed weight of gold.
David Ricardo	David Ricardo (April 18, 1772 – September 11, 1823), a political economist, is often credited with systematizing economics, and was one of the most influential of the classical economists.
Trade theory	The body of economic thought that seeks to explain why and how countries engage in international trade and the welfare implication of that trade, encompassing especially the Ricardian Model, the Heckscher-Ohlin Model, and the New Trade Theory.
Adam Smith	Adam Smith (baptized June 5, 1723 O.S. (June 16 N.S.) – July 17, 1790) was a Scottish political economist and moral philosopher. His Inquiry into the Nature and Causes of the Wealth of Nations was one of the earliest attempts to study the historical development of industry and commerce in Europe. That work helped to create the modern academic discipline of economics

34

Go to **Cram101.com** for the Practice Tests for this Chapter.

Competitiveness	Competitiveness usually refers to characteristics that permit a firm to compete effectively with other firms due to low cost or superior technology, perhaps internationally.
Import quota	Import quota refers to a limit imposed by a nation on the quantity of a good that may be imported during some period of time.
Customs	Customs is an authority or agency in a country responsible for collecting customs duties and for controlling the flow of people, animals and goods (including personal effects and hazardous items) in and out of the country.
Appeal	Appeal refers to the act of asking an appellate court to overturn a decision after the trial court's final judgment has been entered.
Countervailing duties	countervailing duties are tariffs imposed by a country on imported goods in cases where imports have been unfairly subsidized by a foreign government and hurt domestic producers. Antidumping duties are referred to as countervailing duties.
Countervailing duty	A tariff levied against imports that are subsidized by the exporting country's government, designed to offset the effect of the subsidy, is referred to as countervailing duty.
Declining industry	An industry in which economic profits are negative and that will, therefore, decrease its output as firms leave it is called declining industry.
Nontariff barrier	Any policy that interferes with exports or imports other than a simple tariff, prominently including quotas and vers is referred to as nontariff barrier.
Boycott	To protest by refusing to purchase from someone, or otherwise do business with them. In international trade, a boycott most often takes the form of refusal to import a country's goods.
Reciprocal demand	Reciprocal demand refers to the concept in international trade, that it is not just supply and demand that interact, but demand and demand. Describes a trading equilibrium in which a reciprocal equilibrium where one country's demand for another country's products matches with the other country's demands for the products of the first.
Gains from trade	The net increase in output that countries experience as a result of lowering import tariffs and otherwise liberalizing trade is referred to as gains from trade.
John Stuart Mill	John Stuart Mill (May 20, 1806 – May 8, 1873), an English philosopher and political economist, was an influential liberal thinker of the 19th century. An important work of his was Utilitarianism
Terms of trade	Terms of trade refers to the rate at which units of one product can be exchanged for units of another product; the price of a good or service; the amount of one good or service that must be given up to obtain 1 unit of another good or service.
Revenue	Revenue is a U.S. business term for the amount of money that a company receives from its activities, mostly from sales of products and/or services to customers.
Accession	Accession refers to the process of adding a country to an international agreement, such as the GATT, WTO, EU, or NAFTA.
Treaties	The first source of international law, consisting of agreements or contracts between two or more nations that are formally signed by an authorized representative and ratified by the supreme power of each nation are called treaties.
Consideration	Consideration in contract law, a basic requirement for an enforceable agreement under traditional contract principles, defined in this text as legal value, bargained for and given in exchange for an act or promise. In corporation law, cash or property contributed to a corporation in exchange for shares, or a promise to contribute such cash or property.

36

Go to **Cram101.com** for the Practice Tests for this Chapter.

Reciprocity	An industrial buying practice in which two organizations agree to purchase each other's products and services is called reciprocity.
Trade war	Trade war refers to generally, a period in which each of two countries alternate in further restricting trade from the other. More specifically, the process of tariffs and retaliation.
Administration	Administration refers to the management and direction of the affairs of governments and institutions; a collective term for all policymaking officials of a government; the execution and implementation of public policy.
Export subsidies	Government payments to domestic producers to enable them to reduce the price of a good or service to foreign buyers are referred to as export subsidies.
Subsidy	Subsidy refers to government financial assistance to a domestic producer.
In kind	Referring to a payment made with goods instead of money is an in kind. An expression relating to the insurer's right in many Property contracts to replace damaged objects with new or equivalent (in kind) material, rather than to pay a cash benefit.
Complaint	The pleading in a civil case in which the plaintiff states his claim and requests relief is called complaint. In the common law, it is a formal legal document that sets out the basic facts and legal reasons that the filing party (the plaintiffs) believes are sufficient to support a claim against another person, persons, entity or entities (the defendants) that entitles the plaintiff(s) to a remedy (either money damages or injunctive relief).
Banana war	Banana war refers to a trade dispute between the EU and the U.S. over EU preferences for bananas from former colonies. On behalf of U.S.-owned companies exporting bananas from South America and the Caribbean, the US complained to the WTO, which ruled in favor of the U.S.
Voluntary export restraint	Voluntary export restraint refers to a restriction on a country's imports that is achieved by negotiating with the foreign exporting country for it to restrict its exports. The restraint agreement may be concluded at either industry or government level. In the latter case, sometimes referred to as an orderly marketing arrangement.
Embargo	Embargo refers to the prohibition of some category of trade. May apply to exports and/or imports, of particular products or of all trade, vis a vis the world or a particular country or countries.
Amway	Amway is a multi-level marketing company founded in 1959 by Jay Van Andel and Rich DeVos. The company's name is a portmanteau of "American Way." .
Slowdown	A slowdown is an industrial action in which employees perform their duties but seek to reduce productivity or efficiency in their performance of these duties. A slowdown may be used as either a prelude or an alternative to a strike, as it is seen as less disruptive as well as less risky and costly for workers and their union.
Caterpillar	Caterpillar is a United States based corporation headquartered in Peoria, Illinois. Caterpillar is "the world's largest manufacturer of construction and mining equipment, diesel and natural gas engines, and industrial gas turbines."
Contract	A contract is a "promise" or an "agreement" that is enforced or recognized by the law. In the civil law, a contract is considered to be part of the general law of obligations.
United Nations	An international organization created by multilateral treaty in 1945 to promote social and economic cooperation among nations and to protect human rights is the United Nations.
Promotion	Promotion refers to all the techniques sellers use to motivate people to buy products or services. An attempt by marketers to inform people about products and to persuade them to participate in an exchange.
Specialist	A specialist is a trader who makes a market in one or several stocks and holds the limit

Go to **Cram101.com** for the Practice Tests for this Chapter.

order book for those stocks.

Intel	Intel Corporation, founded in 1968 and based in Santa Clara, California, USA, is the world's largest semiconductor company. Intel is best known for its PC microprocessors, where it maintains roughly 80% market share.
Negotiation	Negotiation is the process whereby interested parties resolve disputes, agree upon courses of action, bargain for individual or collective advantage, and/or attempt to craft outcomes which serve their mutual interests.
Predatory pricing	Predatory pricing refers to when a company deliberately prices below its costs in an effort to drive out competitors and restrict supply and then raises prices rather than enlarge demand.
Antitrust	Government intervention to alter market structure or prevent abuse of market power is called antitrust.
Wholesale	According to the United Nations Statistics Division Wholesale is the resale of new and used goods to retailers, to industrial, commercial, institutional or professional users, or to other wholesalers, or involves acting as an agent or broker in buying merchandise for, or selling merchandise, to such persons or companies.
Public company	A public company is a company owned by the public rather than by a relatively few individuals. There are two different meanings for this term: (1) A company that is owned by stockholders who are members of the general public and trade shares publicly, often through a listing on a stock exchange. Ownership is open to anyone that has the money and inclination to buy shares in the company. It is differentiated from privately held companies where the shares are held by a small group of individuals, who are often members of one or a small group of families or otherwise related individuals, or other companies. The variant of this type of company in the United Kingdom and Ireland is known as a public limited compan, and (2) A government-owned corporation. This meaning of a "public company" comes from the fact that government debt is sometimes referred to as "public debt" although there are no "public bonds", government finance is sometimes called "public finance", among similar uses. This is the less-common meaning.
Dumping	Dumping refers to a practice of charging a very low price in a foreign market for such economic purposes as putting rival suppliers out of business.
Manufacturing costs	Costs incurred in a manufacturing process, which consist of direct material, direct labor, and manufacturing overhead are referred to as manufacturing costs.
Litigation	The process of bringing, maintaining, and defending a lawsuit is litigation.
Realization	Realization is the sale of assets when an entity is being liquidated.
Market access	The ability of firms from one country to sell in another is market access.
Import relief	Import relief usually refers to some form of restraint of imports in a particular sector in order to assist domestic producers, and with the connotation that these producers have been suffering from the competition with imports.
Licensing	Licensing is a form of strategic alliance which involves the sale of a right to use certain proprietary knowledge (so called intellectual property) in a defined way.
Authority	Authority in agency law, refers to an agent's ability to affect his principal's legal relations with third parties. Also used to refer to an actor's legal power or ability to do something. In addition, sometimes used to refer to a statute, case, or other legal source that justifies a particular result.
Billboard	The most common form of outdoor advertising is called a billboard.

Go to **Cram101.com** for the Practice Tests for this Chapter.

Export promotion	Export promotion refers to a strategy for economic development that stresses expanding exports, often through policies to assist them such as export subsidies.
License	A license in the sphere of Intellectual Property Rights (IPR) is a document, contract or agreement giving permission or the 'right' to a legally-definable entity to do something (such as manufacture a product or to use a service), or to apply something (such as a trademark), with the objective of achieving commercial gain.
Contribution	In business organization law, the cash or property contributed to a business by its owners is referred to as contribution.
Market share	That fraction of an industry's output accounted for by an individual firm or group of firms is called market share.
Petition	A petition is a request to an authority, most commonly a government official or public entity. In the colloquial sense, a petition is a document addressed to some official and signed by numerous individuals.
International Monetary Fund	The International Monetary Fund is the international organization entrusted with overseeing the global financial system by monitoring exchange rates and balance of payments, as well as offering technical and financial assistance when asked.
Trade dispute	Trade dispute refers to any disagreement between nations involving their international trade or trade policies.
Inception	The date and time on which coverage under an insurance policy takes effect is inception. Also refers to the date at which a stock or mutual fund was first traded.
Comprehensive	A comprehensive refers to a layout accurate in size, color, scheme, and other necessary details to show how a final ad will look. For presentation only, never for reproduction.
Government procurement	Government procurement refers to purchase of goods and services by government and by state-owned enterprises.
Customs valuation	Customs valuation refers to the method by which a customs officer determines the amount of duty payable in the importing country.
Procurement	Procurement is the acquisition of goods or services at the best possible total cost of ownership, in the right quantity, at the right time, in the right place for the direct benefit or use of the governments, corporations, or individuals generally via, but not limited to a contract.
Valuation	In finance, valuation is the process of estimating the market value of a financial asset or liability. They can be done on assets (for example, investments in marketable securities such as stocks, options, business enterprises, or intangible assets such as patents and trademarks) or on liabilities (e.g., Bonds issued by a company).
Intellectual property rights	Intellectual property rights, such as patents, copyrights, trademarks, trade secrets, trade names, and domain names are very valuable business assets. Federal and state laws protect intellectual property rights from misappropriation and infringement.
Intellectual property right	Intellectual property right refers to the right to control and derive the benefits from something one has invented, discovered, or created.
Intellectual property	In law, intellectual property is an umbrella term for various legal entitlements which attach to certain types of information, ideas, or other intangibles in their expressed form. The holder of this legal entitlement is generally entitled to exercise various exclusive rights in relation to its subject matter.
Trade in services	Trade in services refers to the provision of a service to buyers within or from one country by a firm in or from another country.

Go to **Cram101.com** for the Practice Tests for this Chapter.

Property rights	Bundle of legal rights over the use to which a resource is put and over the use made of any income that may be derived from that resource are referred to as property rights.
Capital flow	International capital movement is referred to as capital flow.
Property	Assets defined in the broadest legal sense. Property includes the unrealized receivables of a cash basis taxpayer, but not services rendered.
Trade minister	Trade minister refers to the government official, at the ministerial or cabinet level, primarily responsible for issues of international trade policy; the minister of international trade.
Nontariff measure	Nontariff measure refers to any policy or official practice that alters the conditions of international trade, including ones that act to increase trade as well as those that restrict
General Agreement on Trade in Services	The General Agreement on Trade in Services is a treaty of the World Trade Organization that entered into force in January 1995 as a result of the Uruguay Round negotiations. The treaty was created to extend the multilateral trading system to services, in the same way the General Agreement on Tariffs and Trade provides such a system for merchandise trade.
Bureaucracy	Bureaucracy refers to an organization with many layers of managers who set rules and regulations and oversee all decisions.
Trade secret	Trade secret refers to a secret formula, pattern, process, program, device, method, technique, or compilation of information that is used in its owner's business and affords that owner a competitive advantage. Trade secrets are protected by state law.
Copyright	The legal right to the proceeds from and control over the use of a created product, such a written work, audio, video, film, or software is a copyright. This right generally extends over the life of the author plus fifty years.
Patent	The legal right to the proceeds from and control over the use of an invented product or process, granted for a fixed period of time, usually 20 years. Patent is one form of intellectual property that is subject of the TRIPS agreement.
Rules of origin	Rules of origin refer to rules included in a FTA specifying when a good will be regarded as produced within the FTA, so as to cross between members without tariff. Typical rules of origin are based on percentage of value added or on changes in tariff heading.
Level playing field	The objective of those who advocate protection on the grounds the foreign firms have an unfair advantage. A level playing field would remove such advantages, although it is not usually clear what sorts of advantage would be permitted to remain.
Scope	Scope of a project is the sum total of all projects products and their requirements or features.
Compliance	A type of influence process where a receiver accepts the position advocated by a source to obtain favorable outcomes or to avoid punishment is the compliance.
Sovereignty	A country or region's power and ability to rule itself and manage its own affairs. Some feel that membership in international organizations such as the WTO is a threat to their sovereignty.
Information technology	Information technology refers to technology that helps companies change business by allowing them to use new methods.
Open market	In economics, the open market is the term used to refer to the environment in which bonds are bought and sold.
Exchange control	Rationing of foreign exchange, typically used when the exchange rate is fixed and the central bank is unable or unwilling to enforce the rate by exchange-market intervention is an

44

Go to **Cram101.com** for the Practice Tests for this Chapter.

	exchange control.
Product line	A group of products that are physically similar or are intended for a similar market are called the product line.
Foreign exchange control	The control a government may exercise over the quantity of foreign currency demanded by its citizens and firms and over the rates of exchange in order to limit its out-payments to its in-payments is referred to as foreign exchange control.
Harmonization	Harmonization refers to the changing of government regulations and practices, as a result of an international agreement, to make those of different countries the same or more compatible.
Average total cost	Average total cost refers to a firm's total cost divided by output ; equal to average fixed cost plus average variable cost.
Total cost	The sum of fixed cost and variable cost is referred to as total cost.
Tactic	A short-term immediate decision that, in its totality, leads to the achievement of strategic goals is called a tactic.
Concession	A concession is a business operated under a contract or license associated with a degree of exclusivity in exploiting a business within a certain geographical area. For example, sports arenas or public parks may have concession stands; and public services such as water supply may be operated as concessions.
Financial market	In economics, a financial market is a mechanism which allows people to trade money for securities or commodities such as gold or other precious metals. In general, any commodity market might be considered to be a financial market, if the usual purpose of traders is not the immediate consumption of the commodity, but rather as a means of delaying or accelerating consumption over time.
Freely convertible currency	A country's currency is freely convertible when the government of that country allows both residents and nonresidents to purchase unlimited amounts of foreign currency with the domestic currency is referred to as freely convertible currency.
Convertible currency	Convertible currency refers to a currency that can legally be exchanged for another or for gold.
Floating exchange rate	A system under which the exchange rate for converting one currency into another is continuously adjusted depending on the laws of supply and demand is referred to as a floating exchange rate.
Special drawing right	Special drawing right refers to what was originally intended within the IMF as a sort of international money for use among central banks pegging their exchange rates. The special drawing right is a transferable right to acquire another country's currency.
Utility	Utility refers to the want-satisfying power of a good or service; the satisfaction or pleasure a consumer obtains from the consumption of a good or service.
Market price	Market price is an economic concept with commonplace familiarity; it is the price that a good or service is offered at, or will fetch, in the marketplace; it is of interest mainly in the study of microeconomics.
Equity	Equity is the name given to the set of legal principles, in countries following the English common law tradition, which supplement strict rules of law where their application would operate harshly, so as to achieve what is sometimes referred to as "natural justice."
Sustainable growth	A maximum amount of growth a firm can sustain without increasing financial leverage is called sustainable growth.
Globalization	The increasing world-wide integration of markets for goods, services and capital that

attracted special attention in the late 1990s is called globalization.

Antiglobaliz-tion

Antiglobalization is a term most commonly ascribed to the political stance of people and groups who oppose certain aspects of globalization in its current form, often including the domination of current global trade agreements and trade-governing bodies such as the World Trade Organization by powerful corporations.

Coalition

An informal alliance among managers who support a specific goal is called coalition.

Gap

In December of 1995, Gap became the first major North American retailer to accept independent monitoring of the working conditions in a contract factory producing its garments. Gap is the largest specialty retailer in the United States.

Starbucks

Although it has endured much criticism for its purported monopoly on the global coffee-bean market, Starbucks purchases only 3% of the coffee beans grown worldwide. In 2000 the company introduced a line of fair trade products and now offers three options for socially conscious coffee drinkers. According to Starbucks, they purchased 4.8 million pounds of Certified Fair Trade coffee in fiscal year 2004 and 11.5 million pounds in 2005.

Free market

A free market is a market where price is determined by the unregulated interchange of supply and demand rather than set by artificial means.

Factors of production

Economic resources: land, capital, labor, and entrepreneurial ability are called factors of production.

Welfare

Welfare refers to the economic well being of an individual, group, or economy. For individuals, it is conceptualized by a utility function. For groups, including countries and the world, it is a tricky philosophical concept, since individuals fare differently.

Gross domestic product

Gross domestic product refers to the total value of new goods and services produced in a given year within the borders of a country, regardless of by whom.

Go to **Cram101.com** for the Practice Tests for this Chapter.

Delegation	Delegation is the handing of a task over to another person, usually a subordinate. It is the assignment of authority and responsibility to another person to carry out specific activities.
Authority	Authority in agency law, refers to an agent's ability to affect his principal's legal relations with third parties. Also used to refer to an actor's legal power or ability to do something. In addition, sometimes used to refer to a statute, case, or other legal source that justifies a particular result.
Market	A market is, as defined in economics, a social arrangement that allows buyers and sellers to discover information and carry out a voluntary exchange of goods or services.
Appreciation	Appreciation refers to a rise in the value of a country's currency on the exchange market, relative either to a particular other currency or to a weighted average of other currencies. The currency is said to appreciate. Opposite of 'depreciation.' Appreciation can also refer to the increase in value of any asset.
Points	Loan origination fees that may be deductible as interest by a buyer of property. A seller of property who pays points reduces the selling price by the amount of the points paid for the buyer.
Foreign corporation	Foreign corporation refers to a corporation incorporated in one state doing business in another state. A corporation doing business in a jurisdiction in which it was not formed.
Corporation	A legal entity chartered by a state or the Federal government that is distinct and separate from the individuals who own it is a corporation. This separation gives the corporation unique powers which other legal entities lack.
Management	Management characterizes the process of leading and directing all or part of an organization, often a business, through the deployment and manipulation of resources. Early twentieth-century management writer Mary Parker Follett defined management as "the art of getting things done through people."
Jurisdiction	The power of a court to hear and decide a case is called jurisdiction. It is the practical authority granted to a formally constituted body or to a person to deal with and make pronouncements on legal matters and, by implication, to administer justice within a defined area of responsibility.
Treaties	The first source of international law, consisting of agreements or contracts between two or more nations that are formally signed by an authorized representative and ratified by the supreme power of each nation are called treaties.
Arbitrate	To submit some disputed matter to selected persons and to accept their decision or award as a substitute for the decision of a judicial tribunal is called the arbitrate.
Loyalty	Marketers tend to define customer loyalty as making repeat purchases. Some argue that it should be defined attitudinally as a strongly positive feeling about the brand.
Service	Service refers to a "non tangible product" that is not embodied in a physical good and that typically effects some change in another product, person, or institution. Contrasts with good.
Collective good	A collective good is defined in economics as public goods that could be delivered as private goods, but are delivered instead by the government for various reasons (usually social policy) and financed from public funds like taxes.
Channel	Channel, in communications (sometimes called communications channel), refers to the medium used to convey information from a sender (or transmitter) to a receiver.
Interest	In finance and economics, interest is the price paid by a borrower for the use of a lender's

money. In other words, interest is the amount of paid to "rent" money for a period of time.

Grant
Grant refers to an intergovernmental transfer of funds . Since the New Deal, state and local governments have become increasingly dependent upon federal grants for an almost infinite variety of programs.

Entrepreneur
The owner/operator. The person who organizes, manages, and assumes the risks of a firm, taking a new idea or a new product and turning it into a successful business is an entrepreneur.

Cabinet
The heads of the executive departments of a jurisdiction who report to and advise its chief executive; examples would include the president's cabinet, the governor's cabinet, and the mayor's cabinet.

Policy
Similar to a script in that a policy can be a less than completely rational decision-making method. Involves the use of a pre-existing set of decision steps for any problem that presents itself.

Extension
Extension refers to an out-of-court settlement in which creditors agree to allow the firm more time to meet its financial obligations. A new repayment schedule will be developed, subject to the acceptance of creditors.

Acquisition
A company's purchase of the property and obligations of another company is an acquisition.

Union
A worker association that bargains with employers over wages and working conditions is called a union.

Imperialism
Imperialism is a policy of extending control or authority over foreign entities as a means of acquisition and/or maintenance of empires. This is either through direct territorial conquest or settlement, or through indirect methods of exerting control on the politics and/or economy of these other entities. The term is often used to describe the policy of a nation's dominance over distant lands, regardless of whether the nation considers itself part of the empire.

Intervention
Intervention refers to an activity in which a government buys or sells its currency in the foreign exchange market in order to affect its currency's exchange rate.

Trial
An examination before a competent tribunal, according to the law of the land, of the facts or law put in issue in a cause, for the purpose of determining such issue is a trial. When the court hears and determines any issue of fact or law for the purpose of determining the rights of the parties, it may be considered a trial.

Corruption
The unauthorized use of public office for private gain. The most common forms of corruption are bribery, extortion, and the misuse of inside information.

Sovereignty
A country or region's power and ability to rule itself and manage its own affairs. Some feel that membership in international organizations such as the WTO is a threat to their sovereignty.

Expropriation
Expropriation is the act of removing from control the owner of an item of property. The term is used to both refer to acts by a government or by any group of people.

Contribution
In business organization law, the cash or property contributed to a business by its owners is referred to as contribution.

Investment
Investment refers to spending for the production and accumulation of capital and additions to inventories. In a financial sense, buying an asset with the expectation of making a return.

Economy
The income, expenditures, and resources that affect the cost of running a business and household are called an economy.

Prejudice	Prejudice is, as the name implies, the process of "pre-judging" something. It implies coming to a judgment on a subject before learning where the preponderance of evidence actually lies, or forming a judgment without direct experience.
Wall Street Journal	Dow Jones & Company was founded in 1882 by reporters Charles Dow, Edward Jones and Charles Bergstresser. Jones converted the small Customers' Afternoon Letter into The Wall Street Journal, first published in 1889, and began delivery of the Dow Jones News Service via telegraph. The Journal featured the Jones 'Average', the first of several indexes of stock and bond prices on the New York Stock Exchange.
Security	Security refers to a claim on the borrower future income that is sold by the borrower to the lender. A security is a type of transferable interest representing financial value.
Journal	Book of original entry, in which transactions are recorded in a general ledger system, is referred to as a journal.
North American Free Trade Agreement	A 1993 agreement establishing, over a 15-year period, a free trade zone composed of Canada, Mexico, and the United States is referred to as the North American Free Trade Agreement.
Bay of Pigs invasion	The 1961 Bay of Pigs invasion was a United States-planned and funded attempted invasion by armed Cuban exiles in southwest Cuba. An attempt to overthrow the government of Fidel Castro, the action marked the climax of anti-Cuban US actions.
Free trade	Free trade refers to a situation in which there are no artificial barriers to trade, such as tariffs and quotas. Usually used, often only implicitly, with frictionless trade, so that it implies that there are no barriers to trade of any kind.
Embargo	Embargo refers to the prohibition of some category of trade. May apply to exports and/or imports, of particular products or of all trade, vis a vis the world or a particular country or countries.
Fund	Independent accounting entity with a self-balancing set of accounts segregated for the purposes of carrying on specific activities is referred to as a fund.
Microsoft	Microsoft is a multinational computer technology corporation with 2004 global annual sales of US$39.79 billion and 71,553 employees in 102 countries and regions as of July 2006. It develops, manufactures, licenses, and supports a wide range of software products for computing devices.
Context	The effect of the background under which a message often takes on more and richer meaning is a context. Context is especially important in cross-cultural interactions because some cultures are said to be high context or low context.
Marketing	Promoting and selling products or services to customers, or prospective customers, is referred to as marketing.
Agent	A person who makes economic decisions for another economic actor. A hired manager operates as an agent for a firm's owner.
Capital	Capital generally refers to financial wealth, especially that used to start or maintain a business. In classical economics, capital is one of four factors of production, the others being land and labor and entrepreneurship.
Supply	Supply is the aggregate amount of any material good that can be called into being at a certain price point; it comprises one half of the equation of supply and demand. In classical economic theory, a curve representing supply is one of the factors that produce price.
Brief	Brief refers to a statement of a party's case or legal arguments, usually prepared by an attorney. Also used to make legal arguments before appellate courts.

Buyer	A buyer refers to a role in the buying center with formal authority and responsibility to select the supplier and negotiate the terms of the contract.
Users	Users refer to people in the organization who actually use the product or service purchased by the buying center.
Global strategy	Global strategy refers to strategy focusing on increasing profitability by reaping cost reductions from experience curve and location economies.
Consideration	Consideration in contract law, a basic requirement for an enforceable agreement under traditional contract principles, defined in this text as legal value, bargained for and given in exchange for an act or promise. In corporation law, cash or property contributed to a corporation in exchange for shares, or a promise to contribute such cash or property.
Business Week	Business Week is a business magazine published by McGraw-Hill. It was first published in 1929 under the direction of Malcolm Muir, who was serving as president of the McGraw-Hill Publishing company at the time. It is considered to be the standard both in industry and among students.
Speculation	The purchase or sale of an asset in hopes that its price will rise or fall respectively, in order to make a profit is called speculation.
Trust	An arrangement in which shareholders of independent firms agree to give up their stock in exchange for trust certificates that entitle them to a share of the trust's common profits.
Tangible	Having a physical existence is referred to as the tangible. Personal property other than real estate, such as cars, boats, stocks, or other assets.
Distribution	Distribution in economics, the manner in which total output and income is distributed among individuals or factors.
Margin	A deposit by a buyer in stocks with a seller or a stockbroker, as security to cover fluctuations in the market in reference to stocks that the buyer has purchased but for which he has not paid is a margin. Commodities are also traded on margin.
Economic stagnation	Economic stagnation, often called simply stagnation is a prolonged period of slow economic growth (traditionally measured in terms of the GDP growth). By some definitions, "slow" means that it is significantly slower than a potential growth as estimated by experts in macroeconomics. By others, the growth less than 2-3% per year is a sign of stagnation.
Economic development	Increase in the economic standard of living of a country's population, normally accomplished by increasing its stocks of physical and human capital and improving its technology is an economic development.
Common market	Common market refers to a group of countries that eliminate all barriers to movement of both goods and factors among themselves, and that also, on each product, agree to levy the same tariff on imports from outside the group.
Sustainable development	Economic development that is achieved without undermining the incomes, resources, or environment of future generations is called sustainable development.
Bid	A bid price is a price offered by a buyer when he/she buys a good. In the context of stock trading on a stock exchange, the bid price is the highest price a buyer of a stock is willing to pay for a share of that given stock.
Industry	A group of firms that produce identical or similar products is an industry. It is also used specifically to refer to an area of economic production focused on manufacturing which involves large amounts of capital investment before any profit can be realized, also called "heavy industry".
Social	Social responsibility is a doctrine that claims that an entity whether it is state,

57

responsibility	government, corporation, organization or individual has a responsibility to society.
Manufacturing	Production of goods primarily by the application of labor and capital to raw materials and other intermediate inputs, in contrast to agriculture, mining, forestry, fishing, and services a manufacturing.
Regulation	Regulation refers to restrictions state and federal laws place on business with regard to the conduct of its activities.
Toxic substance	Any chemical or mixture whose manufacture, processing, distribution, use, or disposal presents an unreasonable risk of harm to human health or the environment is called toxic substance.
Realization	Realization is the sale of assets when an entity is being liquidated.
Controlling	A management function that involves determining whether or not an organization is progressing toward its goals and objectives, and taking corrective action if it is not is called controlling.
Maturity	Maturity refers to the final payment date of a loan or other financial instrument, after which point no further interest or principal need be paid.
Operation	A standardized method or technique that is performed repetitively, often on different materials resulting in different finished goods is called an operation.
International Business	International business refers to any firm that engages in international trade or investment.
Developing country	Developing country refers to a country whose per capita income is low by world standards. Same as LDC. As usually used, it does not necessarily connote that the country's income is rising.
Revenue	Revenue is a U.S. business term for the amount of money that a company receives from its activities, mostly from sales of products and/or services to customers.
Dumping	Dumping refers to a practice of charging a very low price in a foreign market for such economic purposes as putting rival suppliers out of business.
Export	In economics, an export is any good or commodity, shipped or otherwise transported out of a country, province, town to another part of the world in a legitimate fashion, typically for use in trade or sale.
Economic growth	Economic growth refers to the increase over time in the capacity of an economy to produce goods and services and to improve the well-being of its citizens.
Leadership	Management merely consists of leadership applied to business situations; or in other words: management forms a sub-set of the broader process of leadership.
Organization for economic cooperation and development	Organization for economic cooperation and development refers to Paris-based intergovernmental organization of 'wealthy' nations whose purpose is to provide its 29 member states with a forum in which governments can compare their experiences, discuss the problems they share, and seek solutions that can then be applied within their own national contexts.
United Nations	An international organization created by multilateral treaty in 1945 to promote social and economic cooperation among nations and to protect human rights is the United Nations.
Resource management	Resource management is the efficient and effective deployment of an organization's resources when they are needed. Such resources may include financial resources, inventory, human skills, production resources, or information technology.
Balance	In banking and accountancy, the outstanding balance is the amount of money owned, (or due), that remains in a deposit account (or a loan account) at a given date, after all past

Go to Cram101.com for the Practice Tests for this Chapter.

remittances, payments and withdrawal have been accounted for. It can be positive (then, in the balance sheet of a firm, it is an asset) or negative (a liability).

Contract	A contract is a "promise" or an "agreement" that is enforced or recognized by the law. In the civil law, a contract is considered to be part of the general law of obligations.
Foundation	A Foundation is a type of philanthropic organization set up by either individuals or institutions as a legal entity (either as a corporation or trust) with the purpose of distributing grants to support causes in line with the goals of the foundation.
Technology	The body of knowledge and techniques that can be used to combine economic resources to produce goods and services is called technology.
Domestic	From or in one's own country. A domestic producer is one that produces inside the home country. A domestic price is the price inside the home country. Opposite of 'foreign' or 'world.'.
Preponderance	Preponderance of the evidence means that evidence, in the judgment of the juror, is entitled to the greatest weight, appears to be more credible, has greater force, and overcomes not only the opposing presumptions, but also the opposing evidence.
Labor	People's physical and mental talents and efforts that are used to help produce goods and services are called labor.
Consumption	In Keynesian economics consumption refers to personal consumption expenditure, i.e., the purchase of currently produced goods and services out of income, out of savings (net worth), or from borrowed funds. It refers to that part of disposable income that does not go to saving.
Raw material	Raw material refers to a good that has not been transformed by production; a primary product.
Trend	Trend refers to the long-term movement of an economic variable, such as its average rate of increase or decrease over enough years to encompass several business cycles.
Consumer market	All the individuals or households that want goods and services for personal consumption or use are a consumer market.
Composition	An out-of-court settlement in which creditors agree to accept a fractional settlement on their original claim is referred to as composition.
Household	An economic unit that provides the economy with resources and uses the income received to purchase goods and services that satisfy economic wants is called household.
Economics	The social science dealing with the use of scarce resources to obtain the maximum satisfaction of society's virtually unlimited economic wants is an economics.
Prime minister	The Prime Minister of the United Kingdom of Great Britain and Northern Ireland is the head of government and so exercises many of the executive functions nominally vested in the Sovereign, who is head of state. According to custom, the Prime Minister and the Cabinet (which he or she heads) are accountable for their actions to Parliament, of which they are members by (modern) convention.
Principal	In agency law, one under whose direction an agent acts and for whose benefit that agent acts is a principal.
Gain	In finance, gain is a profit or an increase in value of an investment such as a stock or bond. Gain is calculated by fair market value or the proceeds from the sale of the investment minus the sum of the purchase price and all costs associated with it.
Industrial revolution	The Industrial Revolution is the stream of new technology and the resulting growth of output that began in England toward the end of the 18th century.

Go to **Cram101.com** for the Practice Tests for this Chapter.
And, **NEVER** highlight a book again!

Pension	A pension is a steady income given to a person (usually after retirement). Pensions are typically payments made in the form of a guaranteed annuity to a retired or disabled employee.
Welfare	Welfare refers to the economic well being of an individual, group, or economy. For individuals, it is conceptualized by a utility function. For groups, including countries and the world, it is a tricky philosophical concept, since individuals fare differently.
Immigration	Immigration refers to the migration of people into a country.
Argument	The discussion by counsel for the respective parties of their contentions on the law and the facts of the case being tried in order to aid the jury in arriving at a correct and just conclusion is called argument.
Gap	In December of 1995, Gap became the first major North American retailer to accept independent monitoring of the working conditions in a contract factory producing its garments. Gap is the largest specialty retailer in the United States.
World Health Organization	The World Health Organization is a specialized agency of the United Nations, acting as a coordinating authority on international public health, headquartered in Geneva, Switzerland. It's constitution states that its mission "is the attainment by all peoples of the highest possible level of health". Its major task is to combat disease, especially key infectious diseases, and to promote the general health of the peoples of the world.
Reuters	Reuters is best known as a news service that provides reports from around the world to newspapers and broadcasters. Its main focus is on supplying the financial markets with information and trading products.
Exporter	A firm that sells its product in another country is an exporter.
Commodity	Could refer to any good, but in trade a commodity is usually a raw material or primary product that enters into international trade, such as metals or basic agricultural products.
Innovation	Innovation refers to the first commercially successful introduction of a new product, the use of a new method of production, or the creation of a new form of business organization.
Commerce	Commerce is the exchange of something of value between two entities. It is the central mechanism from which capitalism is derived.
Effective communication	When the intended meaning equals the perceived meaning it is called effective communication.
Continuous improvement	The constant effort to eliminate waste, reduce response time, simplify the design of both products and processes, and improve quality and customer service is referred to as continuous improvement.
Business model	A business model is the instrument by which a business intends to generate revenue and profits. It is a summary of how a company means to serve its employees and customers, and involves both strategy (what an business intends to do) as well as an implementation.
Marketing Plan	Marketing plan refers to a road map for the marketing activities of an organization for a specified future period of time, such as one year or five years.
Deposition	A form of discovery consisting of the oral examination of a party or a party's witness by the other party's attorney outside of court is called a deposition.
Scarcity	Scarcity is defined as not having sufficient resources to produce enough to fulfill unlimited subjective wants. Alternatively, scarcity implies that not all of society's goals can be attained at the same time, so that trade-offs one good against others are made.

Capital Outflow	Capital outflow is an economic term describing capital flowing out of (or leaving) a particular economy. Outflowing capital can be caused by any number of economic or political reasons but can often originate from instability in either sphere.
Merrill Lynch	Merrill Lynch through its subsidiaries and affiliates, provides capital markets services, investment banking and advisory services, wealth management, asset management, insurance, banking and related products and services on a global basis. It is best known for its Global Private Client services and its strong sales force.
Goldman Sachs	Goldman Sachs is widely respected as a financial advisor to some of the most important companies, largest governments, and wealthiest families in the world. It is a primary dealer in the U.S. Treasury securities market. It offers its clients mergers & acquisitions advisory, provides underwriting services, engages in proprietary trading, invests in private equity deals, and also manages the wealth of affluent individuals and families.
Time deposit	The technical name for a savings account is a time deposit; the bank can require prior notice before the owner withdraws money from a time deposit.
Investment	Investment refers to spending for the production and accumulation of capital and additions to inventories. In a financial sense, buying an asset with the expectation of making a return.
Service	Service refers to a "non tangible product" that is not embodied in a physical good and that typically effects some change in another product, person, or institution. Contrasts with good.
Capital	Capital generally refers to financial wealth, especially that used to start or maintain a business. In classical economics, capital is one of four factors of production, the others being land and labor and entrepreneurship.
Market	A market is, as defined in economics, a social arrangement that allows buyers and sellers to discover information and carry out a voluntary exchange of goods or services.
Capital market	A financial market in which long-term debt and equity instruments are traded is referred to as a capital market. The capital market includes the stock market and the bond market.
Yield	The interest rate that equates a future value or an annuity to a given present value is a yield.
Stock market	An organized marketplace in which common stocks are traded. In the United States, the largest stock market is the New York Stock Exchange, on which are traded the stocks of the largest U.S. companies.
Stock	In financial terminology, stock is the capital raized by a corporation, through the issuance and sale of shares.
Financial assets	Financial assets refer to monetary claims or obligations by one party against another party. Examples are bonds, mortgages, bank loans, and equities.
Mutual fund	A mutual fund is a form of collective investment that pools money from many investors and invests the money in stocks, bonds, short-term money market instruments, and/or other securities. In a mutual fund, the fund manager trades the fund's underlying securities, realizing capital gains or loss, and collects the dividend or interest income.
Household	An economic unit that provides the economy with resources and uses the income received to purchase goods and services that satisfy economic wants is called household.
Asset	An item of property, such as land, capital, money, a share in ownership, or a claim on others for future payment, such as a bond or a bank deposit is an asset.
Fund	Independent accounting entity with a self-balancing set of accounts segregated for the purposes of carrying on specific activities is referred to as a fund.

Go to **Cram101.com** for the Practice Tests for this Chapter.

Analyst	Analyst refers to a person or tool with a primary function of information analysis, generally with a more limited, practical and short term set of goals than a researcher.
Users	Users refer to people in the organization who actually use the product or service purchased by the buying center.
Equity	Equity is the name given to the set of legal principles, in countries following the English common law tradition, which supplement strict rules of law where their application would operate harshly, so as to achieve what is sometimes referred to as "natural justice."
Firm	An organization that employs resources to produce a good or service for profit and owns and operates one or more plants is referred to as a firm.
WorldCom	WorldCom was the United States' second largest long distance phone company (AT&T was the largest). WorldCom grew largely by acquiring other telecommunications companies, most notably MCI Communications. It also owned the Tier 1 ISP UUNET, a major part of the Internet backbone.
Enron	Enron Corportaion's global reputation was undermined by persistent rumours of bribery and political pressure to secure contracts in Central America, South America, Africa, and the Philippines. Especially controversial was its $3 billion contract with the Maharashtra State Electricity Board in India, where it is alleged that Enron officials used political connections within the Clinton and Bush administrations to exert pressure on the board.
Auction	A preexisting business model that operates successfully on the Internet by announcing an item for sale and permitting multiple purchasers to bid on them under specified rules and condition is an auction.
EBay	eBay manages an online auction and shopping website, where people buy and sell goods and services worldwide.
Operation	A standardized method or technique that is performed repetitively, often on different materials resulting in different finished goods is called an operation.
Cultural values	The values that employees need to have and act on for the organization to act on the strategic values are called cultural values.
Diffusion	Diffusion is the process by which a new idea or new product is accepted by the market. The rate of diffusion is the speed that the new idea spreads from one consumer to the next.
Business Week	Business Week is a business magazine published by McGraw-Hill. It was first published in 1929 under the direction of Malcolm Muir, who was serving as president of the McGraw-Hill Publishing company at the time. It is considered to be the standard both in industry and among students.
Marketing	Promoting and selling products or services to customers, or prospective customers, is referred to as marketing.
Context	The effect of the background under which a message often takes on more and richer meaning is a context. Context is especially important in cross-cultural interactions because some cultures are said to be high context or low context.
Contract	A contract is a "promise" or an "agreement" that is enforced or recognized by the law. In the civil law, a contract is considered to be part of the general law of obligations.
Customs	Customs is an authority or agency in a country responsible for collecting customs duties and for controlling the flow of people, animals and goods (including personal effects and hazardous items) in and out of the country.
Agent	A person who makes economic decisions for another economic actor. A hired manager operates as an agent for a firm's owner.

Go to **Cram101.com** for the Practice Tests for this Chapter.

Go to **Cram101.com** for the Practice Tests for this Chapter.
And, **NEVER** highlight a book again!

Change agent	A change agent is someone who engages either deliberately or whose behavior results in social, cultural or behavioral change. This can be studied scientifically and effective techniques can be discovered and employed.
Service economy	Service economy can refer to one or both of two recent economic developments. One is the increased importance of the service sector in industrialized economies. Also used to refer to the relative importance of service in a product offering.
Economy	The income, expenditures, and resources that affect the cost of running a business and household are called an economy.
Technology	The body of knowledge and techniques that can be used to combine economic resources to produce goods and services is called technology.
Wall Street Journal	Dow Jones & Company was founded in 1882 by reporters Charles Dow, Edward Jones and Charles Bergstresser. Jones converted the small Customers' Afternoon Letter into The Wall Street Journal, first published in 1889, and began delivery of the Dow Jones News Service via telegraph. The Journal featured the Jones 'Average', the first of several indexes of stock and bond prices on the New York Stock Exchange.
Innovation	Innovation refers to the first commercially successful introduction of a new product, the use of a new method of production, or the creation of a new form of business organization.
Journal	Book of original entry, in which transactions are recorded in a general ledger system, is referred to as a journal.
Preference	The act of a debtor in paying or securing one or more of his creditors in a manner more favorable to them than to other creditors or to the exclusion of such other creditors is a preference. In the absence of statute, a preference is perfectly good, but to be legal it must be bona fide, and not a mere subterfuge of the debtor to secure a future benefit to himself or to prevent the application of his property to his debts.
Consumption	In Keynesian economics consumption refers to personal consumption expenditure, i.e., the purchase of currently produced goods and services out of income, out of savings (net worth), or from borrowed funds. It refers to that part of disposable income that does not go to saving.
Advertising	Advertising refers to paid, nonpersonal communication through various media by organizations and individuals who are in some way identified in the advertising message.
Per capita	Per capita refers to per person. Usually used to indicate the average per person of any given statistic, commonly income.
Nestle	Nestle is the world's biggest food and beverage company. In the 1860s, a pharmacist, developed a food for babies who were unable to be breastfed. His first success was a premature infant who could not tolerate his own mother's milk nor any of the usual substitutes. The value of the new product was quickly recognized when his new formula saved the child's life.
Incidence	The ultimate economic effect of a tax on the real incomes of producers or consumers. Thus a sales tax may be paid by a retailer, but it is likely that the incidence falls upon the consumer.
Consultant	A professional that provides expert advice in a particular field or area in which customers occassionaly require this type of knowledge is a consultant.
Global marketing	A strategy of using a common marketing plan and program for all countries in which a company operates, thus selling the product or services the same way everywhere in the world is called global marketing.

Go to Cram101.com for the Practice Tests for this Chapter.

Go to **Cram101.com** for the Practice Tests for this Chapter.
And, **NEVER** highlight a book again!

Possession	Possession refers to respecting real property, exclusive dominion and control such as owners of like property usually exercise over it. Manual control of personal property either as owner or as one having a qualified right in it.
Socialization	Socialization is the process by which human beings or animals learn to adopt the behavior patterns of the community in which they live. For both humans and animals, this is typically thought to occur during the early stages of life, during which individuals develop the skills and knowledge necessary to function within their culture and environment.
Channel	Channel, in communications (sometimes called communications channel), refers to the medium used to convey information from a sender (or transmitter) to a receiver.
Market segmentation	The process of dividing the total market into several groups whose members have similar characteristics is market segmentation.
Management	Management characterizes the process of leading and directing all or part of an organization, often a business, through the deployment and manipulation of resources. Early twentieth-century management writer Mary Parker Follett defined management as "the art of getting things done through people."
Variable	A variable is something measured by a number; it is used to analyze what happens to other things when the size of that number changes.
Adam Smith	Adam Smith (baptized June 5, 1723 O.S. (June 16 N.S.) – July 17, 1790) was a Scottish political economist and moral philosopher. His Inquiry into the Nature and Causes of the Wealth of Nations was one of the earliest attempts to study the historical development of industry and commerce in Europe. That work helped to create the modern academic discipline of economics
Enterprise	Enterprise refers to another name for a business organization. Other similar terms are business firm, sometimes simply business, sometimes simply firm, as well as company, and entity.
Communism	Communism refers to an economic system in which capital is owned by private government. Contrasts with capitalism.
Economics	The social science dealing with the use of scarce resources to obtain the maximum satisfaction of society's virtually unlimited economic wants is an economics.
Free enterprise	Free enterprise refers to a system in which economic agents are free to own property and engage in commercial transactions.
Brand	A name, symbol, or design that identifies the goods or services of one seller or group of sellers and distinguishes them from the goods and services of competitors is a brand.
Production	The creation of finished goods and services using the factors of production: land, labor, capital, entrepreneurship, and knowledge.
Promissory note	Commercial paper or instrument in which the maker promises to pay a specific sum of money to another person, to his order, or to bearer is referred to as a promissory note.
Market share	That fraction of an industry's output accounted for by an individual firm or group of firms is called market share.
Exporter	A firm that sells its product in another country is an exporter.
Distribution	Distribution in economics, the manner in which total output and income is distributed among individuals or factors.
Corporation	A legal entity chartered by a state or the Federal government that is distinct and separate from the individuals who own it is a corporation. This separation gives the corporation

Go to **Cram101.com** for the Practice Tests for this Chapter.

	unique powers which other legal entities lack.
Promotion	Promotion refers to all the techniques sellers use to motivate people to buy products or services. An attempt by marketers to inform people about products and to persuade them to participate in an exchange.
Vendor	A person who sells property to a vendee is a vendor. The words vendor and vendee are more commonly applied to the seller and purchaser of real estate, and the words seller and buyer are more commonly applied to the seller and purchaser of personal property.
Value system	A value system refers to how an individual or a group of individuals organize their ethical or ideological values. A well-defined value system is a moral code.
Hierarchy	A system of grouping people in an organization according to rank from the top down in which all subordinate managers must report to one person is called a hierarchy.
Economic development	Increase in the economic standard of living of a country's population, normally accomplished by increasing its stocks of physical and human capital and improving its technology is an economic development.
Consumer behavior	Consumer behavior refers to the actions a person takes in purchasing and using products and services, including the mental and social processes that precede and follow these actions.
Economic growth	Economic growth refers to the increase over time in the capacity of an economy to produce goods and services and to improve the well-being of its citizens.
World Bank	The World Bank is a group of five international organizations responsible for providing finance and advice to countries for the purposes of economic development and poverty reduction, and for encouraging and safeguarding international investment.
Consideration	Consideration in contract law, a basic requirement for an enforceable agreement under traditional contract principles, defined in this text as legal value, bargained for and given in exchange for an act or promise. In corporation law, cash or property contributed to a corporation in exchange for shares, or a promise to contribute such cash or property.
Uncertainty avoidance	The extent to which people prefer to be in clear and unambiguous situations is referred to as the uncertainty avoidance.
Power distance	Power distance refers to the degree to which the less powerful members of society expect there to be differences in the levels of power. A high score suggests that there is an expectation that some individuals wield larger amounts of power than others. Countries with high power distance rating are often characterized by a high rate of political violence.
Authority	Authority in agency law, refers to an agent's ability to affect his principal's legal relations with third parties. Also used to refer to an actor's legal power or ability to do something. In addition, sometimes used to refer to a statute, case, or other legal source that justifies a particular result.
Marketing research	Marketing research refers to the analysis of markets to determine opportunities and challenges, and to find the information needed to make good decisions.
Bond	Bond refers to a debt instrument, issued by a borrower and promising a specified stream of payments to the purchaser, usually regular interest payments plus a final repayment of principal.
Collectivism	Collectivism is a term used to describe that things should be owned by the group and used for the benefit of all rather than being owned by individuals.
Exchange	The trade of things of value between buyer and seller so that each is better off after the trade is called the exchange.

Loyalty	Marketers tend to define customer loyalty as making repeat purchases. Some argue that it should be defined attitudinally as a strongly positive feeling about the brand.
Privilege	Generally, a legal right to engage in conduct that would otherwise result in legal liability is a privilege. Privileges are commonly classified as absolute or conditional. Occasionally, privilege is also used to denote a legal right to refrain from particular behavior.
Accord	An agreement whereby the parties agree to accept something different in satisfaction of the original contract is an accord.
Stockbroker	A registered representative who works as a market intermediary to buy and sell securities for clients is a stockbroker.
Emotional appeals	Advertising messages that appeal to consumers' feelings and emotions are referred to as emotional appeals.
Appeal	Appeal refers to the act of asking an appellate court to overturn a decision after the trial court's final judgment has been entered.
Empathy	Empathy refers to dimension of service quality-caring individualized attention provided to customers.
Appreciation	Appreciation refers to a rise in the value of a country's currency on the exchange market, relative either to a particular other currency or to a weighted average of other currencies. The currency is said to appreciate. Opposite of 'depreciation.' Appreciation can also refer to the increase in value of any asset.
International Business	International business refers to any firm that engages in international trade or investment.
Negotiation	Negotiation is the process whereby interested parties resolve disputes, agree upon courses of action, bargain for individual or collective advantage, and/or attempt to craft outcomes which serve their mutual interests.
Copywriter	Individual who helps conceive the ideas for ads and commercials and writes the words or copy for them is referred to as copywriter.
Transaction cost	A transaction cost is a cost incurred in making an economic exchange. For example, most people, when buying or selling a stock, must pay a commission to their broker; that commission is a transaction cost of doing the stock deal.
Harvard Business Review	Harvard Business Review is a research-based magazine written for business practitioners, it claims a high ranking business readership and enjoys the reverence of academics, executives, and management consultants. It has been the frequent publishing home for well known scholars and management thinkers.
Advertisement	Advertisement is the promotion of goods, services, companies and ideas, usually by an identified sponsor. Marketers see advertising as part of an overall promotional strategy.
Comprehensive	A comprehensive refers to a layout accurate in size, color, scheme, and other necessary details to show how a final ad will look. For presentation only, never for reproduction.
Advertising campaign	A comprehensive advertising plan that consists of a series of messages in a variety of media that center on a single theme or idea is referred to as an advertising campaign.
Discount	The difference between the face value of a bond and its selling price, when a bond is sold for less than its face value it's referred to as a discount.
Mistake	In contract law a mistake is incorrect understanding by one or more parties to a contract and may be used as grounds to invalidate the agreement. Common law has identified three different types of mistake in contract: unilateral mistake, mutual mistake, and common mistake.

Go to **Cram101.com** for the Practice Tests for this Chapter.

Product development	In business and engineering, new product development is the complete process of bringing a new product to market. There are two parallel aspects to this process : one involves product engineering ; the other marketing analysis. Marketers see new product development as the first stage in product life cycle management, engineers as part of Product Lifecycle Management.
Preparation	Preparation refers to usually the first stage in the creative process. It includes education and formal training.
Value judgment	Value judgment refers to an opinion of what is desirable or undesirable; belief regarding what ought or ought not to be.
Resistance to change	Resistance to change refers to an attitude or behavior that shows unwillingness to make or support a change.
Accumulation	The acquisition of an increasing quantity of something. The accumulation of factors, especially capital, is a primary mechanism for economic growth.
Specie	Specie refers to coins, normally including only those made of precious metal.
Assimilation	Assimilation refers to the process through which a minority group learns the ways of the dominant group. In organizations, this means that when people of different types and backgrounds are hired, the organization attempts to mold them to fit the existing organizational culture.
Subculture	A subgroups within the larger, or national, culture with unique values, ideas, and attitudes is a subculture.
Xerox	Xerox was founded in 1906 as "The Haloid Company" manufacturing photographic paper and equipment. The company came to prominence in 1959 with the introduction of the first plain paper photocopier using the process of xerography (electrophotography) developed by Chester Carlson, the Xerox 914.
Interdependence	The extent to which departments depend on each other for resources or materials to accomplish their tasks is referred to as interdependence.
Common market	Common market refers to a group of countries that eliminate all barriers to movement of both goods and factors among themselves, and that also, on each product, agree to levy the same tariff on imports from outside the group.
Marketing strategy	Marketing strategy refers to the means by which a marketing goal is to be achieved, usually characterized by a specified target market and a marketing program to reach it.
Immigration	Immigration refers to the migration of people into a country.
Interest	In finance and economics, interest is the price paid by a borrower for the use of a lender's money. In other words, interest is the amount of paid to "rent" money for a period of time.
Labor	People's physical and mental talents and efforts that are used to help produce goods and services are called labor.
Ethnocentrism	Ironically, ethnocentrism may be something that all cultures have in common. People often feel this occurring during what some call culture shock. Ethnocentrism often entails the belief that one's own race or ethnic group is the most important and/or that some or all aspects of its culture are superior to those of other groups.
Public relations	Public relations refers to the management function that evaluates public attitudes, changes policies and procedures in response to the public's requests, and executes a program of action and information to earn public understanding and acceptance.
Gain	In finance, gain is a profit or an increase in value of an investment such as a stock or

Go to **Cram101.com** for the Practice Tests for this Chapter.

bond. Gain is calculated by fair market value or the proceeds from the sale of the investment minus the sum of the purchase price and all costs associated with it.

Option	A contract that gives the purchaser the option to buy or sell the underlying financial instrument at a specified price, called the exercise price or strike price, within a specific period of time.
Diffusion of innovation	Diffusion of innovation is a concept suggesting that customers first enter a market at different times, depending on their attitude to innovation and new products, and their willingness to take risks. Customers can thus be classified as innovators, early adopters, early majority, late majority and laggards.
Sticky	Sticky is a term used in economics used to describe a situation in which a variable is resistant to change. For example, nominal wages are often said to be sticky.
Scope	Scope of a project is the sum total of all projects products and their requirements or features.
Adoption	In corporation law, a corporation's acceptance of a pre-incorporation contract by action of its board of directors, by which the corporation becomes liable on the contract, is referred to as adoption.
Developing country	Developing country refers to a country whose per capita income is low by world standards. Same as LDC. As usually used, it does not necessarily connote that the country's income is rising.
Testimonial	Testimonial refers to a statement by a public figure professing the merits of some product or service.
Boycott	To protest by refusing to purchase from someone, or otherwise do business with them. In international trade, a boycott most often takes the form of refusal to import a country's goods.
Product safety	Product safety refers to a multi-step, scientific process to assess the probability that exposure to a product during any stage of its lifecycle will lead to a negative impact on human health or the environment.
Marketing Plan	Marketing plan refers to a road map for the marketing activities of an organization for a specified future period of time, such as one year or five years.
Domestic	From or in one's own country. A domestic producer is one that produces inside the home country. A domestic price is the price inside the home country. Opposite of 'foreign' or 'world.'.
Multinational corporation	An organization that manufactures and markets products in many different countries and has multinational stock ownership and multinational management is referred to as multinational corporation.

Go to **Cram101.com** for the Practice Tests for this Chapter.

General manager	A manager who is responsible for several departments that perform different functions is called general manager.
Operation	A standardized method or technique that is performed repetitively, often on different materials resulting in different finished goods is called an operation.
Industry	A group of firms that produce identical or similar products is an industry. It is also used specifically to refer to an area of economic production focused on manufacturing which involves large amounts of capital investment before any profit can be realized, also called "heavy industry".
Hasbro	Hasbro originated with the Mr. Potato Head toy. Mr. Potato Head was the invention of George Lerner in the late 1940s. The idea was originally sold to a breakfast cereal manufacturer so that the separate parts could be distributed as cereal package premiums.
Marketing	Promoting and selling products or services to customers, or prospective customers, is referred to as marketing.
Wall Street Journal	Dow Jones & Company was founded in 1882 by reporters Charles Dow, Edward Jones and Charles Bergstresser. Jones converted the small Customers' Afternoon Letter into The Wall Street Journal, first published in 1889, and began delivery of the Dow Jones News Service via telegraph. The Journal featured the Jones 'Average', the first of several indexes of stock and bond prices on the New York Stock Exchange.
Journal	Book of original entry, in which transactions are recorded in a general ledger system, is referred to as a journal.
Management	Management characterizes the process of leading and directing all or part of an organization, often a business, through the deployment and manipulation of resources. Early twentieth-century management writer Mary Parker Follett defined management as "the art of getting things done through people."
Market	A market is, as defined in economics, a social arrangement that allows buyers and sellers to discover information and carry out a voluntary exchange of goods or services.
Weber	Weber was a German political economist and sociologist who is considered one of the founders of the modern study of sociology and public administration. His major works deal with rationalization in sociology of religion and government, but he also wrote much in the field of economics. His most popular work is his essay The Protestant Ethic and the Spirit of Capitalism.
Profit	Profit refers to the return to the resource entrepreneurial ability; total revenue minus total cost.
Authority	Authority in agency law, refers to an agent's ability to affect his principal's legal relations with third parties. Also used to refer to an actor's legal power or ability to do something. In addition, sometimes used to refer to a statute, case, or other legal source that justifies a particular result.
Welfare	Welfare refers to the economic well being of an individual, group, or economy. For individuals, it is conceptualized by a utility function. For groups, including countries and the world, it is a tricky philosophical concept, since individuals fare differently.
Interest	In finance and economics, interest is the price paid by a borrower for the use of a lender's money. In other words, interest is the amount of paid to "rent" money for a period of time.
Business opportunity	A business opportunity involves the sale or lease of any product, service, equipment, etc. that will enable the purchaser-licensee to begin a business
Loyalty	Marketers tend to define customer loyalty as making repeat purchases. Some argue that it

Go to **Cram101.com** for the Practice Tests for this Chapter.

Go to **Cram101.com** for the Practice Tests for this Chapter.
And, **NEVER** highlight a book again!

81

should be defined attitudinally as a strongly positive feeling about the brand.

Accommodation	Accommodation is a term used to describe a delivery of nonconforming goods meant as a partial performance of a contract for the sale of goods, where a full performance is not possible.
Capitalism	Capitalism refers to an economic system in which capital is mostly owned by private individuals and corporations. Contrasts with communism.
Tactic	A short-term immediate decision that, in its totality, leads to the achievement of strategic goals is called a tactic.
Empathy	Empathy refers to dimension of service quality-caring individualized attention provided to customers.
Firm	An organization that employs resources to produce a good or service for profit and owns and operates one or more plants is referred to as a firm.
Customs	Customs is an authority or agency in a country responsible for collecting customs duties and for controlling the flow of people, animals and goods (including personal effects and hazardous items) in and out of the country.
Argument	The discussion by counsel for the respective parties of their contentions on the law and the facts of the case being tried in order to aid the jury in arriving at a correct and just conclusion is called argument.
Points	Loan origination fees that may be deductible as interest by a buyer of property. A seller of property who pays points reduces the selling price by the amount of the points paid for the buyer.
Trust	An arrangement in which shareholders of independent firms agree to give up their stock in exchange for trust certificates that entitle them to a share of the trust's common profits.
Trade minister	Trade minister refers to the government official, at the ministerial or cabinet level, primarily responsible for issues of international trade policy; the minister of international trade.
Commerce	Commerce is the exchange of something of value between two entities. It is the central mechanism from which capitalism is derived.
End user	End user refers to the ultimate user of a product or service.
Users	Users refer to people in the organization who actually use the product or service purchased by the buying center.
Agent	A person who makes economic decisions for another economic actor. A hired manager operates as an agent for a firm's owner.
Option	A contract that gives the purchaser the option to buy or sell the underlying financial instrument at a specified price, called the exercise price or strike price, within a specific period of time.
Goodwill	Goodwill is an important accounting concept that describes the value of a business entity not directly attributable to its tangible assets and liabilities.
Negotiation	Negotiation is the process whereby interested parties resolve disputes, agree upon courses of action, bargain for individual or collective advantage, and/or attempt to craft outcomes which serve their mutual interests.
Compliance	A type of influence process where a receiver accepts the position advocated by a source to obtain favorable outcomes or to avoid punishment is the compliance.
Allowance	Reduction in the selling price of goods extended to the buyer because the goods are defective

Go to **Cram101.com** for the Practice Tests for this Chapter.
And, **NEVER** highlight a book again!

83

or of lower quality than the buyer ordered and to encourage a buyer to keep merchandise that would otherwise be returned is the allowance.

Export
In economics, an export is any good or commodity, shipped or otherwise transported out of a country, province, town to another part of the world in a legitimate fashion, typically for use in trade or sale.

Drucker
Drucker as a business thinker took off in the 1940s, when his initial writings on politics and society won him access to the internal workings of General Motors, which was one of the largest companies in the world at that time. His experiences in Europe had left him fascinated with the problem of authority.

Futures
Futures refer to contracts for the sale and future delivery of stocks or commodities, wherein either party may waive delivery, and receive or pay, as the case may be, the difference in market price at the time set for delivery.

Corporation
A legal entity chartered by a state or the Federal government that is distinct and separate from the individuals who own it is a corporation. This separation gives the corporation unique powers which other legal entities lack.

Enterprise
Enterprise refers to another name for a business organization. Other similar terms are business firm, sometimes simply business, sometimes simply firm, as well as company, and entity.

Instrument
Instrument refers to an economic variable that is controlled by policy makers and can be used to influence other variables, called targets. Examples are monetary and fiscal policies used to achieve external and internal balance.

Continuity
A media scheduling strategy where a continuous pattern of advertising is used over the time span of the advertising campaign is continuity.

Personnel
A collective term for all of the employees of an organization. Personnel is also commonly used to refer to the personnel management function or the organizational unit responsible for administering personnel programs.

Promotion
Promotion refers to all the techniques sellers use to motivate people to buy products or services. An attempt by marketers to inform people about products and to persuade them to participate in an exchange.

Openness
Openness refers to the extent to which an economy is open, often measured by the ratio of its trade to GDP.

Status quo
Status quo is a Latin term meaning the present, current, existing state of affairs.

Adam Smith
Adam Smith (baptized June 5, 1723 O.S. (June 16 N.S.) – July 17, 1790) was a Scottish political economist and moral philosopher. His Inquiry into the Nature and Causes of the Wealth of Nations was one of the earliest attempts to study the historical development of industry and commerce in Europe. That work helped to create the modern academic discipline of economics

Invisible hand
Invisible hand refers to a phrase coined by Adam Smith to describe the process that turns self-directed gain into social and economic benefits for all.

Transaction cost
A transaction cost is a cost incurred in making an economic exchange. For example, most people, when buying or selling a stock, must pay a commission to their broker; that commission is a transaction cost of doing the stock deal.

International Business
International business refers to any firm that engages in international trade or investment.

Cultural values
The values that employees need to have and act on for the organization to act on the

Go to **Cram101.com** for the Practice Tests for this Chapter.

85

strategic values are called cultural values.

Committee	A long-lasting, sometimes permanent team in the organization structure created to deal with tasks that recur regularly is the committee.
Middle management	Middle management refers to the level of management that includes general managers, division managers, and branch and plant managers who are responsible for tactical planning and controlling.
Holding	The holding is a court's determination of a matter of law based on the issue presented in the particular case. In other words: under this law, with these facts, this result.
Collectivism	Collectivism is a term used to describe that things should be owned by the group and used for the benefit of all rather than being owned by individuals.
Hierarchy	A system of grouping people in an organization according to rank from the top down in which all subordinate managers must report to one person is called a hierarchy.
Foundation	A Foundation is a type of philanthropic organization set up by either individuals or institutions as a legal entity (either as a corporation or trust) with the purpose of distributing grants to support causes in line with the goals of the foundation.
Power distance	Power distance refers to the degree to which the less powerful members of society expect there to be differences in the levels of power. A high score suggests that there is an expectation that some individuals wield larger amounts of power than others. Countries with high power distance rating are often characterized by a high rate of political violence.
Security	Security refers to a claim on the borrower future income that is sold by the borrower to the lender. A security is a type of transferable interest representing financial value.
Standard of living	Standard of living refers to the level of consumption that people enjoy, on the average, and is measured by average income per person.
Economy	The income, expenditures, and resources that affect the cost of running a business and household are called an economy.
Supervisor	A Supervisor is an employee of an organization with some of the powers and responsibilities of management, occupying a role between true manager and a regular employee. A Supervisor position is typically the first step towards being promoted into a management role.
Harvard Business Review	Harvard Business Review is a research-based magazine written for business practitioners, it claims a high ranking business readership and enjoys the reverence of academics, executives, and management consultants. It has been the frequent publishing home for well known scholars and management thinkers.
Mitsubishi	In a statement, the Mitsubishi says that forced labor is inconsistent with the company's values, and that the various lawsuits targeting Mitsubishi are misdirected. Instead, a spokesman says the Mitsubishi of World War II is not the same Mitsubishi of today. The conglomerate also rejected a Chinese slave labor lawsuit demand by saying it bore no responsibility since it was national policy to employ Chinese laborers."
Consultant	A professional that provides expert advice in a particular field or area in which customers occasionaly require this type of knowledge is a consultant.
Innovation	Innovation refers to the first commercially successful introduction of a new product, the use of a new method of production, or the creation of a new form of business organization.
Brief	Brief refers to a statement of a party's case or legal arguments, usually prepared by an attorney. Also used to make legal arguments before appellate courts.
Extension	Extension refers to an out-of-court settlement in which creditors agree to allow the firm

Go to **Cram101.com** for the Practice Tests for this Chapter.

	more time to meet its financial obligations. A new repayment schedule will be developed, subject to the acceptance of creditors.
Prime minister	The Prime Minister of the United Kingdom of Great Britain and Northern Ireland is the head of government and so exercises many of the executive functions nominally vested in the Sovereign, who is head of state. According to custom, the Prime Minister and the Cabinet (which he or she heads) are accountable for their actions to Parliament, of which they are members by (modern) convention.
Microsoft	Microsoft is a multinational computer technology corporation with 2004 global annual sales of US$39.79 billion and 71,553 employees in 102 countries and regions as of July 2006. It develops, manufactures, licenses, and supports a wide range of software products for computing devices.
Dell Computer	Dell Computer, formerly PC's Limited, was founded on the principle that by selling personal computer systems directly to customers, PC's Limited could best understand their needs and provide the most effective computing solutions to meet those needs.
Boot	Boot is any type of personal property received in a real property transaction that is not like kind, such as cash, mortgage notes, a boat or stock. The exchanger pays taxes on the boot to the extent of recognized capital gain. In an exchange if any funds are not used in purchasing the replacement property, that also will be called boot.
Technology	The body of knowledge and techniques that can be used to combine economic resources to produce goods and services is called technology.
Diffusion	Diffusion is the process by which a new idea or new product is accepted by the market. The rate of diffusion is the speed that the new idea spreads from one consumer to the next.
Buyer	A buyer refers to a role in the buying center with formal authority and responsibility to select the supplier and negotiate the terms of the contract.
Variable	A variable is something measured by a number; it is used to analyze what happens to other things when the size of that number changes.
Global marketing	A strategy of using a common marketing plan and program for all countries in which a company operates, thus selling the product or services the same way everywhere in the world is called global marketing.
Common mistake	A common mistake is where both parties hold the same mistaken belief of the facts.
Mistake	In contract law a mistake is incorrect understanding by one or more parties to a contract and may be used as grounds to invalidate the agreement. Common law has identified three different types of mistake in contract: unilateral mistake, mutual mistake, and common mistake.
Polychronic	In The Silent Language (1959), Hall coined the term polychronic to describe the ability to attend to multiple events simultaneously.
Tangible	Having a physical existence is referred to as the tangible. Personal property other than real estate, such as cars, boats, stocks, or other assets.
Context	The effect of the background under which a message often takes on more and richer meaning is a context. Context is especially important in cross-cultural interactions because some cultures are said to be high context or low context.
Service	Service refers to a "non tangible product" that is not embodied in a physical good and that typically effects some change in another product, person, or institution. Contrasts with good.
Demographic	A demographic is a term used in marketing and broadcasting, to describe a demographic grouping or a market segment.

Go to Cram101.com for the Practice Tests for this Chapter.

Vendor	A person who sells property to a vendee is a vendor. The words vendor and vendee are more commonly applied to the seller and purchaser of real estate, and the words seller and buyer are more commonly applied to the seller and purchaser of personal property.
Assignment	A transfer of property or some right or interest is referred to as assignment.
Prejudice	Prejudice is, as the name implies, the process of "pre-judging" something. It implies coming to a judgment on a subject before learning where the preponderance of evidence actually lies, or forming a judgment without direct experience.
Labor	People's physical and mental talents and efforts that are used to help produce goods and services are called labor.
Organizational Behavior	The study of human behavior in organizational settings, the interface between human behavior and the organization, and the organization itself is called organizational behavior.
International dimension	Portion of the external environment that represents events originating in foreign countries as well as opportunities for domestic companies in other countries is called international dimension.
Lufthansa	Lufthansa is a founding member of Star Alliance, the largest airline alliance in the world. The Lufthansa Group operates more than 400 aircraft and employs nearly 100,000 people worldwide.
Glass ceiling	Glass ceiling refers to a term that refers to the many barriers that can exist to thwart a woman's rise to the top of an organization; one that provides a view of the top, but a ceiling on how far a woman can go.
Domestic	From or in one's own country. A domestic producer is one that produces inside the home country. A domestic price is the price inside the home country. Opposite of 'foreign' or 'world.'.
Business ethics	The study of what makes up good and bad conduct as related to business activities and values is business ethics.
Value judgment	Value judgment refers to an opinion of what is desirable or undesirable; belief regarding what ought or ought not to be.
Corruption	The unauthorized use of public office for private gain. The most common forms of corruption are bribery, extortion, and the misuse of inside information.
Marxism	The set of social, political, and economic doctrines developed by Karl Marx in the nineteenth century. As an economic theory, Marxism predicted that capitalism would collapse as a result of its own internal contradictions.
Reuters	Reuters is best known as a news service that provides reports from around the world to newspapers and broadcasters. Its main focus is on supplying the financial markets with information and trading products.
Consumerism	Consumerism is a term used to describe the effects of equating personal happiness with purchasing material possessions and consumption.
Intellectual property	In law, intellectual property is an umbrella term for various legal entitlements which attach to certain types of information, ideas, or other intangibles in their expressed form. The holder of this legal entitlement is generally entitled to exercise various exclusive rights in relation to its subject matter.
Property	Assets defined in the broadest legal sense. Property includes the unrealized receivables of a cash basis taxpayer, but not services rendered.
Aid	Assistance provided by countries and by international institutions such as the World Bank to

developing countries in the form of monetary grants, loans at low interest rates, in kind, or a combination of these is called aid. Aid can also refer to assistance of any type rendered to benefit some group or individual.

Financial crisis
A loss of confidence in a country's currency or other financial assets causing international investors to withdraw their funds from the country is referred to as a financial crisis.

Marketing research
Marketing research refers to the analysis of markets to determine opportunities and challenges, and to find the information needed to make good decisions.

WorldCom
WorldCom was the United States' second largest long distance phone company (AT&T was the largest). WorldCom grew largely by acquiring other telecommunications companies, most notably MCI Communications. It also owned the Tier 1 ISP UUNET, a major part of the Internet backbone.

Bribery
When one person gives another person money, property, favors, or anything else of value for a favor in return, we have bribery. Often referred to as a payoff or 'kickback.'

Enron
Enron Corportaion's global reputation was undermined by persistent rumours of bribery and political pressure to secure contracts in Central America, South America, Africa, and the Philippines. Especially controversial was its $3 billion contract with the Maharashtra State Electricity Board in India, where it is alleged that Enron officials used political connections within the Clinton and Bush administrations to exert pressure on the board.

Fraud
Tax fraud falls into two categories: civil and criminal. Under civil fraud, the IRS may impose as a penalty of an amount equal to as much as 75 percent of the underpayment.

Publicly held corporation
Publicly held corporation refers to a corporation that may have thousands of stockholders and whose stock is regularly traded on a national securities market.

Exchange
The trade of things of value between buyer and seller so that each is better off after the trade is called the exchange.

Regulation
Regulation refers to restrictions state and federal laws place on business with regard to the conduct of its activities.

Corporate tax
Corporate tax refers to a direct tax levied by various jurisdictions on the profits made by companies or associations. As a general principle, this varies substantially between jurisdictions.

Contract A
Contract A is a concept applied in Canadian contract law (a Common Law system country) which has recently been applied by courts regarding the fairness and equal treatment of bidders in a contract tendering process. Essentially this concept formalises previously applied precedents and strengthens the protection afforded to Contractors in the tendering process.

Contract
A contract is a "promise" or an "agreement" that is enforced or recognized by the law. In the civil law, a contract is considered to be part of the general law of obligations.

Expense
In accounting, an expense represents an event in which an asset is used up or a liability is incurred. In terms of the accounting equation, expenses reduce owners' equity.

Competitor
Other organizations in the same industry or type of business that provide a good or service to the same set of customers is referred to as a competitor.

Complaint
The pleading in a civil case in which the plaintiff states his claim and requests relief is called complaint. In the common law, it is a formal legal document that sets out the basic facts and legal reasons that the filing party (the plaintiffs) believes are sufficient to support a claim against another person, persons, entity or entities (the defendants) that entitles the plaintiff(s) to a remedy (either money damages or injunctive relief).

Organization
Organization for economic cooperation and development refers to Paris-based intergovernmental

for economic cooperation and development	organization of 'wealthy' nations whose purpose is to provide its 29 member states with a forum in which governments can compare their experiences, discuss the problems they share, and seek solutions that can then be applied within their own national contexts.
Accord	An agreement whereby the parties agree to accept something different in satisfaction of the original contract is an accord.
Transparency	Transparency refers to a concept that describes a company being so open to other companies working with it that the once-solid barriers between them become see-through and electronic information is shared as if the companies were one.
Coalition	An informal alliance among managers who support a specific goal is called coalition.
Policy	Similar to a script in that a policy can be a less than completely rational decision-making method. Involves the use of a pre-existing set of decision steps for any problem that presents itself.
Analyst	Analyst refers to a person or tool with a primary function of information analysis, generally with a more limited, practical and short term set of goals than a researcher.
Transparency International	Transparency International is an international organization addressing corruption, including, but not limited to, political corruption.
Hearing	A hearing is a proceeding before a court or other decision-making body or officer. A hearing is generally distinguished from a trial in that it is usually shorter and often less formal.
Political economy	Early name for the discipline of economics. A field within economics encompassing several alternatives to neoclassical economics, including Marxist economics. Also called radical political economy.
Consumption	In Keynesian economics consumption refers to personal consumption expenditure, i.e., the purchase of currently produced goods and services out of income, out of savings (net worth), or from borrowed funds. It refers to that part of disposable income that does not go to saving.
Communism	Communism refers to an economic system in which capital is owned by private government. Contrasts with capitalism.
Direct investment	Direct investment refers to a domestic firm actually investing in and owning a foreign subsidiary or division.
Investment	Investment refers to spending for the production and accumulation of capital and additions to inventories. In a financial sense, buying an asset with the expectation of making a return.
Foreign direct investment	Foreign direct investment refers to the buying of permanent property and businesses in foreign nations.
Capital	Capital generally refers to financial wealth, especially that used to start or maintain a business. In classical economics, capital is one of four factors of production, the others being land and labor and entrepreneurship.
Allegation	An allegation is a statement of a fact by a party in a pleading, which the party claims it will prove. Allegations remain assertions without proof, only claims until they are proved.
Foreign Corrupt Practices Act	The Foreign Corrupt Practices Act of 1977 is a United States federal law requiring any company that has publicly-traded stock to maintain records that accurately and fairly represent the company's transactions; additionally, requires any publicly-traded company to have an adequate system of internal accounting controls.
Comprehensive	A comprehensive refers to a layout accurate in size, color, scheme, and other necessary details to show how a final ad will look. For presentation only, never for reproduction.

Business operations	Business operations are those activities involved in the running of a business for the purpose of producing value for the stakeholders. The outcome of business operations is the harvesting of value from assets owned by a business.
Consumer protection	Consumer protection is government regulation to protect the interests of consumers, for example by requiring businesses to disclose detailed information about products, particularly in areas where safety or public health is an issue, such as food.
Social responsibility	Social responsibility is a doctrine that claims that an entity whether it is state, government, corporation, organization or individual has a responsibility to society.
Controlling	A management function that involves determining whether or not an organization is progressing toward its goals and objectives, and taking corrective action if it is not is called controlling.
Business strategy	Business strategy, which refers to the aggregated operational strategies of single business firm or that of an SBU in a diversified corporation refers to the way in which a firm competes in its chosen arenas.
Revenue	Revenue is a U.S. business term for the amount of money that a company receives from its activities, mostly from sales of products and/or services to customers.
Boeing	Boeing is the world's largest aircraft manufacturer by revenue. Headquartered in Chicago, Illinois, Boeing is the second-largest defense contractor in the world. In 2005, the company was the world's largest civil aircraft manufacturer in terms of value.
Layoff	A layoff is the termination of an employee or (more commonly) a group of employees for business reasons, such as the decision that certain positions are no longer necessary.
Reciprocity	An industrial buying practice in which two organizations agree to purchase each other's products and services is called reciprocity.
Frequency	Frequency refers to the speed of the up and down movements of a fluctuating economic variable; that is, the number of times per unit of time that the variable completes a cycle of up and down movement.
Cost advantage	Possession of a lower cost of production or operation than a competing firm or country is cost advantage.
Closing	The finalization of a real estate sales transaction that passes title to the property from the seller to the buyer is referred to as a closing. Closing is a sales term which refers to the process of making a sale. It refers to reaching the final step, which may be an exchange of money or acquiring a signature.
Subculture	A subgroups within the larger, or national, culture with unique values, ideas, and attitudes is a subculture.
Consideration	Consideration in contract law, a basic requirement for an enforceable agreement under traditional contract principles, defined in this text as legal value, bargained for and given in exchange for an act or promise. In corporation law, cash or property contributed to a corporation in exchange for shares, or a promise to contribute such cash or property.
Decentralization	Decentralization is the process of redistributing decision-making closer to the point of service or action. This gives freedom to managers at lower levels of the organization to make decisions.
Scope	Scope of a project is the sum total of all projects products and their requirements or features.
Shell	One of the original Seven Sisters, Royal Dutch/Shell is the world's third-largest oil company by revenue, and a major player in the petrochemical industry and the solar energy business.

Shell has six core businesses: Exploration and Production, Gas and Power, Downstream, Chemicals, Renewables, and Trading/Shipping, and operates in more than 140 countries.

Nike   Because Nike creates goods for a wide range of sports, they have competition from every sports and sports fashion brand there is. Nike has no direct competitors because there is no single brand which can compete directly with their range of sports and non-sports oriented gear, except for Reebok.

Go to **Cram101.com** for the Practice Tests for this Chapter.
And, **NEVER** highlight a book again!

Retaliation	The use of an increased trade barrier in response to another country increasing its trade barrier, either as a way of undoing the adverse effects of the latter's action or of punishing it is retaliation.
Tariff	A tax imposed by a nation on an imported good is called a tariff.
Union	A worker association that bargains with employers over wages and working conditions is called a union.
Trade war	Trade war refers to generally, a period in which each of two countries alternate in further restricting trade from the other. More specifically, the process of tariffs and retaliation.
Dealer	People who link buyers with sellers by buying and selling securities at stated prices are referred to as a dealer.
Enterprise	Enterprise refers to another name for a business organization. Other similar terms are business firm, sometimes simply business, sometimes simply firm, as well as company, and entity.
Supply	Supply is the aggregate amount of any material good that can be called into being at a certain price point; it comprises one half of the equation of supply and demand. In classical economic theory, a curve representing supply is one of the factors that produce price.
Customs	Customs is an authority or agency in a country responsible for collecting customs duties and for controlling the flow of people, animals and goods (including personal effects and hazardous items) in and out of the country.
Banana war	Banana war refers to a trade dispute between the EU and the U.S. over EU preferences for bananas from former colonies. On behalf of U.S.-owned companies exporting bananas from South America and the Caribbean, the US complained to the WTO, which ruled in favor of the U.S.
Industry	A group of firms that produce identical or similar products is an industry. It is also used specifically to refer to an area of economic production focused on manufacturing which involves large amounts of capital investment before any profit can be realized, also called "heavy industry".
Corporation	A legal entity chartered by a state or the Federal government that is distinct and separate from the individuals who own it is a corporation. This separation gives the corporation unique powers which other legal entities lack.
Export	In economics, an export is any good or commodity, shipped or otherwise transported out of a country, province, town to another part of the world in a legitimate fashion, typically for use in trade or sale.
Quota	A government-imposed restriction on quantity, or sometimes on total value, used to restrict the import of something to a specific quantity is called a quota.
Firm	An organization that employs resources to produce a good or service for profit and owns and operates one or more plants is referred to as a firm.
Trade barrier	An artificial disincentive to export and/or import, such as a tariff, quota, or other NTB is called a trade barrier.
Brand	A name, symbol, or design that identifies the goods or services of one seller or group of sellers and distinguishes them from the goods and services of competitors is a brand.
Contribution	In business organization law, the cash or property contributed to a business by its owners is referred to as contribution.
Grievance	A charge by employees that management is not abiding by the terms of the negotiated labormanagement agreement is the grievance.

Compliance	A type of influence process where a receiver accepts the position advocated by a source to obtain favorable outcomes or to avoid punishment is the compliance.
Market	A market is, as defined in economics, a social arrangement that allows buyers and sellers to discover information and carry out a voluntary exchange of goods or services.
Production	The creation of finished goods and services using the factors of production: land, labor, capital, entrepreneurship, and knowledge.
Domestic	From or in one's own country. A domestic producer is one that produces inside the home country. A domestic price is the price inside the home country. Opposite of 'foreign' or 'world.'.
Business plan	A detailed written statement that describes the nature of the business, the target market, the advantages the business will have in relation to competition, and the resources and qualifications of the owner is referred to as a business plan.
International Business	International business refers to any firm that engages in international trade or investment.
Policy	Similar to a script in that a policy can be a less than completely rational decision-making method. Involves the use of a pre-existing set of decision steps for any problem that presents itself.
Interest	In finance and economics, interest is the price paid by a borrower for the use of a lender's money. In other words, interest is the amount of paid to "rent" money for a period of time.
International law	Law that governs affairs between nations and that regulates transactions between individuals and businesses of different countries is an international law.
Grant	Grant refers to an intergovernmental transfer of funds . Since the New Deal, state and local governments have become increasingly dependent upon federal grants for an almost infinite variety of programs.
Sovereignty	A country or region's power and ability to rule itself and manage its own affairs. Some feel that membership in international organizations such as the WTO is a threat to their sovereignty.
Context	The effect of the background under which a message often takes on more and richer meaning is a context. Context is especially important in cross-cultural interactions because some cultures are said to be high context or low context.
Extension	Extension refers to an out-of-court settlement in which creditors agree to allow the firm more time to meet its financial obligations. A new repayment schedule will be developed, subject to the acceptance of creditors.
Gain	In finance, gain is a profit or an increase in value of an investment such as a stock or bond. Gain is calculated by fair market value or the proceeds from the sale of the investment minus the sum of the purchase price and all costs associated with it.
Arbitration	Arbitration is a form of mediation or conciliation, where the mediating party is given power by the disputant parties to settle the dispute by making a finding. In practice arbitration is generally used as a substitute for judicial systems, particularly when the judicial processes are viewed as too slow, expensive or biased. Arbitration is also used by communities which lack formal law, as a substitute for formal law.
Covenant	A covenant is a signed written agreement between two or more parties. Also referred to as a contract.
Investment	Investment refers to spending for the production and accumulation of capital and additions to inventories. In a financial sense, buying an asset with the expectation of making a return.

Go to **Cram101.com** for the Practice Tests for this Chapter.

Go to **Cram101.com** for the Practice Tests for this Chapter.
And, **NEVER** highlight a book again!

Monopoly	A monopoly is defined as a persistent market situation where there is only one provider of a kind of product or service.
Assault	An intentional tort that prohibits any attempt or offer to cause harmful or offensive contact with another if it results in a well-grounded apprehension of imminent battery in the mind of the threatened person is called assault.
Variable	A variable is something measured by a number; it is used to analyze what happens to other things when the size of that number changes.
Multinational corporation	An organization that manufactures and markets products in many different countries and has multinational stock ownership and multinational management is referred to as multinational corporation.
Political risk	Refers to the many different actions of people, subgroups, and whole countries that have the potential to affect the financial status of a firm is called political risk.
Rule of law	A legal system in which rules are clear, well-understood, and fairly enforced, including property rights and enforcement of contracts is called rule of law.
Continuity	A media scheduling strategy where a continuous pattern of advertising is used over the time span of the advertising campaign is continuity.
Open market	In economics, the open market is the term used to refer to the environment in which bonds are bought and sold.
Bureaucracy	Bureaucracy refers to an organization with many layers of managers who set rules and regulations and oversee all decisions.
Analogy	Analogy is either the cognitive process of transferring information from a particular subject to another particular subject (the target), or a linguistic expression corresponding to such a process. In a narrower sense, analogy is an inference or an argument from a particular to another particular, as opposed to deduction, induction, and abduction, where at least one of the premises or the conclusion is general.
Reuters	Reuters is best known as a news service that provides reports from around the world to newspapers and broadcasters. Its main focus is on supplying the financial markets with information and trading products.
Expropriation	Expropriation is the act of removing from control the owner of an item of property. The term is used to both refer to acts by a government or by any group of people.
Administration	Administration refers to the management and direction of the affairs of governments and institutions; a collective term for all policymaking officials of a government; the execution and implementation of public policy.
Gross domestic product	Gross domestic product refers to the total value of new goods and services produced in a given year within the borders of a country, regardless of by whom.
Trade association	An industry trade group or trade association is generally a public relations organization founded and funded by corporations that operate in a specific industry. Its purpose is generally to promote that industry through PR activities such as advertizing, education, political donations, political pressure, publishing, and astroturfing.
Free trade	Free trade refers to a situation in which there are no artificial barriers to trade, such as tariffs and quotas. Usually used, often only implicitly, with frictionless trade, so that it implies that there are no barriers to trade of any kind.
Brief	Brief refers to a statement of a party's case or legal arguments, usually prepared by an attorney. Also used to make legal arguments before appellate courts.

Go to **Cram101.com** for the Practice Tests for this Chapter.
And, **NEVER** highlight a book again!

105

Appeal	Appeal refers to the act of asking an appellate court to overturn a decision after the trial court's final judgment has been entered.
World Bank	The World Bank is a group of five international organizations responsible for providing finance and advice to countries for the purposes of economic development and poverty reduction, and for encouraging and safeguarding international investment.
Profit	Profit refers to the return to the resource entrepreneurial ability; total revenue minus total cost.
PepsiCo	In many ways, PepsiCo differs from its main competitor, having three times as many employees, larger revenues, but a smaller net profit.
Disintegration	Disintegration is an organization of production in which different stages of production are divided among different suppliers that are located in different countries.
Hearing	A hearing is a proceeding before a court or other decision-making body or officer. A hearing is generally distinguished from a trial in that it is usually shorter and often less formal.
Economic nationalism	Economic nationalism is a term used to describe policies which are guided by the idea of protecting domestic consumption, labor and capital formation, even if this requires the imposition of tariffs and other restrictions on the movement of labor, goods and capital. Economic nationalism may include such doctrines as protectionism and import substitution.
Consideration	Consideration in contract law, a basic requirement for an enforceable agreement under traditional contract principles, defined in this text as legal value, bargained for and given in exchange for an act or promise. In corporation law, cash or property contributed to a corporation in exchange for shares, or a promise to contribute such cash or property.
Security	Security refers to a claim on the borrower future income that is sold by the borrower to the lender. A security is a type of transferable interest representing financial value.
Economic development	Increase in the economic standard of living of a country's population, normally accomplished by increasing its stocks of physical and human capital and improving its technology is an economic development.
Capital	Capital generally refers to financial wealth, especially that used to start or maintain a business. In classical economics, capital is one of four factors of production, the others being land and labor and entrepreneurship.
Marketing management	Marketing management refers to the process of planning and executing the conception, pricing, promotion, and distribution of ideas, goods, and services to create mutually beneficial exchanges.
Purchasing	Purchasing refers to the function in a firm that searches for quality material resources, finds the best suppliers, and negotiates the best price for goods and services.
Management	Management characterizes the process of leading and directing all or part of an organization, often a business, through the deployment and manipulation of resources. Early twentieth-century management writer Mary Parker Follett defined management as "the art of getting things done through people."
Marketing	Promoting and selling products or services to customers, or prospective customers, is referred to as marketing.
Journal	Book of original entry, in which transactions are recorded in a general ledger system, is referred to as a journal.
Draft	A signed, written order by which one party instructs another party to pay a specified sum to a third party, at sight or at a specific date is a draft.

Antiglobaliz-tion	Antiglobalization is a term most commonly ascribed to the political stance of people and groups who oppose certain aspects of globalization in its current form, often including the domination of current global trade agreements and trade-governing bodies such as the World Trade Organization by powerful corporations.
Great Depression	The period of severe economic contraction and high unemployment that began in 1929 and continued throughout the 1930s is referred to as the Great Depression.
Globalization	The increasing world-wide integration of markets for goods, services and capital that attracted special attention in the late 1990s is called globalization.
Depression	Depression refers to a prolonged period characterized by high unemployment, low output and investment, depressed business confidence, falling prices, and widespread business failures. A milder form of business downturn is a recession.
Equity	Equity is the name given to the set of legal principles, in countries following the English common law tradition, which supplement strict rules of law where their application would operate harshly, so as to achieve what is sometimes referred to as "natural justice."
Shares	Shares refer to an equity security, representing a shareholder's ownership of a corporation. Shares are one of a finite number of equal portions in the capital of a company, entitling the owner to a proportion of distributed, non-reinvested profits known as dividends and to a portion of the value of the company in case of liquidation.
Multinational corporations	Firms that own production facilities in two or more countries and produce and sell their products globally are referred to as multinational corporations.
Developing country	Developing country refers to a country whose per capita income is low by world standards. Same as LDC. As usually used, it does not necessarily connote that the country's income is rising.
Market share	That fraction of an industry's output accounted for by an individual firm or group of firms is called market share.
Consumption	In Keynesian economics consumption refers to personal consumption expenditure, i.e., the purchase of currently produced goods and services out of income, out of savings (net worth), or from borrowed funds. It refers to that part of disposable income that does not go to saving.
Subsidiary	A company that is controlled by another company or corporation is a subsidiary.
Per capita	Per capita refers to per person. Usually used to indicate the average per person of any given statistic, commonly income.
Institutional investors	Institutional investors refers to large organizations such as pension funds, mutual funds, insurance companies, and banks that invest their own funds or the funds of others.
Wall Street Journal	Dow Jones & Company was founded in 1882 by reporters Charles Dow, Edward Jones and Charles Bergstresser. Jones converted the small Customers' Afternoon Letter into The Wall Street Journal, first published in 1889, and began delivery of the Dow Jones News Service via telegraph. The Journal featured the Jones 'Average', the first of several indexes of stock and bond prices on the New York Stock Exchange.
Bid	A bid price is a price offered by a buyer when he/she buys a good. In the context of stock trading on a stock exchange, the bid price is the highest price a buyer of a stock is willing to pay for a share of that given stock.
Business Week	Business Week is a business magazine published by McGraw-Hill. It was first published in 1929 under the direction of Malcolm Muir, who was serving as president of the McGraw-Hill Publishing company at the time. It is considered to be the standard both in industry and

Go to **Cram101.com** for the Practice Tests for this Chapter.

among students.

Trade deficit	The amount by which imports exceed exports of goods and services is referred to as trade deficit.
Deficit	The deficit is the amount by which expenditure exceed revenue.
Balance	In banking and accountancy, the outstanding balance is the amount of money owned, (or due), that remains in a deposit account (or a loan account) at a given date, after all past remittances, payments and withdrawal have been accounted for. It can be positive (then, in the balance sheet of a firm, it is an asset) or negative (a liability).
Welfare	Welfare refers to the economic well being of an individual, group, or economy. For individuals, it is conceptualized by a utility function. For groups, including countries and the world, it is a tricky philosophical concept, since individuals fare differently.
Press release	A written public news announcement normally distributed to major news services is referred to as press release.
News release	A publicity tool consisting of an announcement regarding changes in the company or the product line is called a news release.
Boycott	To protest by refusing to purchase from someone, or otherwise do business with them. In international trade, a boycott most often takes the form of refusal to import a country's goods.
Economy	The income, expenditures, and resources that affect the cost of running a business and household are called an economy.
Exchange control	Rationing of foreign exchange, typically used when the exchange rate is fixed and the central bank is unable or unwilling to enforce the rate by exchange-market intervention is an exchange control.
Regulation	Regulation refers to restrictions state and federal laws place on business with regard to the conduct of its activities.
Exchange	The trade of things of value between buyer and seller so that each is better off after the trade is called the exchange.
Asset	An item of property, such as land, capital, money, a share in ownership, or a claim on others for future payment, such as a bond or a bank deposit is an asset.
Property	Assets defined in the broadest legal sense. Property includes the unrealized receivables of a cash basis taxpayer, but not services rendered.
Economic growth	Economic growth refers to the increase over time in the capacity of an economy to produce goods and services and to improve the well-being of its citizens.
Host country	The country in which the parent-country organization seeks to locate or has already located a facility is a host country.
Takeover	A takeover in business refers to one company (the acquirer) purchasing another (the target). Such events resemble mergers, but without the formation of a new company.
Labor	People's physical and mental talents and efforts that are used to help produce goods and services are called labor.
Technology	The body of knowledge and techniques that can be used to combine economic resources to produce goods and services is called technology.
Privatization	A process in which investment bankers take companies that were previously owned by the government to the public markets is referred to as privatization.

Foreign exchange	In finance, foreign exchange means currencies, such as U.S. Dollars and Euros. These are traded on foreign exchange markets.
Exchange rate	Exchange rate refers to the price at which one country's currency trades for another, typically on the exchange market.
Official rate	Official rate refers to the par value of a pegged exchange rate.
Liability	A liability is a present obligation of the enterprise arizing from past events, the settlement of which is expected to result in an outflow from the enterprise of resources embodying economic benefits.
Economic risk	The likelihood that events, including economic mismanagement, will cause drastic changes in a country's business environment that adversely affects the profit and other goals of a particular business enterprise is referred to as economic risk.
Infant industry	Infant industry refers to a young industry that may need temporary protection from competition from the established industries of other countries to develop an acquired comparative advantage.
Revenue	Revenue is a U.S. business term for the amount of money that a company receives from its activities, mostly from sales of products and/or services to customers.
Foreign exchange reserves	Foreign exchange reserves are the foreign currency deposits held by national banks of different nations. These are assets of governments which are held in different reserve currencies such as the dollar, euro and yen.
Operation	A standardized method or technique that is performed repetitively, often on different materials resulting in different finished goods is called an operation.
Currency control	Currency control is a system whereby a country tries to regulate the value of money (currency) within its borders. From simple to complex policy changes, it can be characterized as a government initiated system to control currency fluctuations through interest rates, bonds, laws, money printing, and many more.
General Motors	General Motors is the world's largest automaker. Founded in 1908, today it employs about 327,000 people around the world. With global headquarters in Detroit, it manufactures its cars and trucks in 33 countries.
Creditor	A person to whom a debt or legal obligation is owed, and who has the right to enforce payment of that debt or obligation is referred to as creditor.
Cabinet	The heads of the executive departments of a jurisdiction who report to and advise its chief executive; examples would include the president's cabinet, the governor's cabinet, and the mayor's cabinet.
Trade union	A Trade Union, as we understand the term, is a continuous association of wage-earners for the purpose of maintaining or improving the conditions of their employment. They may organise strikes or resistance to lockouts in furtherance of particular goals.
Layoff	A layoff is the termination of an employee or (more commonly) a group of employees for business reasons, such as the decision that certain positions are no longer necessary.
Controlling	A management function that involves determining whether or not an organization is progressing toward its goals and objectives, and taking corrective action if it is not is called controlling.
Service	Service refers to a "non tangible product" that is not embodied in a physical good and that typically effects some change in another product, person, or institution. Contrasts with good.

Go to **Cram101.com** for the Practice Tests for this Chapter.

Go to **Cram101.com** for the Practice Tests for this Chapter.
And, **NEVER** highlight a book again!

Agent	A person who makes economic decisions for another economic actor. A hired manager operates as an agent for a firm's owner.
Fund	Independent accounting entity with a self-balancing set of accounts segregated for the purposes of carrying on specific activities is referred to as a fund.
Public interest	The universal label that political actors wrap around the policies and programs that they advocate is referred to as public interest.
Cost of living	The amount of money it takes to buy the goods and services that a typical family consumes is the cost of living.
Labor union	A group of workers organized to advance the interests of the group is called a labor union.
Concession	A concession is a business operated under a contract or license associated with a degree of exclusivity in exploiting a business within a certain geographical area. For example, sports arenas or public parks may have concession stands; and public services such as water supply may be operated as concessions.
Wage	The payment for the service of a unit of labor, per unit time. In trade theory, it is the only payment to labor, usually unskilled labor. In empirical work, wage data may exclude other compenzation, which must be added to get the total cost of employment.
Kmart	Kmart is an international chain of discount department stores in the United States, Australia, and New Zealand. Kmart merged with Sears in early 2005, creating the Sears Holdings Corporation.
Publicity	Publicity refers to any information about an individual, product, or organization that's distributed to the public through the media and that's not paid for or controlled by the seller.
Full employment	Full employment refers to the unemployment rate at which there is no cyclical unemployment of the labor force; equal to between 4 and 5 percent in the United States because some frictional and structural unemployment is unavoidable.
Nestle	Nestle is the world's biggest food and beverage company. In the 1860s, a pharmacist, developed a food for babies who were unable to be breastfed. His first success was a premature infant who could not tolerate his own mother's milk nor any of the usual substitutes. The value of the new product was quickly recognized when his new formula saved the child's life.
Pizza Hut	Pizza Hut is the world's largest pizza restaurant chain with nearly 34,000 restaurants, delivery-carry out units, and kiosks in 100 countries
Joint venture	Joint venture refers to an undertaking by two parties for a specific purpose and duration, taking any of several legal forms.
International Monetary Fund	The International Monetary Fund is the international organization entrusted with overseeing the global financial system by monitoring exchange rates and balance of payments, as well as offering technical and financial assistance when asked.
Nike	Because Nike creates goods for a wide range of sports, they have competition from every sports and sports fashion brand there is. Nike has no direct competitors because there is no single brand which can compete directly with their range of sports and non-sports oriented gear, except for Reebok.
Aid	Assistance provided by countries and by international institutions such as the World Bank to developing countries in the form of monetary grants, loans at low interest rates, in kind, or a combination of these is called aid. Aid can also refer to assistance of any type rendered to benefit some group or individual.

Michelin	Incorporated on May 28, 1888, Michelin's activities date back to 1830 in vulcanized rubber, before they moved into tires for bicycles and later for cars. Michelin owned the automobile manufacturer Citroën between 1934 and 1976.
Commerce	Commerce is the exchange of something of value between two entities. It is the central mechanism from which capitalism is derived.
Pawn	In law a pledge (also pawn) is a bailment of personal property as a security for some debt or engagement
Emerging markets	The term emerging markets is commonly used to describe business and market activity in industrializing or emerging regions of the world. It is sometimes loosely used as a replacement for emerging economies, but really signifies a business phenomenon that is not fully described by or constrained to geography or economic strength; such countries are considered to be in a transitional phase between developing and developed status.
Emerging market	The term emerging market is commonly used to describe business and market activity in industrializing or emerging regions of the world.
Yahoo	Yahoo is an American computer services company. It operates an Internet portal, the Yahoo Directory and a host of other services including the popular Yahoo Mail. Yahoo is the most visited website on the Internet today with more than 400 million unique users. The global network of Yahoo! websites received 3.4 billion page views per day on average as of October 2005.
Manufacturing	Production of goods primarily by the application of labor and capital to raw materials and other intermediate inputs, in contrast to agriculture, mining, forestry, fishing, and services a manufacturing.
Users	Users refer to people in the organization who actually use the product or service purchased by the buying center.
Petition	A petition is a request to an authority, most commonly a government official or public entity. In the colloquial sense, a petition is a document addressed to some official and signed by numerous individuals.
Google	As it has grown, Google has found itself the focus of various controversies related to its business practices and services. For example, Google Print's effort to digitize millions of books and make the full text searchable has led to copyright disputes with the Authors Guild, cooperation with the governments of China, France and Germany to filter search results in accordance to regional laws and regulations has led to claims of censorship.
Customs duty	A customs duty is a tariff or tax on the import or export of goods.
Accounting	A system that collects and processes financial information about an organization and reports that information to decision makers is referred to as accounting.
Authority	Authority in agency law, refers to an agent's ability to affect his principal's legal relations with third parties. Also used to refer to an actor's legal power or ability to do something. In addition, sometimes used to refer to a statute, case, or other legal source that justifies a particular result.
Political instability	Events such as riots, revolutions, or government upheavals that affect the operations of an international company is called political instability.
Assessment	Collecting information and providing feedback to employees about their behavior, communication style, or skills is an assessment.
Child labor	Originally, the employment of children in a manner detrimental to their health and social development. Now that the law contains strong child labor prohibitions, the term refers to

Go to **Cram101.com** for the Practice Tests for this Chapter.
And, **NEVER** highlight a book again!

the employment of children below the legal age limit.

Developed country

A developed country is one that enjoys a relatively high standard of living derived through an industrialized, diversified economy. Countries with a very high Human Development Index are generally considered developed countries.

Evaluation

The consumer's appraisal of the product or brand on important attributes is called evaluation.

Labor force

In economics the labor force is the group of people who have a potential for being employed.

Gap

In December of 1995, Gap became the first major North American retailer to accept independent monitoring of the working conditions in a contract factory producing its garments. Gap is the largest specialty retailer in the United States.

Maquiladora

A maquiladora is a factory that imports materials and equipment on a duty-free and tariff-free basis for assembly or manufacturing and then re-exports the assembled product usually back to the originating country.

Incentive

An incentive is any factor (financial or non-financial) that provides a motive for a particular course of action, or counts as a reason for preferring one choice to the alternatives.

Import substitution

Import substitution refers to a strategy for economic development that replaces imports with domestic production. It may be motivated by the infant industry argument, or simply by the desire to mimic the industrial structure of advanced countries.

Balance of payments

Balance of payments refers to a list, or accounting, of all of a country's international transactions for a given time period, usually one year.

Social responsibility

Social responsibility is a doctrine that claims that an entity whether it is state, government, corporation, organization or individual has a responsibility to society.

Expense

In accounting, an expense represents an event in which an asset is used up or a liability is incurred. In terms of the accounting equation, expenses reduce owners' equity.

Compaq

Compaq was founded in February 1982 by Rod Canion, Jim Harris and Bill Murto, three senior managers from semiconductor manufacturer Texas Instruments. Each invested $1,000 to form the company. Their first venture capital came from Ben Rosen and Sevin-Rosen partners. It is often told that the architecture of the original PC was first sketched out on a placemat by the founders while dining in the Houston restaurant, House of Pies.

Strike

The withholding of labor services by an organized group of workers is referred to as a strike.

Marketing strategy

Marketing strategy refers to the means by which a marketing goal is to be achieved, usually characterized by a specified target market and a marketing program to reach it.

Managing director

Managing director is the term used for the chief executive of many limited companies in the United Kingdom, Commonwealth and some other English speaking countries. The title reflects their role as both a member of the Board of Directors but also as the senior manager.

Logo

Logo refers to device or other brand name that cannot be spoken.

Global citizenship

Global citizenship is a person's obligation to respect and protect their environment and people around them while thinking on a global scale. This can be related to globalization.

Bargaining power

Bargaining power refers to the ability to influence the setting of prices or wages, usually arising from some sort of monopoly or monopsony position

Licensing

Licensing is a form of strategic alliance which involves the sale of a right to use certain proprietary knowledge (so called intellectual property) in a defined way.

Go to **Cram101.com** for the Practice Tests for this Chapter.

License	A license in the sphere of Intellectual Property Rights (IPR) is a document, contract or agreement giving permission or the 'right' to a legally-definable entity to do something (such as manufacture a product or to use a service), or to apply something (such as a trademark), with the objective of achieving commercial gain.
Bribery	When one person gives another person money, property, favors, or anything else of value for a favor in return, we have bribery. Often referred to as a payoff or 'kickback.'
Contract	A contract is a "promise" or an "agreement" that is enforced or recognized by the law. In the civil law, a contract is considered to be part of the general law of obligations.
Long run	In economic models, the long run time frame assumes no fixed factors of production. Firms can enter or leave the marketplace, and the cost (and availability) of land, labor, raw materials, and capital goods can be assumed to vary.
Corruption	The unauthorized use of public office for private gain. The most common forms of corruption are bribery, extortion, and the misuse of inside information.
Business opportunity	A business opportunity involves the sale or lease of any product, service, equipment, etc. that will enable the purchaser-licensee to begin a business
Insurance	Insurance refers to a system by which individuals can reduce their exposure to risk of large losses by spreading the risks among a large number of persons.
International management	International management refers to the management of business operations conducted in more than one country.

Foreign subsidiary	A company owned in a foreign country by another company is referred to as foreign subsidiary.
Subsidiary	A company that is controlled by another company or corporation is a subsidiary.
Policy	Similar to a script in that a policy can be a less than completely rational decision-making method. Involves the use of a pre-existing set of decision steps for any problem that presents itself.
Authority	Authority in agency law, refers to an agent's ability to affect his principal's legal relations with third parties. Also used to refer to an actor's legal power or ability to do something. In addition, sometimes used to refer to a statute, case, or other legal source that justifies a particular result.
Boycott	To protest by refusing to purchase from someone, or otherwise do business with them. In international trade, a boycott most often takes the form of refusal to import a country's goods.
Marketing	Promoting and selling products or services to customers, or prospective customers, is referred to as marketing.
Federal government	Federal government refers to the government of the United States, as distinct from the state and local governments.
Commercial law	The law that relates to the rights of property and persons engaged in trade or commerce and regulates corporate contracts, hiring practices, and the manufacture and sales of consumer goods is called commercial law.
Legal system	Legal system refers to system of rules that regulate behavior and the processes by which the laws of a country are enforced and through which redress of grievances is obtained.
Jurisdiction	The power of a court to hear and decide a case is called jurisdiction. It is the practical authority granted to a formally constituted body or to a person to deal with and make pronouncements on legal matters and, by implication, to administer justice within a defined area of responsibility.
Regulation	Regulation refers to restrictions state and federal laws place on business with regard to the conduct of its activities.
International Business	International business refers to any firm that engages in international trade or investment.
Foundation	A Foundation is a type of philanthropic organization set up by either individuals or institutions as a legal entity (either as a corporation or trust) with the purpose of distributing grants to support causes in line with the goals of the foundation.
Common law	The legal system that is based on the judgement and decree of courts rather than legislative action is called common law.
Economy	The income, expenditures, and resources that affect the cost of running a business and household are called an economy.
Union	A worker association that bargains with employers over wages and working conditions is called a union.
Market system	All the product and resource markets of a market economy and the relationships among them are called a market system.
Free market	A free market is a market where price is determined by the unregulated interchange of supply and demand rather than set by artificial means.
Market	A market is, as defined in economics, a social arrangement that allows buyers and sellers to

Go to **Cram101.com** for the Practice Tests for this Chapter.

discover information and carry out a voluntary exchange of goods or services.

Due process	Due process of law is a legal concept that ensures the government will respect all of a person's legal rights instead of just some or most of those legal rights when the government deprives a person of life, liberty, or property.
Journal	Book of original entry, in which transactions are recorded in a general ledger system, is referred to as a journal.
Firm	An organization that employs resources to produce a good or service for profit and owns and operates one or more plants is referred to as a firm.
Technology	The body of knowledge and techniques that can be used to combine economic resources to produce goods and services is called technology.
Patent	The legal right to the proceeds from and control over the use of an invented product or process, granted for a fixed period of time, usually 20 years. Patent is one form of intellectual property that is subject of the TRIPS agreement.
Entrepreneurship	The assembling of resources to produce new or improved products and technologies is referred to as entrepreneurship.
Intellectual property	In law, intellectual property is an umbrella term for various legal entitlements which attach to certain types of information, ideas, or other intangibles in their expressed form. The holder of this legal entitlement is generally entitled to exercise various exclusive rights in relation to its subject matter.
Electronic business	Electronic business is any business process that is empowered by an information system. Today, this is mostly done with Web-based technologies.
Business Week	Business Week is a business magazine published by McGraw-Hill. It was first published in 1929 under the direction of Malcolm Muir, who was serving as president of the McGraw-Hill Publishing company at the time. It is considered to be the standard both in industry and among students.
Innovation	Innovation refers to the first commercially successful introduction of a new product, the use of a new method of production, or the creation of a new form of business organization.
Precedent	A previously decided court decision that is recognized as authority for the disposition of future decisions is a precedent.
Contract	A contract is a "promise" or an "agreement" that is enforced or recognized by the law. In the civil law, a contract is considered to be part of the general law of obligations.
Property	Assets defined in the broadest legal sense. Property includes the unrealized receivables of a cash basis taxpayer, but not services rendered.
Statute	A statute is a formal, written law of a country or state, written and enacted by its legislative authority, perhaps to then be ratified by the highest executive in the government, and finally published.
Uniform Commercial Code	Uniform commercial code refers to a comprehensive commercial law adopted by every state in the United States; it covers sales laws and other commercial laws.
Aid	Assistance provided by countries and by international institutions such as the World Bank to developing countries in the form of monetary grants, loans at low interest rates, in kind, or a combination of these is called aid. Aid can also refer to assistance of any type rendered to benefit some group or individual.
Impossibility of performance	Impossibility of performance refers to nonperformance that is excused if the contract becomes impossible to perform; must be objective impossibility, not subjective.

Go to **Cram101.com** for the Practice Tests for this Chapter.

Impossibility	A doctrine under which a party to a contract is relieved of his or her duty to perform when that performance has become impossible because of the occurrence of an event unforeseen at the time of contracting is referred to as impossibility.
Compliance	A type of influence process where a receiver accepts the position advocated by a source to obtain favorable outcomes or to avoid punishment is the compliance.
Strike	The withholding of labor services by an organized group of workers is referred to as a strike.
Labor	People's physical and mental talents and efforts that are used to help produce goods and services are called labor.
Scope	Scope of a project is the sum total of all projects products and their requirements or features.
Economic freedom	Freedom to engage in economic transactions, without government interference but with government support of the institutions necessary for that freedom, including rule of law, sound money, and open markets is referred to as economic freedom.
Property rights	Bundle of legal rights over the use to which a resource is put and over the use made of any income that may be derived from that resource are referred to as property rights.
Prohibition	Prohibition refers to denial of the right to import or export, applying to particular products and/or particular countries. Includes embargo.
Interest	In finance and economics, interest is the price paid by a borrower for the use of a lender's money. In other words, interest is the amount of paid to "rent" money for a period of time.
Usury	Usury refers to the taking of more than the law allows on a loan or for forbearance of a debt. Illegal interest.
Mortgage	Mortgage refers to a note payable issued for property, such as a house, usually repaid in equal installments consisting of part principle and part interest, over a specified period.
Real property	Real property is a legal term encompassing real estate and ownership interests in real estate (immovable property).
Capital	Capital generally refers to financial wealth, especially that used to start or maintain a business. In classical economics, capital is one of four factors of production, the others being land and labor and entrepreneurship.
Buyer	A buyer refers to a role in the buying center with formal authority and responsibility to select the supplier and negotiate the terms of the contract.
Margin	A deposit by a buyer in stocks with a seller or a stockbroker, as security to cover fluctuations in the market in reference to stocks that the buyer has purchased but for which he has not paid is a margin. Commodities are also traded on margin.
Commerce	Commerce is the exchange of something of value between two entities. It is the central mechanism from which capitalism is derived.
Economic model	Economic model refers to a simplified picture of economic reality; an abstract generalization.
Rule of law	A legal system in which rules are clear, well-understood, and fairly enforced, including property rights and enforcement of contracts is called rule of law.
Management	Management characterizes the process of leading and directing all or part of an organization, often a business, through the deployment and manipulation of resources. Early twentieth-century management writer Mary Parker Follett defined management as "the art of getting things done through people."

Go to **Cram101.com** for the Practice Tests for this Chapter.
And, **NEVER** highlight a book again!

127

Insurance	Insurance refers to a system by which individuals can reduce their exposure to risk of large losses by spreading the risks among a large number of persons.
Customs	Customs is an authority or agency in a country responsible for collecting customs duties and for controlling the flow of people, animals and goods (including personal effects and hazardous items) in and out of the country.
Investment	Investment refers to spending for the production and accumulation of capital and additions to inventories. In a financial sense, buying an asset with the expectation of making a return.
Economic growth	Economic growth refers to the increase over time in the capacity of an economy to produce goods and services and to improve the well-being of its citizens.
Private sector	The households and business firms of the economy are referred to as private sector.
Mixed economy	An economy in which some production is done by the private sector and some by the state, in state-owned enterprises is called mixed economy.
Principal	In agency law, one under whose direction an agent acts and for whose benefit that agent acts is a principal.
United Nations	An international organization created by multilateral treaty in 1945 to promote social and economic cooperation among nations and to protect human rights is the United Nations.
Arbitration	Arbitration is a form of mediation or conciliation, where the mediating party is given power by the disputant parties to settle the dispute by making a finding. In practice arbitration is generally used as a substitute for judicial systems, particularly when the judicial processes are viewed as too slow, expensive or biased. Arbitration is also used by communities which lack formal law, as a substitute for formal law.
Adjudicate	To settle a case or claim is to adjudicate.
Entrepreneur	The owner/operator. The person who organizes, manages, and assumes the risks of a firm, taking a new idea or a new product and turning it into a successful business is an entrepreneur.
Prime minister	The Prime Minister of the United Kingdom of Great Britain and Northern Ireland is the head of government and so exercises many of the executive functions nominally vested in the Sovereign, who is head of state. According to custom, the Prime Minister and the Cabinet (which he or she heads) are accountable for their actions to Parliament, of which they are members by (modern) convention.
Privatization	A process in which investment bankers take companies that were previously owned by the government to the public markets is referred to as privatization.
Brand	A name, symbol, or design that identifies the goods or services of one seller or group of sellers and distinguishes them from the goods and services of competitors is a brand.
Export	In economics, an export is any good or commodity, shipped or otherwise transported out of a country, province, town to another part of the world in a legitimate fashion, typically for use in trade or sale.
Grant	Grant refers to an intergovernmental transfer of funds . Since the New Deal, state and local governments have become increasingly dependent upon federal grants for an almost infinite variety of programs.
Complaint	The pleading in a civil case in which the plaintiff states his claim and requests relief is called complaint. In the common law, it is a formal legal document that sets out the basic facts and legal reasons that the filing party (the plaintiffs) believes are sufficient to support a claim against another person, persons, entity or entities (the defendants) that entitles the plaintiff(s) to a remedy (either money damages or injunctive relief).

Conciliation	A form of mediation in which the parties choose an interested third party to act as the mediator is referred to as conciliation.
Mediation	Mediation consists of a process of alternative dispute resolution in which a (generally) neutral third party using appropriate techniques, assists two or more parties to help them negotiate an agreement, with concrete effects, on a matter of common interest.
Option	A contract that gives the purchaser the option to buy or sell the underlying financial instrument at a specified price, called the exercise price or strike price, within a specific period of time.
Litigation	The process of bringing, maintaining, and defending a lawsuit is litigation.
Negotiation	Negotiation is the process whereby interested parties resolve disputes, agree upon courses of action, bargain for individual or collective advantage, and/or attempt to craft outcomes which serve their mutual interests.
Domestic	From or in one's own country. A domestic producer is one that produces inside the home country. A domestic price is the price inside the home country. Opposite of 'foreign' or 'world.'.
Plaintiff	A plaintiff is the party who initiates a lawsuit (also known as an action) before a court. By doing so, the plaintiff seeks a legal remedy, and if successful, the court will issue judgment in favour of the plaintiff and make the appropriate court order.
Arbitrate	To submit some disputed matter to selected persons and to accept their decision or award as a substitute for the decision of a judicial tribunal is called the arbitrate.
Bilateral agreement	A bilateral agreement is between two countries or organizations, as opposed to several countries.
Breach of contract	When one party fails to follow the terms of a contract, we have breach of contract.
Jury	A body of lay persons, selected by lot, or by some other fair and impartial means, to ascertain, under the guidance of the judge, the truth in questions of fact arising either in civil litigation or a criminal process is referred to as jury.
Manufacturing	Production of goods primarily by the application of labor and capital to raw materials and other intermediate inputs, in contrast to agriculture, mining, forestry, fishing, and services a manufacturing.
Nike	Because Nike creates goods for a wide range of sports, they have competition from every sports and sports fashion brand there is. Nike has no direct competitors because there is no single brand which can compete directly with their range of sports and non-sports oriented gear, except for Reebok.
Honda	With more than 14 million internal combustion engines built each year, Honda is the largest engine-maker in the world. In 2004, the company began to produce diesel motors, which were both very quiet whilst not requiring particulate filters to pass pollution standards. It is arguable, however, that the foundation of their success is the motorcycle division.
Wall Street Journal	Dow Jones & Company was founded in 1882 by reporters Charles Dow, Edward Jones and Charles Bergstresser. Jones converted the small Customers' Afternoon Letter into The Wall Street Journal, first published in 1889, and began delivery of the Dow Jones News Service via telegraph. The Journal featured the Jones 'Average', the first of several indexes of stock and bond prices on the New York Stock Exchange.
Competitor	Other organizations in the same industry or type of business that provide a good or service to the same set of customers is referred to as a competitor.

Go to **Cram101.com** for the Practice Tests for this Chapter.
And, **NEVER** highlight a book again!

Gucci	Gucci, or the House of Gucci, is an Italian fashion and leather goods label. It was founded by Guccio Gucci (1881-1953) in Florence in 1921. In the late 1980s made Gucci one of the world's most influential fashion houses and a highly profitable business operation. In October of 1995 Gucci decided to go public and had its first initial public offering on the AEX and NYSE for $22 per share..
Intellectual property rights	Intellectual property rights, such as patents, copyrights, trademarks, trade secrets, trade names, and domain names are very valuable business assets. Federal and state laws protect intellectual property rights from misappropriation and infringement.
Intellectual property right	Intellectual property right refers to the right to control and derive the benefits from something one has invented, discovered, or created.
Microsoft	Microsoft is a multinational computer technology corporation with 2004 global annual sales of US$39.79 billion and 71,553 employees in 102 countries and regions as of July 2006. It develops, manufactures, licenses, and supports a wide range of software products for computing devices.
Asset	An item of property, such as land, capital, money, a share in ownership, or a claim on others for future payment, such as a bond or a bank deposit is an asset.
Industry	A group of firms that produce identical or similar products is an industry. It is also used specifically to refer to an area of economic production focused on manufacturing which involves large amounts of capital investment before any profit can be realized, also called "heavy industry".
Profit	Profit refers to the return to the resource entrepreneurial ability; total revenue minus total cost.
Trademark	A distinctive word, name, symbol, device, or combination thereof, which enables consumers to identify favored products or services and which may find protection under state or federal law is a trademark.
Copyright	The legal right to the proceeds from and control over the use of a created product, such a written work, audio, video, film, or software is a copyright. This right generally extends over the life of the author plus fifty years.
Logo	Logo refers to device or other brand name that cannot be spoken.
Brand image	The advertising metric that measures the type and favorability of consumer perceptions of the brand is referred to as the brand image.
Revenue	Revenue is a U.S. business term for the amount of money that a company receives from its activities, mostly from sales of products and/or services to customers.
Operation	A standardized method or technique that is performed repetitively, often on different materials resulting in different finished goods is called an operation.
Pfizer	Pfizer is the world's largest pharmaceutical company based in New York City. It produces the number-one selling drug Lipitor (atorvastatin, used to lower blood cholesterol).
Composition	An out-of-court settlement in which creditors agree to accept a fractional settlement on their original claim is referred to as composition.
Churning	Churning is the practice of executing trades for an investment account by a salesman or broker in order to generate commissions from the account. It is a breach of securities law in many jurisdictions, and it is generally actionable by the account holder for the return of the commissions paid.
Collusion	Collusion refers to cooperation among firms to raise price and otherwise increase their profits.

Go to **Cram101.com** for the Practice Tests for this Chapter.

World Health Organization	The World Health Organization is a specialized agency of the United Nations, acting as a coordinating authority on international public health, headquartered in Geneva, Switzerland. It's constitution states that its mission "is the attainment by all peoples of the highest possible level of health". Its major task is to combat disease, especially key infectious diseases, and to promote the general health of the peoples of the world.
Balance	In banking and accountancy, the outstanding balance is the amount of money owned, (or due), that remains in a deposit account (or a loan account) at a given date, after all past remittances, payments and withdrawal have been accounted for. It can be positive (then, in the balance sheet of a firm, it is an asset) or negative (a liability).
License	A license in the sphere of Intellectual Property Rights (IPR) is a document, contract or agreement giving permission or the 'right' to a legally-definable entity to do something (such as manufacture a product or to use a service), or to apply something (such as a trademark), with the objective of achieving commercial gain.
Royalties	Remuneration paid to the owners of technology, patents, or trade names for the use of same name are called royalties.
Licensing agreement	Detailed and comprehensive written agreement between the licensor and licensee that sets forth the express terms of their agreement is called a licensing agreement.
Distribution	Distribution in economics, the manner in which total output and income is distributed among individuals or factors.
Licensing	Licensing is a form of strategic alliance which involves the sale of a right to use certain proprietary knowledge (so called intellectual property) in a defined way.
Leverage	Leverage is using given resources in such a way that the potential positive or negative outcome is magnified. In finance, this generally refers to borrowing.
Applicant	In many tribunal and administrative law suits, the person who initiates the claim is called the applicant.
Mutual recognition	The acceptance by one country of another country's certification that a satisfactory standard has been met for ability, performance, safety, etc a mutual recognition.
Administration	Administration refers to the management and direction of the affairs of governments and institutions; a collective term for all policymaking officials of a government; the execution and implementation of public policy.
Promotion	Promotion refers to all the techniques sellers use to motivate people to buy products or services. An attempt by marketers to inform people about products and to persuade them to participate in an exchange.
Treaties	The first source of international law, consisting of agreements or contracts between two or more nations that are formally signed by an authorized representative and ratified by the supreme power of each nation are called treaties.
Bayer	Bayer is a German chemical and pharmaceutical company founded in 1863. By 1899, their trademark Aspirin was registered worldwide for the Bayer brand of acetylsalicylic acid, but through the widespread use to describe all brands of the compound, and Bayer's inability to protect its trademark the word "aspirin" lost its trademark status in the United States and some other countries.
Comprehensive	A comprehensive refers to a layout accurate in size, color, scheme, and other necessary details to show how a final ad will look. For presentation only, never for reproduction.
World Trade Organization	The World Trade Organization is an international, multilateral organization, which sets the rules for the global trading system and resolves disputes between its member states, all of

Go to **Cram101.com** for the Practice Tests for this Chapter.
And, **NEVER** highlight a book again!

135

whom are signatories to its approximately 30 agreements.

Vendor

A person who sells property to a vendee is a vendor. The words vendor and vendee are more commonly applied to the seller and purchaser of real estate, and the words seller and buyer are more commonly applied to the seller and purchaser of personal property.

Corporation

A legal entity chartered by a state or the Federal government that is distinct and separate from the individuals who own it is a corporation. This separation gives the corporation unique powers which other legal entities lack.

Agent

A person who makes economic decisions for another economic actor. A hired manager operates as an agent for a firm's owner.

Cooperative

A business owned and controlled by the people who use it, producers, consumers, or workers with similar needs who pool their resources for mutual gain is called cooperative.

Product development

In business and engineering, new product development is the complete process of bringing a new product to market. There are two parallel aspects to this process : one involves product engineering ; the other marketing analysis. Marketers see new product development as the first stage in product life cycle management, engineers as part of Product Lifecycle Management.

Channel

Channel, in communications (sometimes called communications channel), refers to the medium used to convey information from a sender (or transmitter) to a receiver.

Cash discount

Cash discount refers to a discount offered on merchandise sold to encourage prompt payment; offered by sellers of merchandise and represents sales discounts to the seller when they are used and purchase discounts to the purchaser of the merchandise.

Discount

The difference between the face value of a bond and its selling price, when a bond is sold for less than its face value it's referred to as a discount.

Premium

Premium refers to the fee charged by an insurance company for an insurance policy. The rate of losses must be relatively predictable: In order to set the premium (prices) insurers must be able to estimate them accurately.

Coupon

In finance, a coupon is "attached" to a bond, either physically (as with old bonds) or electronically. Each coupon represents a predetermined payment promized to the bond-holder in return for his or her loan of money to the bond-issuer. .

Rebate

Rebate refers to a sales promotion in which money is returned to the consumer based on proof of purchase.

Unfair competition

Antitrust or competition laws, legislate against trade practices that undermine competitiveness or are considered to be unfair competition. The term antitrust derives from the U.S. law that was originally formulated to combat business trusts - now commonly known as cartels.

Incentive

An incentive is any factor (financial or non-financial) that provides a motive for a particular course of action, or counts as a reason for preferring one choice to the alternatives.

Advertising

Advertising refers to paid, nonpersonal communication through various media by organizations and individuals who are in some way identified in the advertising message.

Puffery

Advertising or other sales presentations that praise the item to be sold using subjective opinions, superlatives, or exaggerations, vaguely and generally, stating no specific facts is called puffery.

Status quo

Status quo is a Latin term meaning the present, current, existing state of affairs.

Go to **Cram101.com** for the Practice Tests for this Chapter.
And, **NEVER** highlight a book again!

Integration	Economic integration refers to reducing barriers among countries to transactions and to movements of goods, capital, and labor, including harmonization of laws, regulations, and standards. Integrated markets theoretically function as a unified market.
Consumer protection	Consumer protection is government regulation to protect the interests of consumers, for example by requiring businesses to disclose detailed information about products, particularly in areas where safety or public health is an issue, such as food.
Multinational corporations	Firms that own production facilities in two or more countries and produce and sell their products globally are referred to as multinational corporations.
Multinational corporation	An organization that manufactures and markets products in many different countries and has multinational stock ownership and multinational management is referred to as multinational corporation.
Points	Loan origination fees that may be deductible as interest by a buyer of property. A seller of property who pays points reduces the selling price by the amount of the points paid for the buyer.
Antitrust laws	Legislation that prohibits anticompetitive business activities such as price fixing, bid rigging, monopolization, and tying contracts is referred to as antitrust laws.
Antitrust	Government intervention to alter market structure or prevent abuse of market power is called antitrust.
Acquisition	A company's purchase of the property and obligations of another company is an acquisition.
Nestle	Nestle is the world's biggest food and beverage company. In the 1860s, a pharmacist, developed a food for babies who were unable to be breastfed. His first success was a premature infant who could not tolerate his own mother's milk nor any of the usual substitutes. The value of the new product was quickly recognized when his new formula saved the child's life.
Trust	An arrangement in which shareholders of independent firms agree to give up their stock in exchange for trust certificates that entitle them to a share of the trust's common profits.
Antitrust legislation	Antitrust legislation refers to laws prohibiting monopolization, restraints of trade, and collusion among firms to raise prices or inhibit competition.
Exchange	The trade of things of value between buyer and seller so that each is better off after the trade is called the exchange.
Tactic	A short-term immediate decision that, in its totality, leads to the achievement of strategic goals is called a tactic.
Exempt	Employees who are not covered by the Fair Labor Standards Act are exempt. Exempt employees are not eligible for overtime pay.
Licensee	A person lawfully on land in possession of another for purposes unconnected with the business interests of the possessor is referred to as the licensee.
International law	Law that governs affairs between nations and that regulates transactions between individuals and businesses of different countries is an international law.
Foreign Corrupt Practices Act	The Foreign Corrupt Practices Act of 1977 is a United States federal law requiring any company that has publicly-traded stock to maintain records that accurately and fairly represent the company's transactions; additionally, requires any publicly-traded company to have an adequate system of internal accounting controls.
Competitiveness	Competitiveness usually refers to characteristics that permit a firm to compete effectively with other firms due to low cost or superior technology, perhaps internationally.

138

Go to **Cram101.com** for the Practice Tests for this Chapter.

Liability	A liability is a present obligation of the enterprise arizing from past events, the settlement of which is expected to result in an outflow from the enterprise of resources embodying economic benefits.
Bribery	When one person gives another person money, property, favors, or anything else of value for a favor in return, we have bribery. Often referred to as a payoff or 'kickback.'
Developing country	Developing country refers to a country whose per capita income is low by world standards. Same as LDC. As usually used, it does not necessarily connote that the country's income is rising.
Department of Justice	The United States Department of Justice is a Cabinet department in the United States government designed to enforce the law and defend the interests of the United States according to the law and to ensure fair and impartial administration of justice for all Americans. This department is administered by the United States Attorney General, one of the original members of the cabinet.
Control system	A control system is a device or set of devices that manage the behavior of other devices. Some devices or systems are not controllable.A control system is an interconnection of components connected or related in such a manner as to command, direct, or regulate itself or another system.
Security	Security refers to a claim on the borrower future income that is sold by the borrower to the lender. A security is a type of transferable interest representing financial value.
Embargo	Embargo refers to the prohibition of some category of trade. May apply to exports and/or imports, of particular products or of all trade, vis a vis the world or a particular country or countries.
Economic sanction	A economic sanction can vary from imposing import duties on goods from, or blocking the export of certain goods to the target country, to a full naval blockade of its ports in an effort to verify, and curb or block specified imported goods.
Joint venture	Joint venture refers to an undertaking by two parties for a specific purpose and duration, taking any of several legal forms.
Service	Service refers to a "non tangible product" that is not embodied in a physical good and that typically effects some change in another product, person, or institution. Contrasts with good.
Sherman Act	Federal antitrust act of 1890 that makes monopoly and conspiracies to restrain trade criminal offenses is the Sherman Act.
Starbucks	Although it has endured much criticism for its purported monopoly on the global coffee-bean market, Starbucks purchases only 3% of the coffee beans grown worldwide. In 2000 the company introduced a line of fair trade products and now offers three options for socially conscious coffee drinkers. According to Starbucks, they purchased 4.8 million pounds of Certified Fair Trade coffee in fiscal year 2004 and 11.5 million pounds in 2005.
Secondary boycott	Secondary boycott refers to an attempt by labor to convince others to stop doing business with a firm that is the subject of a primary boycott; prohibited by the Taft-Hartley Act.
Primary boycott	When a union encourages both its members and the general public not to buy the products of a firm involved in a labor dispute, we have primary boycott.
Invoice	The itemized bill for a transaction, stating the nature of the transaction and its cost. In international trade, the invoice price is often the preferred basis for levying an ad valorem tariff.
Raw material	Raw material refers to a good that has not been transformed by production; a primary product.

Freight forwarder	An organization that puts many small shipments together to create a single large shipment that can be transported cost-effectively to the final destination is called freight forwarder.
Host country	The country in which the parent-country organization seeks to locate or has already located a facility is a host country.
Damages	The sum of money recoverable by a plaintiff who has received a judgment in a civil case is called damages.
Citibank	In April of 2006, Citibank struck a deal with 7-Eleven to put its ATMs in over 5,500 convenience stores in the U.S. In the same month, it also announced it would sell all of its Buffalo and Rochester New York branches and accounts to M&T Bank.
Enterprise	Enterprise refers to another name for a business organization. Other similar terms are business firm, sometimes simply business, sometimes simply firm, as well as company, and entity.
Testimony	In some contexts, the word bears the same import as the word evidence, but in most connections it has a much narrower meaning. Testimony are the words heard from the witness in court, and evidence is what the jury considers it worth.
Committee	A long-lasting, sometimes permanent team in the organization structure created to deal with tasks that recur regularly is the committee.
Appeal	Appeal refers to the act of asking an appellate court to overturn a decision after the trial court's final judgment has been entered.
Extraterritorial income	Extraterritorial income refers to taxpayer gross income attributed to foreign trading.
Cybersquatters	Cybersquatters are individuals or businesses that intentionally obtain a domain name registration for a company's trademark so that it can sell the domain name back to the trademark owner.
Hasbro	Hasbro originated with the Mr. Potato Head toy. Mr. Potato Head was the invention of George Lerner in the late 1940s. The idea was originally sold to a breakfast cereal manufacturer so that the separate parts could be distributed as cereal package premiums.
Trade name	A commercial legal name under which a company does business is referred to as the trade name.
Trademark infringement	Trademark infringement refers to unauthorized use of another's mark. The holder may recover damages and other remedies from the infringer.
Injunction	Injunction refers to a court order directing a person or organization not to perform a certain act because the act would do irreparable damage to some other person or persons; a restraining order.
Respondent	Respondent refers to a term often used to describe the party charged in an administrative proceeding. The party adverse to the appellant in a case appealed to a higher court.
Product liability	Part of tort law that holds businesses liable for harm that results from the production, design, sale, or use of products they market is referred to as product liability.
Defamation	An intentional tort that prohibits the publication of false and defamatory statements concerning another is defamation.
Libel	Libel refers to the defamation action appropriate to printed or written defamations, or to those that have a physical form.
Users	Users refer to people in the organization who actually use the product or service purchased by the buying center.

Burden of proof	Used to refer both to the necessity or obligation of proving the facts needed to support a party's claim, and the persuasiveness of the evidence used to do so is a burden of proof. Regarding the second sense of the term, the usual burden of proof in a civil case is a preponderance of the evidence.
Reuters	Reuters is best known as a news service that provides reports from around the world to newspapers and broadcasters. Its main focus is on supplying the financial markets with information and trading products.
Merchant	Under the Uniform Commercial Code, one who regularly deals in goods of the kind sold in the contract at issue, or holds himself out as having special knowledge or skill relevant to such goods, or who makes the sale through an agent who regularly deals in such goods or claims such knowledge or skill is referred to as merchant.
Consideration	Consideration in contract law, a basic requirement for an enforceable agreement under traditional contract principles, defined in this text as legal value, bargained for and given in exchange for an act or promise. In corporation law, cash or property contributed to a corporation in exchange for shares, or a promise to contribute such cash or property.
Credit	Credit refers to a recording as positive in the balance of payments, any transaction that gives rise to a payment into the country, such as an export, the sale of an asset, or borrowing from abroad.
Euro	The common currency of a subset of the countries of the EU, adopted January 1, 1999 is called euro.
Levy	Levy refers to imposing and collecting a tax or tariff.
Duty free	Duty Free is the term that is often used to describe goods bought at ports and airports that do not attract the usual government taxes and customs duties.
Digital signature	Digital signature is an encryption scheme for authenticating digital information that should not be confused with ordinary physical signatures on paper or with an electronic signature, but implemented using techniques from the field of public-key cryptography.
Economic development	Increase in the economic standard of living of a country's population, normally accomplished by increasing its stocks of physical and human capital and improving its technology is an economic development.

Go to **Cram101.com** for the Practice Tests for this Chapter.

Marketing strategy	Marketing strategy refers to the means by which a marketing goal is to be achieved, usually characterized by a specified target market and a marketing program to reach it.
Marketing	Promoting and selling products or services to customers, or prospective customers, is referred to as marketing.
Buyer	A buyer refers to a role in the buying center with formal authority and responsibility to select the supplier and negotiate the terms of the contract.
Customs	Customs is an authority or agency in a country responsible for collecting customs duties and for controlling the flow of people, animals and goods (including personal effects and hazardous items) in and out of the country.
Preference	The act of a debtor in paying or securing one or more of his creditors in a manner more favorable to them than to other creditors or to the exclusion of such other creditors is a preference. In the absence of statute, a preference is perfectly good, but to be legal it must be bona fide, and not a mere subterfuge of the debtor to secure a future benefit to himself or to prevent the application of his property to his debts.
Recession	A significant decline in economic activity. In the U.S., recession is approximately defined as two successive quarters of falling GDP, as judged by NBER.
Market	A market is, as defined in economics, a social arrangement that allows buyers and sellers to discover information and carry out a voluntary exchange of goods or services.
World Trade Organization	The World Trade Organization is an international, multilateral organization, which sets the rules for the global trading system and resolves disputes between its member states, all of whom are signatories to its approximately 30 agreements.
Apple Computer	Apple Computer has been a major player in the evolution of personal computing since its founding in 1976. The Apple II microcomputer, introduced in 1977, was a hit with home users.
Market share	That fraction of an industry's output accounted for by an individual firm or group of firms is called market share.
Industry	A group of firms that produce identical or similar products is an industry. It is also used specifically to refer to an area of economic production focused on manufacturing which involves large amounts of capital investment before any profit can be realized, also called "heavy industry".
Productivity	Productivity refers to the total output of goods and services in a given period of time divided by work hours.
Marketing research	Marketing research refers to the analysis of markets to determine opportunities and challenges, and to find the information needed to make good decisions.
Firm	An organization that employs resources to produce a good or service for profit and owns and operates one or more plants is referred to as a firm.
Budget	Budget refers to an account, usually for a year, of the planned expenditures and the expected receipts of an entity. For a government, the receipts are tax revenues.
Commodity	Could refer to any good, but in trade a commodity is usually a raw material or primary product that enters into international trade, such as metals or basic agricultural products.
Service	Service refers to a "non tangible product" that is not embodied in a physical good and that typically effects some change in another product, person, or institution. Contrasts with good.
Market opportunities	Market opportunities refer to areas where a company believes there are favorable demand trends, needs, and/or wants that are not being satisfied, and where it can compete

Go to **Cram101.com** for the Practice Tests for this Chapter.

	effectively.
Annual report	An annual report is prepared by corporate management that presents financial information including financial statements, footnotes, and the management discussion and analysis.
Distribution	Distribution in economics, the manner in which total output and income is distributed among individuals or factors.
Promotion	Promotion refers to all the techniques sellers use to motivate people to buy products or services. An attempt by marketers to inform people about products and to persuade them to participate in an exchange.
Vendor	A person who sells property to a vendee is a vendor. The words vendor and vendee are more commonly applied to the seller and purchaser of real estate, and the words seller and buyer are more commonly applied to the seller and purchaser of personal property.
Operation	A standardized method or technique that is performed repetitively, often on different materials resulting in different finished goods is called an operation.
Scope	Scope of a project is the sum total of all projects products and their requirements or features.
Effective communication	When the intended meaning equals the perceived meaning it is called effective communication.
Senior executive	Senior executive means a chief executive officer, chief operating officer, chief financial officer and anyone in charge of a principal business unit or function.
Communication task	Under the DAGMAR approach to setting advertising goals and objectives, something that can be performed by and attributed to advertising such as awareness, comprehension, conviction, and action is a communication task.
Drucker	Drucker as a business thinker took off in the 1940s, when his initial writings on politics and society won him access to the internal workings of General Motors, which was one of the largest companies in the world at that time. His experiences in Europe had left him fascinated with the problem of authority.
Wall Street Journal	Dow Jones & Company was founded in 1882 by reporters Charles Dow, Edward Jones and Charles Bergstresser. Jones converted the small Customers' Afternoon Letter into The Wall Street Journal, first published in 1889, and began delivery of the Dow Jones News Service via telegraph. The Journal featured the Jones 'Average', the first of several indexes of stock and bond prices on the New York Stock Exchange.
Journal	Book of original entry, in which transactions are recorded in a general ledger system, is referred to as a journal.
Marketing Plan	Marketing plan refers to a road map for the marketing activities of an organization for a specified future period of time, such as one year or five years.
Trend	Trend refers to the long-term movement of an economic variable, such as its average rate of increase or decrease over enough years to encompass several business cycles.
Domestic	From or in one's own country. A domestic producer is one that produces inside the home country. A domestic price is the price inside the home country. Opposite of 'foreign' or 'world.'.
Assessment	Collecting information and providing feedback to employees about their behavior, communication style, or skills is an assessment.
Profitability analysis	A means of measuring the profitability of the firm's products, customer groups, sales territories, channels of distribution, and order sizes is called profitability analysis.

Go to **Cram101.com** for the Practice Tests for this Chapter.

149

Business cycle	Business cycle refers to the pattern followed by macroeconommic variables, such as GDP and unemployment that rise and fall irregularly over time, relative to trend.
Inflation	An increase in the overall price level of an economy, usually as measured by the CPI or by the implicit price deflator is called inflation.
Economy	The income, expenditures, and resources that affect the cost of running a business and household are called an economy.
Market segmentation	The process of dividing the total market into several groups whose members have similar characteristics is market segmentation.
Single market	A single market is a customs union with common policies on product regulation, and freedom of movement of all the four factors of production (goods, services, capital and labor).
Competitor	Other organizations in the same industry or type of business that provide a good or service to the same set of customers is referred to as a competitor.
Revenue	Revenue is a U.S. business term for the amount of money that a company receives from its activities, mostly from sales of products and/or services to customers.
Variable	A variable is something measured by a number; it is used to analyze what happens to other things when the size of that number changes.
Appreciation	Appreciation refers to a rise in the value of a country's currency on the exchange market, relative either to a particular other currency or to a weighted average of other currencies. The currency is said to appreciate. Opposite of 'depreciation.' Appreciation can also refer to the increase in value of any asset.
Competitive intelligence	Competitive Intelligence is defined as business intelligence focusing on the external competitive environment.
Trade secret	Trade secret refers to a secret formula, pattern, process, program, device, method, technique, or compilation of information that is used in its owner's business and affords that owner a competitive advantage. Trade secrets are protected by state law.
Compromise	Compromise occurs when the interaction is moderately important to meeting goals and the goals are neither completely compatible nor completely incompatible.
Economic development	Increase in the economic standard of living of a country's population, normally accomplished by increasing its stocks of physical and human capital and improving its technology is an economic development.
Rebranding	Rebranding, is the process by which a product or service developed with one brand or company or product line affiliation is marketed or distributed with a different identity. This involves radical changes to the brand's logo, brand name, image, marketing strategy, and advertising themes.
American Marketing Association	The American Marketing Association is a professional association for marketers. It has approximately 38,000 members. It was formed in 1937 from the merger of two predecessor organizations.
Homogeneous	In the context of procurement/purchasing, homogeneous is used to describe goods that do not vary in their essential characteristic irrespective of the source of supply.
Cooperative	A business owned and controlled by the people who use it, producers, consumers, or workers with similar needs who pool their resources for mutual gain is called cooperative.
Customer service	The ability of logistics management to satisfy users in terms of time, dependability, communication, and convenience is called the customer service.
Consumption	In Keynesian economics consumption refers to personal consumption expenditure, i.e., the

Go to Cram101.com for the Practice Tests for this Chapter.

purchase of currently produced goods and services out of income, out of savings (net worth), or from borrowed funds. It refers to that part of disposable income that does not go to saving.

Property	Assets defined in the broadest legal sense. Property includes the unrealized receivables of a cash basis taxpayer, but not services rendered.
Focus group	A small group of people who meet under the direction of a discussion leader to communicate their opinions about an organization, its products, or other given issues is a focus group.
Comprehensive	A comprehensive refers to a layout accurate in size, color, scheme, and other necessary details to show how a final ad will look. For presentation only, never for reproduction.
Trade association	An industry trade group or trade association is generally a public relations organization founded and funded by corporations that operate in a specific industry. Its purpose is generally to promote that industry through PR activities such as advertizing, education, political donations, political pressure, publishing, and astroturfing.
Management	Management characterizes the process of leading and directing all or part of an organization, often a business, through the deployment and manipulation of resources. Early twentieth-century management writer Mary Parker Follett defined management as "the art of getting things done through people."
Organization for economic cooperation and development	Organization for economic cooperation and development refers to Paris-based intergovernmental organization of 'wealthy' nations whose purpose is to provide its 29 member states with a forum in which governments can compare their experiences, discuss the problems they share, and seek solutions that can then be applied within their own national contexts.
United Nations	An international organization created by multilateral treaty in 1945 to promote social and economic cooperation among nations and to protect human rights is the United Nations.
Corporate level	Corporate level refers to level at which top management directs overall strategy for the entire organization.
Market research	Market research is the process of systematic gathering, recording and analyzing of data about customers, competitors and the market. Market research can help create a business plan, launch a new product or service, fine tune existing products and services, expand into new markets etc. It can be used to determine which portion of the population will purchase the product/service, based on variables like age, gender, location and income level. It can be found out what market characteristics your target market has.
Consumer good	Products and services that are ultimately consumed rather than used in the production of another good are a consumer good.
Enterprise	Enterprise refers to another name for a business organization. Other similar terms are business firm, sometimes simply business, sometimes simply firm, as well as company, and entity.
Production	The creation of finished goods and services using the factors of production: land, labor, capital, entrepreneurship, and knowledge.
Profit	Profit refers to the return to the resource entrepreneurial ability; total revenue minus total cost.
Bayer	Bayer is a German chemical and pharmaceutical company founded in 1863. By 1899, their trademark Aspirin was registered worldwide for the Bayer brand of acetylsalicylic acid, but through the widespread use to describe all brands of the compound, and Bayer's inability to protect its trademark the word "aspirin" lost its trademark status in the United States and some other countries.

Policy	Similar to a script in that a policy can be a less than completely rational decision-making method. Involves the use of a pre-existing set of decision steps for any problem that presents itself.
Union	A worker association that bargains with employers over wages and working conditions is called a union.
Comparability	Ability to compare the accounting information of different companies because they use the same accounting principles is known as comparability.
Preparation	Preparation refers to usually the first stage in the creative process. It includes education and formal training.
Economic growth	Economic growth refers to the increase over time in the capacity of an economy to produce goods and services and to improve the well-being of its citizens.
Interest	In finance and economics, interest is the price paid by a borrower for the use of a lender's money. In other words, interest is the amount of paid to "rent" money for a period of time.
Primary data	Facts and figures that are newly collected for the project are referred to as primary data.
Respondent	Respondent refers to a term often used to describe the party charged in an administrative proceeding. The party adverse to the appellant in a case appealed to a higher court.
Quantitative research	Quantitative research is the systematic scientific investigation of quantitative properties and phenomena and their relationships. The objective of quantitative research is to develop and employ mathematical models, theories and hypotheses pertaining to natural phenomena. The process of measurement is central to quantitative research because it provides the fundamental connection between empirical observation and mathematical expression of quantitative relationships.
Microsoft	Microsoft is a multinational computer technology corporation with 2004 global annual sales of US$39.79 billion and 71,553 employees in 102 countries and regions as of July 2006. It develops, manufactures, licenses, and supports a wide range of software products for computing devices.
Users	Users refer to people in the organization who actually use the product or service purchased by the buying center.
Demographic characteristic	The vital statistics of a population group or a derived sample, such as: age, sex, education, ethnic heritage, education, income, housing is referred to as a demographic characteristic.
Demographic	A demographic is a term used in marketing and broadcasting, to describe a demographic grouping or a market segment.
Technology	The body of knowledge and techniques that can be used to combine economic resources to produce goods and services is called technology.
Instrument	Instrument refers to an economic variable that is controlled by policy makers and can be used to influence other variables, called targets. Examples are monetary and fiscal policies used to achieve external and internal balance.
Product design	Product Design is defined as the idea generation, concept development, testing and manufacturing or implementation of a physical object or service. It is possibly the evolution of former discipline name - Industrial Design.
Export	In economics, an export is any good or commodity, shipped or otherwise transported out of a country, province, town to another part of the world in a legitimate fashion, typically for use in trade or sale.
Gain	In finance, gain is a profit or an increase in value of an investment such as a stock or

	bond. Gain is calculated by fair market value or the proceeds from the sale of the investment minus the sum of the purchase price and all costs associated with it.
Nissan	Nissan is Japan's second largest car company after Toyota. Nissan is among the top three Asian rivals of the "big three" in the US.
Commerce	Commerce is the exchange of something of value between two entities. It is the central mechanism from which capitalism is derived.
Confirmed	When the seller's bank agrees to assume liability on the letter of credit issued by the buyer's bank the transaction is confirmed. The term means that the credit is not only backed up by the issuing foreign bank, but that payment is also guaranteed by the notifying American bank.
News conference	A publicity tool consisting of an informational meeting with representatives of the media who are sent advance materials on the content is a news conference.
Security	Security refers to a claim on the borrower future income that is sold by the borrower to the lender. A security is a type of transferable interest representing financial value.
Partnership	In the common law, a partnership is a type of business entity in which partners share with each other the profits or losses of the business undertaking in which they have all invested.
Incentive	An incentive is any factor (financial or non-financial) that provides a motive for a particular course of action, or counts as a reason for preferring one choice to the alternatives.
International Business	International business refers to any firm that engages in international trade or investment.
Job satisfaction	Job satisfaction describes how content an individual is with his or her job. It is a relatively recent term since in previous centuries the jobs available to a particular person were often predetermined by the occupation of that person's parent.
Gerber	Gerber is perhaps the most well-known purveyor of baby food and baby products in the world. The company was founded in 1927 in Fremont, Michigan by Daniel Frank Gerber, owner of the Fremont Canning Company.
Agent	A person who makes economic decisions for another economic actor. A hired manager operates as an agent for a firm's owner.
Tenant	The party to whom the leasehold is transferred is a tenant. A leasehold estate is an ownership interest in land in which a lessee or a tenant holds real property by some form of title from a lessor or landlord.
Accommodation	Accommodation is a term used to describe a delivery of nonconforming goods meant as a partial performance of a contract for the sale of goods, where a full performance is not possible.
Securities and exchange commission	Securities and exchange commission refers to U.S. government agency that determines the financial statements that public companies must provide to stockholders and the measurement rules that they must use in producing those statements.
Publicly held corporation	Publicly held corporation refers to a corporation that may have thousands of stockholders and whose stock is regularly traded on a national securities market.
Corporation	A legal entity chartered by a state or the Federal government that is distinct and separate from the individuals who own it is a corporation. This separation gives the corporation unique powers which other legal entities lack.
Exchange	The trade of things of value between buyer and seller so that each is better off after the trade is called the exchange.

Go to **Cram101.com** for the Practice Tests for this Chapter.

157

Inventory	Tangible property held for sale in the normal course of business or used in producing goods or services for sale is an inventory.
Merchant	Under the Uniform Commercial Code, one who regularly deals in goods of the kind sold in the contract at issue, or holds himself out as having special knowledge or skill relevant to such goods, or who makes the sale through an agent who regularly deals in such goods or claims such knowledge or skill is referred to as merchant.
Outsourcing	Outsourcing refers to a production activity that was previously done inside a firm or plant that is now conducted outside that firm or plant.
Brand	A name, symbol, or design that identifies the goods or services of one seller or group of sellers and distinguishes them from the goods and services of competitors is a brand.
Household	An economic unit that provides the economy with resources and uses the income received to purchase goods and services that satisfy economic wants is called household.
Logo	Logo refers to device or other brand name that cannot be spoken.
Postal Service	The postal service was created in Philadelphia under Benjamin Franklin on July 26, 1775 by decree of the Second Continental Congress. Based on a clause in the United States Constitution empowering Congress "To establish Post Offices and post Roads."
Expected return	Expected return refers to the return on an asset expected over the next period.
Context	The effect of the background under which a message often takes on more and richer meaning is a context. Context is especially important in cross-cultural interactions because some cultures are said to be high context or low context.
Brand preference	When all marketing conditions are equal, a consumer will choose a preferred brand over another, we have brand preference.
Customer satisfaction	Customer satisfaction is a business term which is used to capture the idea of measuring how satisfied an enterprise's customers are with the organization's efforts in a marketplace.
American Airlines	American Airlines developed from a conglomeration of about 82 small airlines through a series of corporate acquisitions and reorganizations: initially, the name American Airways was used as a common brand by a number of independent air carriers. American Airlines is the largest airline in the world in terms of total passengers transported and fleet size, and the second-largest airline in the world.
Advertising	Advertising refers to paid, nonpersonal communication through various media by organizations and individuals who are in some way identified in the advertising message.
Consumer behavior	Consumer behavior refers to the actions a person takes in purchasing and using products and services, including the mental and social processes that precede and follow these actions.
Standardization	Standardization, in the context related to technologies and industries, is the process of establishing a technical standard among competing entities in a market, where this will bring benefits without hurting competition.
Post hoc	Post hoc refers to literally, 'after this, therefore because of this."
Marketing mix	The marketing mix approach to marketing is a model of crafting and implementing marketing strategies. It stresses the "mixing" or blending of various factors in such a way that both organizational and consumer (target markets) objectives are attained.
Globalization	The increasing world-wide integration of markets for goods, services and capital that attracted special attention in the late 1990s is called globalization.
Tariff	A tax imposed by a nation on an imported good is called a tariff.

Go to **Cram101.com** for the Practice Tests for this Chapter.
And, **NEVER** highlight a book again!

Product concept	The verbal and perhaps pictorial description of the benefits and features of a proposed product; also the early stage of the product development process in which only the product concept exists.
Direct marketing	Promotional element that uses direct communication with consumers to generate a response in the form of an order, a request for further information, or a visit to a retail outlet is direct marketing.
Product development	In business and engineering, new product development is the complete process of bringing a new product to market. There are two parallel aspects to this process : one involves product engineering ; the other marketing analysis. Marketers see new product development as the first stage in product life cycle management, engineers as part of Product Lifecycle Management.
Option	A contract that gives the purchaser the option to buy or sell the underlying financial instrument at a specified price, called the exercise price or strike price, within a specific period of time.
Product innovation	The development and sale of a new or improved product is a product innovation. Production of a new product on a commercial basis.
Concept testing	Concept testing is the process of using quantitative methods and qualitative methods to evaluate consumer response to a product idea prior to the introduction of a product to the market. It can also be used to generate communication designed to alter consumer attitudes toward existing products.
Innovation	Innovation refers to the first commercially successful introduction of a new product, the use of a new method of production, or the creation of a new form of business organization.
Application service provider	An application service provider is a business that provides computer-based services to customers over a network.
License	A license in the sphere of Intellectual Property Rights (IPR) is a document, contract or agreement giving permission or the 'right' to a legally-definable entity to do something (such as manufacture a product or to use a service), or to apply something (such as a trademark), with the objective of achieving commercial gain.
Insurance	Insurance refers to a system by which individuals can reduce their exposure to risk of large losses by spreading the risks among a large number of persons.
Staffing	Staffing refers to a management function that includes hiring, motivating, and retaining the best people available to accomplish the company's objectives.
Aid	Assistance provided by countries and by international institutions such as the World Bank to developing countries in the form of monetary grants, loans at low interest rates, in kind, or a combination of these is called aid. Aid can also refer to assistance of any type rendered to benefit some group or individual.
Market niche	A market niche or niche market is a focused, targetable portion of a market. By definition, then, a business that focuses on a niche market is addressing a need for a product or service that is not being addressed by mainstream providers.
Niche	In industry, a niche is a situation or an activity perfectly suited to a person. A niche can imply a working position or an area suited to a person who occupies it. Basically, a job where a person is able to succeed and thrive.
Analogy	Analogy is either the cognitive process of transferring information from a particular subject to another particular subject (the target), or a linguistic expression corresponding to such a process. In a narrower sense, analogy is an inference or an argument from a particular to

101

161

	another particular, as opposed to deduction, induction, and abduction, where at least one of the premises or the conclusion is general.
Emerging markets	The term emerging markets is commonly used to describe business and market activity in industrializing or emerging regions of the world. It is sometimes loosely used as a replacement for emerging economies, but really signifies a business phenomenon that is not fully described by or constrained to geography or economic strength; such countries are considered to be in a transitional phase between developing and developed status.
Emerging market	The term emerging market is commonly used to describe business and market activity in industrializing or emerging regions of the world.
Accounting	A system that collects and processes financial information about an organization and reports that information to decision makers is referred to as accounting.
Drawback	Drawback refers to rebate of import duties when the imported good is re-exported or used as input to the production of an exported good.
Regression analysis	Regression analysis refers to the statistical technique of finding a straight line that approximates the information in a group of data points. Used throughout empirical economics, including both international trade and finance.
Developed country	A developed country is one that enjoys a relatively high standard of living derived through an industrialized, diversified economy. Countries with a very high Human Development Index are generally considered developed countries.
Business plan	A detailed written statement that describes the nature of the business, the target market, the advantages the business will have in relation to competition, and the resources and qualifications of the owner is referred to as a business plan.
Usage rate	Usage rate refers to quantity consumed or patronage-store visits during a specific period; varies significantly among different customer groups.
Consideration	Consideration in contract law, a basic requirement for an enforceable agreement under traditional contract principles, defined in this text as legal value, bargained for and given in exchange for an act or promise. In corporation law, cash or property contributed to a corporation in exchange for shares, or a promise to contribute such cash or property.
Face value	The nominal or par value of an instrument as expressed on its face is referred to as the face value.
Disparity	Disparity refers to the regional and economic differences in a country, province, state, or continent
Asset	An item of property, such as land, capital, money, a share in ownership, or a claim on others for future payment, such as a bond or a bank deposit is an asset.
Specialist	A specialist is a trader who makes a market in one or several stocks and holds the limit order book for those stocks.
Decentralization	Decentralization is the process of redistributing decision-making closer to the point of service or action. This gives freedom to managers at lower levels of the organization to make decisions.
Analyst	Analyst refers to a person or tool with a primary function of information analysis, generally with a more limited, practical and short term set of goals than a researcher.
Personnel	A collective term for all of the employees of an organization. Personnel is also commonly used to refer to the personnel management function or the organizational unit responsible for administering personnel programs.

Go to **Cram101.com** for the Practice Tests for this Chapter.

Go to **Cram101.com** for the Practice Tests for this Chapter.
And, **NEVER** highlight a book again!

163

Advertising agency	A firm that specializes in the creation, production, and placement of advertising messages and may provide other services that facilitate the marketing communications process is an advertising agency.
Distribution channel	A distribution channel is a chain of intermediaries, each passing a product down the chain to the next organization, before it finally reaches the consumer or end-user.
Channel	Channel, in communications (sometimes called communications channel), refers to the medium used to convey information from a sender (or transmitter) to a receiver.
Consumer privacy	Consumer privacy laws and regulations seek to protect any individual from loss of privacy due to failures or limitations of corporate customer privacy measures.
Information system	An information system is a system whether automated or manual, that comprises people, machines, and/or methods organized to collect, process, transmit, and disseminate data that represent user information.
Systems design	Systems design is the process or art of defining the hardware and software architecture, components, modules, interfaces, and data for a computer system to satisfy specified requirements.
Voice of the customer	A term that refers to the wants, opinions, perceptions, and desires of the customer is a voice of the customer.
Hearing	A hearing is a proceeding before a court or other decision-making body or officer. A hearing is generally distinguished from a trial in that it is usually shorter and often less formal.
Gap	In December of 1995, Gap became the first major North American retailer to accept independent monitoring of the working conditions in a contract factory producing its garments. Gap is the largest specialty retailer in the United States.
Principal	In agency law, one under whose direction an agent acts and for whose benefit that agent acts is a principal.
International Monetary Fund	The International Monetary Fund is the international organization entrusted with overseeing the global financial system by monitoring exchange rates and balance of payments, as well as offering technical and financial assistance when asked.
Fund	Independent accounting entity with a self-balancing set of accounts segregated for the purposes of carrying on specific activities is referred to as a fund.
International trade	The export of goods and services from a country and the import of goods and services into a country is referred to as the international trade.
Gross National Product	Gross National Product is the total value of final goods and services produced in a year by a country's nationals (including profits from capital held abroad).
Labor	People's physical and mental talents and efforts that are used to help produce goods and services are called labor.
Business opportunity	A business opportunity involves the sale or lease of any product, service, equipment, etc. that will enable the purchaser-licensee to begin a business
Export promotion	Export promotion refers to a strategy for economic development that stresses expanding exports, often through policies to assist them such as export subsidies.
Central Intelligence Agency	The primary function of the Central Intelligence Agency is obtaining and analyzing information about foreign governments, corporations, and individuals, and reporting such information to the various branches of the Government. A second function is overtly and covertly disseminating information, both true and false, that influences others to make decisions favorable to the United States Government.

Go to **Cram101.com** for the Practice Tests for this Chapter.

Go to **Cram101.com** for the Practice Tests for this Chapter.
And, **NEVER** highlight a book again!

165

Research report	A research report is a business report produced by business research firms by their financial analysts. They are designed to dig out the important pieces of companies operational and financial reporting to paint a picture of the future of companies to assist debt and equity investing.
Economic policy	Economic policy refers to the actions that governments take in the economic field. It covers the systems for setting interest rates and government deficit as well as the labor market, national ownership, and many other areas of government.
Trade barrier	An artificial disincentive to export and/or import, such as a tariff, quota, or other NTB is called a trade barrier.
Exporting	Selling products to another country is called exporting.
Administration	Administration refers to the management and direction of the affairs of governments and institutions; a collective term for all policymaking officials of a government; the execution and implementation of public policy.
Brief	Brief refers to a statement of a party's case or legal arguments, usually prepared by an attorney. Also used to make legal arguments before appellate courts.
International division	Division responsible for a firm's international activities is an international division.
Manufacturing	Production of goods primarily by the application of labor and capital to raw materials and other intermediate inputs, in contrast to agriculture, mining, forestry, fishing, and services a manufacturing.
Foreign subsidiary	A company owned in a foreign country by another company is referred to as foreign subsidiary.
Affiliates	Local television stations that are associated with a major network are called affiliates. Affiliates agree to preempt time during specified hours for programming provided by the network and carry the advertising contained in the program.
Subsidiary	A company that is controlled by another company or corporation is a subsidiary.
Trade name	A commercial legal name under which a company does business is referred to as the trade name.
Franchising	Franchising is a method of doing business wherein a franchisor licenses trademarks and tried and proven methods of doing business to a franchisee in exchange for a recurring payment, and usually a percentage piece of gross sales or gross profits as well as the annual fees. The term " franchising " is used to describe a wide variety of business systems which may or may not fall into the legal definition provided above.
Product line	A group of products that are physically similar or are intended for a similar market are called the product line.
Regulation	Regulation refers to restrictions state and federal laws place on business with regard to the conduct of its activities.
Exporter	A firm that sells its product in another country is an exporter.
Broker	In commerce, a broker is a party that mediates between a buyer and a seller. A broker who also acts as a seller or as a buyer becomes a principal party to the deal.
Market share data	A comparative measure that determines relative positions of firms in the marketplace is called market share data.
Common market	Common market refers to a group of countries that eliminate all barriers to movement of both goods and factors among themselves, and that also, on each product, agree to levy the same tariff on imports from outside the group.

Business intelligence	Business intelligence refers to data about the past history, present status, or future projections for a business organization.
Business development	Business development emcompasses a number of techniques designed to grow an economic enterprise. Such techniques include, but are not limited to, assessments of marketing opportunities and target markets, intelligence gathering on customers and competitors, generating leads for possible sales, followup sales activity, and formal proposal writing.
Joint venture	Joint venture refers to an undertaking by two parties for a specific purpose and duration, taking any of several legal forms.
Licensing	Licensing is a form of strategic alliance which involves the sale of a right to use certain proprietary knowledge (so called intellectual property) in a defined way.

168

Go to **Cram101.com** for the Practice Tests for this Chapter.

Go to **Cram101.com** for the Practice Tests for this Chapter.
And, **NEVER** highlight a book again!

169

Discount	The difference between the face value of a bond and its selling price, when a bond is sold for less than its face value it's referred to as a discount.
Brand	A name, symbol, or design that identifies the goods or services of one seller or group of sellers and distinguishes them from the goods and services of competitors is a brand.
Operation	A standardized method or technique that is performed repetitively, often on different materials resulting in different finished goods is called an operation.
Revenue	Revenue is a U.S. business term for the amount of money that a company receives from its activities, mostly from sales of products and/or services to customers.
Profit	Profit refers to the return to the resource entrepreneurial ability; total revenue minus total cost.
World Trade Organization	The World Trade Organization is an international, multilateral organization, which sets the rules for the global trading system and resolves disputes between its member states, all of whom are signatories to its approximately 30 agreements.
Market	A market is, as defined in economics, a social arrangement that allows buyers and sellers to discover information and carry out a voluntary exchange of goods or services.
Anticipation	In finance, anticipation is where debts are paid off early, generally in order to pay less interest.
Business plan	A detailed written statement that describes the nature of the business, the target market, the advantages the business will have in relation to competition, and the resources and qualifications of the owner is referred to as a business plan.
Regulation	Regulation refers to restrictions state and federal laws place on business with regard to the conduct of its activities.
Consumption	In Keynesian economics consumption refers to personal consumption expenditure, i.e., the purchase of currently produced goods and services out of income, out of savings (net worth), or from borrowed funds. It refers to that part of disposable income that does not go to saving.
Marketing	Promoting and selling products or services to customers, or prospective customers, is referred to as marketing.
Conspicuous consumption	Conspicuous consumption is a term introduced by the American economist and sociologist Thorstein Veblen, in The Theory of the Leisure Class (1899). It is used to describe the obvious consumption of goods, commodities and services for the sake of displaying income or wealth in order to acquire social status.
Market opportunities	Market opportunities refer to areas where a company believes there are favorable demand trends, needs, and/or wants that are not being satisfied, and where it can compete effectively.
Investment	Investment refers to spending for the production and accumulation of capital and additions to inventories. In a financial sense, buying an asset with the expectation of making a return.
Commerce	Commerce is the exchange of something of value between two entities. It is the central mechanism from which capitalism is derived.
Developing country	Developing country refers to a country whose per capita income is low by world standards. Same as LDC. As usually used, it does not necessarily connote that the country's income is rising.
Private sector	The households and business firms of the economy are referred to as private sector.
Enterprise	Enterprise refers to another name for a business organization. Other similar terms are

	business firm, sometimes simply business, sometimes simply firm, as well as company, and entity.
Economy	The income, expenditures, and resources that affect the cost of running a business and household are called an economy.
Service	Service refers to a "non tangible product" that is not embodied in a physical good and that typically effects some change in another product, person, or institution. Contrasts with good.
Consumer behavior	Consumer behavior refers to the actions a person takes in purchasing and using products and services, including the mental and social processes that precede and follow these actions.
Emerging markets	The term emerging markets is commonly used to describe business and market activity in industrializing or emerging regions of the world. It is sometimes loosely used as a replacement for emerging economies, but really signifies a business phenomenon that is not fully described by or constrained to geography or economic strength; such countries are considered to be in a transitional phase between developing and developed status.
Emerging market	The term emerging market is commonly used to describe business and market activity in industrializing or emerging regions of the world.
Amway	Amway is a multi-level marketing company founded in 1959 by Jay Van Andel and Rich DeVos. The company's name is a portmanteau of "American Way." .
Avon	Avon is an American cosmetics, perfume and toy seller with markets in over 135 countries across the world and a sales of $7.74 billion worldwide.
Sony	Sony is a multinational corporation and one of the world's largest media conglomerates founded in Tokyo, Japan. One of its divisions Sony Electronics is one of the leading manufacturers of electronics, video, communications, and information technology products for the consumer and professional markets.
Economic growth	Economic growth refers to the increase over time in the capacity of an economy to produce goods and services and to improve the well-being of its citizens.
Trading bloc	Trading bloc refers to a group of countries that are somehow closely associated in international trade, usually in some sort of PTA.
Economic development	Increase in the economic standard of living of a country's population, normally accomplished by increasing its stocks of physical and human capital and improving its technology is an economic development.
Distribution	Distribution in economics, the manner in which total output and income is distributed among individuals or factors.
Supply	Supply is the aggregate amount of any material good that can be called into being at a certain price point; it comprises one half of the equation of supply and demand. In classical economic theory, a curve representing supply is one of the factors that produce price.
Free enterprise	Free enterprise refers to a system in which economic agents are free to own property and engage in commercial transactions.
Command economy	A command economy refers to an economy in which a central government either directly or indirectly sets output targets, incomes, and prices.
Gross domestic product	Gross domestic product refers to the total value of new goods and services produced in a given year within the borders of a country, regardless of by whom.
Production	The creation of finished goods and services using the factors of production: land, labor, capital, entrepreneurship, and knowledge.

Per capita	Per capita refers to per person. Usually used to indicate the average per person of any given statistic, commonly income.
Domestic	From or in one's own country. A domestic producer is one that produces inside the home country. A domestic price is the price inside the home country. Opposite of 'foreign' or 'world.'.
Consumer demand	Consumer demand or consumption is also known as personal consumption expenditure. It is the largest part of aggregate demand or effective demand at the macroeconomic level.There are two variants of consumption in the aggregate demand model, including induced consumption and autonomous consumption.
Interest rate	The rate of return on bonds, loans, or deposits. When one speaks of 'the' interest rate, it is usually in a model where there is only one.
Interest	In finance and economics, interest is the price paid by a borrower for the use of a lender's money. In other words, interest is the amount of paid to "rent" money for a period of time.
Labor	People's physical and mental talents and efforts that are used to help produce goods and services are called labor.
Buyer	A buyer refers to a role in the buying center with formal authority and responsibility to select the supplier and negotiate the terms of the contract.
Productivity	Productivity refers to the total output of goods and services in a given period of time divided by work hours.
Technology	The body of knowledge and techniques that can be used to combine economic resources to produce goods and services is called technology.
Human resources	Human resources refers to the individuals within the firm, and to the portion of the firm's organization that deals with hiring, firing, training, and other personnel issues.
Consumer good	Products and services that are ultimately consumed rather than used in the production of another good are a consumer good.
Real income	Real income refers to the amount of goods and services that can be purchased with nominal income during some period of time; nominal income adjusted for inflation.
United Nations	An international organization created by multilateral treaty in 1945 to promote social and economic cooperation among nations and to protect human rights is the United Nations.
Gross National Product	Gross National Product is the total value of final goods and services produced in a year by a country's nationals (including profits from capital held abroad).
Market value	Market value refers to the price of an asset agreed on between a willing buyer and a willing seller; the price an asset could demand if it is sold on the open market.
Asset	An item of property, such as land, capital, money, a share in ownership, or a claim on others for future payment, such as a bond or a bank deposit is an asset.
Business operations	Business operations are those activities involved in the running of a business for the purpose of producing value for the stakeholders. The outcome of business operations is the harvesting of value from assets owned by a business.
Domestic corporation	A corporation in the state in which it was formed is a domestic corporation.
Corporation	A legal entity chartered by a state or the Federal government that is distinct and separate from the individuals who own it is a corporation. This separation gives the corporation unique powers which other legal entities lack.

Go to **Cram101.com** for the Practice Tests for this Chapter.

Affiliates	Local television stations that are associated with a major network are called affiliates. Affiliates agree to preempt time during specified hours for programming provided by the network and carry the advertising contained in the program.
Per capita income	The per capita income for a group of people may be defined as their total personal income, divided by the total population. Per capita income is usually reported in units of currency per year.
World Bank	The World Bank is a group of five international organizations responsible for providing finance and advice to countries for the purposes of economic development and poverty reduction, and for encouraging and safeguarding international investment.
Economic expansion	The upward phase of the business cycle, in which GDP is rising and unemployment is falling over time is called economic expansion.
Industry	A group of firms that produce identical or similar products is an industry. It is also used specifically to refer to an area of economic production focused on manufacturing which involves large amounts of capital investment before any profit can be realized, also called "heavy industry".
Exporter	A firm that sells its product in another country is an exporter.
Exporting	Selling products to another country is called exporting.
Volkswagen	Volkswagen or VW is an automobile manufacturer based in Wolfsburg, Germany in the state of Lower Saxony. It forms the core of this Group, one of the world's four largest car producers. Its German tagline is "Aus Liebe zum Automobil", which is translated as "For the love of the car" - or, For Love of the People's Cars,".
World price	The price of a good on the 'world market,' meaning the price outside of any country's borders and therefore exclusive of any trade taxes or subsidies is the world price.
Free trade	Free trade refers to a situation in which there are no artificial barriers to trade, such as tariffs and quotas. Usually used, often only implicitly, with frictionless trade, so that it implies that there are no barriers to trade of any kind.
Export	In economics, an export is any good or commodity, shipped or otherwise transported out of a country, province, town to another part of the world in a legitimate fashion, typically for use in trade or sale.
Standard of living	Standard of living refers to the level of consumption that people enjoy, on the average, and is measured by average income per person.
Samsung	On November 30, 2005 Samsung pleaded guilty to a charge it participated in a worldwide DRAM price fixing conspiracy during 1999-2002 that damaged competition and raized PC prices.
Zenith	Zenith is an American manufacturer of televisions headquartered in Lincolnshire, Illinois. It was the inventor of the modern remote control, and it introduced HDTV in North America.
Cultural values	The values that employees need to have and act on for the organization to act on the strategic values are called cultural values.
Economic policy	Economic policy refers to the actions that governments take in the economic field. It covers the systems for setting interest rates and government deficit as well as the labor market, national ownership, and many other areas of government.
Policy	Similar to a script in that a policy can be a less than completely rational decision-making method. Involves the use of a pre-existing set of decision steps for any problem that presents itself.
Property rights	Bundle of legal rights over the use to which a resource is put and over the use made of any

Go to **Cram101.com** for the Practice Tests for this Chapter.
And, **NEVER** highlight a book again!

177

	income that may be derived from that resource are referred to as property rights.
Contract	A contract is a "promise" or an "agreement" that is enforced or recognized by the law. In the civil law, a contract is considered to be part of the general law of obligations.
Property	Assets defined in the broadest legal sense. Property includes the unrealized receivables of a cash basis taxpayer, but not services rendered.
Factors of production	Economic resources: land, capital, labor, and entrepreneurial ability are called factors of production.
Raw material	Raw material refers to a good that has not been transformed by production; a primary product.
Management	Management characterizes the process of leading and directing all or part of an organization, often a business, through the deployment and manipulation of resources. Early twentieth-century management writer Mary Parker Follett defined management as "the art of getting things done through people."
Capital	Capital generally refers to financial wealth, especially that used to start or maintain a business. In classical economics, capital is one of four factors of production, the others being land and labor and entrepreneurship.
International trade	The export of goods and services from a country and the import of goods and services into a country is referred to as the international trade.
Incentive	An incentive is any factor (financial or non-financial) that provides a motive for a particular course of action, or counts as a reason for preferring one choice to the alternatives.
Privatization	A process in which investment bankers take companies that were previously owned by the government to the public markets is referred to as privatization.
Budget	Budget refers to an account, usually for a year, of the planned expenditures and the expected receipts of an entity. For a government, the receipts are tax revenues.
Tariff	A tax imposed by a nation on an imported good is called a tariff.
Early growth	Early growth refers to the first stage of the retail life cycle, when a new outlet emerges as a sharp departure from competitive forms.
Open market	In economics, the open market is the term used to refer to the environment in which bonds are bought and sold.
Manufacturing	Production of goods primarily by the application of labor and capital to raw materials and other intermediate inputs, in contrast to agriculture, mining, forestry, fishing, and services a manufacturing.
Vertical integration	Vertical integration refers to production of different stages of processing of a product within the same firm.
Economies of scale	In economics, returns to scale and economies of scale are related terms that describe what happens as the scale of production increases. They are different terms and not to be used interchangeably.
Transaction cost	A transaction cost is a cost incurred in making an economic exchange. For example, most people, when buying or selling a stock, must pay a commission to their broker; that commission is a transaction cost of doing the stock deal.
Integration	Economic integration refers to reducing barriers among countries to transactions and to movements of goods, capital, and labor, including harmonization of laws, regulations, and standards. Integrated markets theoretically function as a unified market.

Go to **Cram101.com** for the Practice Tests for this Chapter.
And, **NEVER** highlight a book again!

Firm	An organization that employs resources to produce a good or service for profit and owns and operates one or more plants is referred to as a firm.
Diffusion	Diffusion is the process by which a new idea or new product is accepted by the market. The rate of diffusion is the speed that the new idea spreads from one consumer to the next.
Intellectual property	In law, intellectual property is an umbrella term for various legal entitlements which attach to certain types of information, ideas, or other intangibles in their expressed form. The holder of this legal entitlement is generally entitled to exercise various exclusive rights in relation to its subject matter.
Innovation	Innovation refers to the first commercially successful introduction of a new product, the use of a new method of production, or the creation of a new form of business organization.
Accord	An agreement whereby the parties agree to accept something different in satisfaction of the original contract is an accord.
Grant	Grant refers to an intergovernmental transfer of funds . Since the New Deal, state and local governments have become increasingly dependent upon federal grants for an almost infinite variety of programs.
Entrepreneur	The owner/operator. The person who organizes, manages, and assumes the risks of a firm, taking a new idea or a new product and turning it into a successful business is an entrepreneur.
Specialist	A specialist is a trader who makes a market in one or several stocks and holds the limit order book for those stocks.
Journal	Book of original entry, in which transactions are recorded in a general ledger system, is referred to as a journal.
Information technology	Information technology refers to technology that helps companies change business by allowing them to use new methods.
Hyperinflation	Hyperinflation refers to a very rapid rise in the price level; an extremely high rate of inflation.
Assessment	Collecting information and providing feedback to employees about their behavior, communication style, or skills is an assessment.
Brief	Brief refers to a statement of a party's case or legal arguments, usually prepared by an attorney. Also used to make legal arguments before appellate courts.
Market price	Market price is an economic concept with commonplace familiarity; it is the price that a good or service is offered at, or will fetch, in the marketplace; it is of interest mainly in the study of microeconomics.
Fair value	Fair value is a concept used in finance and economics, defined as a rational and unbiased estimate of the potential market price of a good, service, or asset.
Cooperative	A business owned and controlled by the people who use it, producers, consumers, or workers with similar needs who pool their resources for mutual gain is called cooperative.
Wall Street Journal	Dow Jones & Company was founded in 1882 by reporters Charles Dow, Edward Jones and Charles Bergstresser. Jones converted the small Customers' Afternoon Letter into The Wall Street Journal, first published in 1889, and began delivery of the Dow Jones News Service via telegraph. The Journal featured the Jones 'Average', the first of several indexes of stock and bond prices on the New York Stock Exchange.
Host country	The country in which the parent-country organization seeks to locate or has already located a facility is a host country.

Leverage	Leverage is using given resources in such a way that the potential positive or negative outcome is magnified. In finance, this generally refers to borrowing.
Trade barrier	An artificial disincentive to export and/or import, such as a tariff, quota, or other NTB is called a trade barrier.
Trend	Trend refers to the long-term movement of an economic variable, such as its average rate of increase or decrease over enough years to encompass several business cycles.
Social overhead capital	Basic infrastructure projects such as roads, power generation, and irrigation systems are referred to as social overhead capital.
Advertising agency	A firm that specializes in the creation, production, and placement of advertising messages and may provide other services that facilitate the marketing communications process is an advertising agency.
Marketing research	Marketing research refers to the analysis of markets to determine opportunities and challenges, and to find the information needed to make good decisions.
Advertising	Advertising refers to paid, nonpersonal communication through various media by organizations and individuals who are in some way identified in the advertising message.
Credit	Credit refers to a recording as positive in the balance of payments, any transaction that gives rise to a payment into the country, such as an export, the sale of an asset, or borrowing from abroad.
Commodity	Could refer to any good, but in trade a commodity is usually a raw material or primary product that enters into international trade, such as metals or basic agricultural products.
Contribution	In business organization law, the cash or property contributed to a business by its owners is referred to as contribution.
Economic system	Economic system refers to a particular set of institutional arrangements and a coordinating mechanism for solving the economizing problem; a method of organizing an economy, of which the market system and the command system are the two general types.
Inventory	Tangible property held for sale in the normal course of business or used in producing goods or services for sale is an inventory.
Household	An economic unit that provides the economy with resources and uses the income received to purchase goods and services that satisfy economic wants is called household.
Draft	A signed, written order by which one party instructs another party to pay a specified sum to a third party, at sight or at a specific date is a draft.
Manufacturing costs	Costs incurred in a manufacturing process, which consist of direct material, direct labor, and manufacturing overhead are referred to as manufacturing costs.
Facilitating agent	A facilitating agent is a business firm that assists in the performance of distribution tasks other than buying, selling, and transferring title (e.g., bank, transportation company, warehouse).
Disposable income	Disposable income is income minus taxes. More accurately, income minus direct taxes plus transfer payments; that is, the income available to be spent and saved.
Agent	A person who makes economic decisions for another economic actor. A hired manager operates as an agent for a firm's owner.
Union	A worker association that bargains with employers over wages and working conditions is called a union.
Channel	Channel, in communications (sometimes called communications channel), refers to the medium

Go to **Cram101.com** for the Practice Tests for this Chapter.
And, **NEVER** highlight a book again!

183

	used to convey information from a sender (or transmitter) to a receiver.
Competitor	Other organizations in the same industry or type of business that provide a good or service to the same set of customers is referred to as a competitor.
Customer service	The ability of logistics management to satisfy users in terms of time, dependability, communication, and convenience is called the customer service.
Pizza Hut	Pizza Hut is the world's largest pizza restaurant chain with nearly 34,000 restaurants, delivery-carry out units, and kiosks in 100 countries
Franchise	A contractual right to sell certain products or services, use certain trademarks, or perform activities in a geographical region is called a franchise.
Purchasing power	The amount of goods that money will buy, usually measured by the CPI is referred to as purchasing power.
Purchasing	Purchasing refers to the function in a firm that searches for quality material resources, finds the best suppliers, and negotiates the best price for goods and services.
Marketing strategy	Marketing strategy refers to the means by which a marketing goal is to be achieved, usually characterized by a specified target market and a marketing program to reach it.
Optimum	Optimum refers to the best. Usually refers to a most preferred choice by consumers subject to a budget constraint or a profit maximizing choice by firms or industry subject to a technological constraint.
Utility	Utility refers to the want-satisfying power of a good or service; the satisfaction or pleasure a consumer obtains from the consumption of a good or service.
Market development	Selling existing products to new markets is called market development.
Hypermarket	A large retail store offering a mix of food products and general merchandise products under one roof is called a hypermarket.
Market system	All the product and resource markets of a market economy and the relationships among them are called a market system.
Foundation	A Foundation is a type of philanthropic organization set up by either individuals or institutions as a legal entity (either as a corporation or trust) with the purpose of distributing grants to support causes in line with the goals of the foundation.
Growth stage	The second stage of the product life cycle characterized by rapid increases in sales and by the appearance of competitors is referred to as the growth stage.
Acceleration	Acceleration refers to the shortening of the time for the performance of a contract or the payment of a note by the operation of some provision in the contract or note itself.
Market potential	Market potential refers to maximum total sales of a product by all firms to a segment during a specified time period under specified environmental conditions and marketing efforts of the firms.
Product innovation	The development and sale of a new or improved product is a product innovation. Production of a new product on a commercial basis.
Labor intensive	Describing an industry or sector of the economy that relies relatively heavily on inputs of labor, usually relative to capital but sometimes to human capital or skilled labor, compared to other industries or sectors is labor intensive.
Standardization	Standardization, in the context related to technologies and industries, is the process of establishing a technical standard among competing entities in a market, where this will bring

benefits without hurting competition.

PepsiCo	In many ways, PepsiCo differs from its main competitor, having three times as many employees, larger revenues, but a smaller net profit.
Product differentiation	A strategy in which one firm's product is distinguished from competing products by means of its design, related services, quality, location, or other attributes is called product differentiation.
Committee	A long-lasting, sometimes permanent team in the organization structure created to deal with tasks that recur regularly is the committee.
Authority	Authority in agency law, refers to an agent's ability to affect his principal's legal relations with third parties. Also used to refer to an actor's legal power or ability to do something. In addition, sometimes used to refer to a statute, case, or other legal source that justifies a particular result.
Vendor	A person who sells property to a vendee is a vendor. The words vendor and vendee are more commonly applied to the seller and purchaser of real estate, and the words seller and buyer are more commonly applied to the seller and purchaser of personal property.
Billboard	The most common form of outdoor advertising is called a billboard.
Middle class	Colloquially, the term is often applied to people who have a degree of economic independence, but not a great deal of social influence or power in their society. The term often encompasses merchants and professionals, bureaucrats, and some farmers and skilled workers[citation needed]. While most Americans identify themselves as middle class, only 20% live the lifestyle indicative of the American middle class.
Market segments	Market segments refer to the groups that result from the process of market segmentation; these groups ideally have common needs and will respond similarly to a marketing action.
Mixed economy	An economy in which some production is done by the private sector and some by the state, in state-owned enterprises is called mixed economy.
Sponsorship	When the advertiser assumes responsibility for the production and usually the content of a television program as well as the advertising that appears within it, we have sponsorship.
Advertising Age	Advertising Age is the world's leading source of news, analysis, information and data on advertising, marketing and media. The magazine was started as a broadsheet newspaper in Chicago in 1930.
Accounting	A system that collects and processes financial information about an organization and reports that information to decision makers is referred to as accounting.
A share	In finance the term A share has two distinct meanings, both relating to securities. The first is a designation for a 'class' of common or preferred stock. A share of common or preferred stock typically has enhanced voting rights or other benefits compared to the other forms of shares that may have been created. The equity structure, or how many types of shares are offered, is determined by the corporate charter.
Insurance	Insurance refers to a system by which individuals can reduce their exposure to risk of large losses by spreading the risks among a large number of persons.
Harvard Business Review	Harvard Business Review is a research-based magazine written for business practitioners, it claims a high ranking business readership and enjoys the reverence of academics, executives, and management consultants. It has been the frequent publishing home for well known scholars and management thinkers.
Principal	In agency law, one under whose direction an agent acts and for whose benefit that agent acts is a principal.

Trade liberalization	Reduction of tariffs and removal or relaxation of NTBs is referred to as trade liberalization.
Economic model	Economic model refers to a simplified picture of economic reality; an abstract generalization.
Import substitution	Import substitution refers to a strategy for economic development that replaces imports with domestic production. It may be motivated by the infant industry argument, or simply by the desire to mimic the industrial structure of advanced countries.
Protectionism	Protectionism refers to advocacy of protection. The word has a negative connotation, and few advocates of protection in particular situations will acknowledge being protectionists.
Growth strategy	A strategy based on investing in companies and sectors which are growing faster than their peers is a growth strategy. The benefits are usually in the form of capital gains rather than dividends.
Gillette	On October 1, 2005, Gillette finalized its purchase by Procter & Gamble. As a result of this merger, the Gillette Company no longer exists. Its last day of market trading - symbol G on the New York Stock Exchange - was September 30, 2005. The merger created the world's largest personal care and household products company.
Infomercial	An infomercials is a television commercial that runs as long as a typical television program. Also known as paid programming (or teleshopping in Europe), they are normally shown outside of peak hours, such as late at night or early in the morning.
Tactic	A short-term immediate decision that, in its totality, leads to the achievement of strategic goals is called a tactic.
Average revenue	Average revenue refers to total revenue from the sale of a product divided by the quantity of the product sold ; equal to the price at which the product is sold when all units of the product are sold at the same price.
Users	Users refer to people in the organization who actually use the product or service purchased by the buying center.
Installations	Support goods, consisting of buildings and fixed equipment are called installations.
Financial crisis	A loss of confidence in a country's currency or other financial assets causing international investors to withdraw their funds from the country is referred to as a financial crisis.
Devaluation	Lowering the value of a nation's currency relative to other currencies is called devaluation.
Default	In finance, default occurs when a debtor has not met its legal obligations according to the debt contract, e.g. it has not made a scheduled payment, or violated a covenant (condition) of the debt contract.
Recession	A significant decline in economic activity. In the U.S., recession is approximately defined as two successive quarters of falling GDP, as judged by NBER.
Restructuring	Restructuring is the corporate management term for the act of partially dismantling and reorganizing a company for the purpose of making it more efficient and therefore more profitable.
Business opportunity	A business opportunity involves the sale or lease of any product, service, equipment, etc. that will enable the purchaser-licensee to begin a business
Free market	A free market is a market where price is determined by the unregulated interchange of supply and demand rather than set by artificial means.
Capitalism	Capitalism refers to an economic system in which capital is mostly owned by private individuals and corporations. Contrasts with communism.

Long run	In economic models, the long run time frame assumes no fixed factors of production. Firms can enter or leave the marketplace, and the cost (and availability) of land, labor, raw materials, and capital goods can be assumed to vary.
Stabilization policy	Stabilization policy refers to the use of monetary and fiscal policies to reduce business fluctuations in aggregate employment and prices.
Trade pattern	What goods a country trades, with whom, and in what direction. Explaining the trade pattern is one of the major purposes of trade theory, especially which goods a country will export and which it will import.
Inflation	An increase in the overall price level of an economy, usually as measured by the CPI or by the implicit price deflator is called inflation.
Market economy	A market economy is an economic system in which the production and distribution of goods and services takes place through the mechanism of free markets guided by a free price system rather than by the state in a planned economy.
Single market	A single market is a customs union with common policies on product regulation, and freedom of movement of all the four factors of production (goods, services, capital and labor).
Business Week	Business Week is a business magazine published by McGraw-Hill. It was first published in 1929 under the direction of Malcolm Muir, who was serving as president of the McGraw-Hill Publishing company at the time. It is considered to be the standard both in industry and among students.
Bureaucracy	Bureaucracy refers to an organization with many layers of managers who set rules and regulations and oversee all decisions.
Corruption	The unauthorized use of public office for private gain. The most common forms of corruption are bribery, extortion, and the misuse of inside information.
Downturn	A decline in a stock market or economic cycle is a downturn.
Monetary policy	The use of the money supply and/or the interest rate to influence the level of economic activity and other policy objectives including the balance of payments or the exchange rate is called monetary policy.
International Monetary Fund	The International Monetary Fund is the international organization entrusted with overseeing the global financial system by monitoring exchange rates and balance of payments, as well as offering technical and financial assistance when asked.
Fund	Independent accounting entity with a self-balancing set of accounts segregated for the purposes of carrying on specific activities is referred to as a fund.
Special economic zone	A Special Economic Zone is a geographical region that has economic laws different from a country's typical economic laws. Usually the goal is an increase in foreign investment.
Socialism	An economic system under which the state owns the resources and makes the economic decisions is called socialism.
Analyst	Analyst refers to a person or tool with a primary function of information analysis, generally with a more limited, practical and short term set of goals than a researcher.
Market access	The ability of firms from one country to sell in another is market access.
Compliance	A type of influence process where a receiver accepts the position advocated by a source to obtain favorable outcomes or to avoid punishment is the compliance.
Concession	A concession is a business operated under a contract or license associated with a degree of exclusivity in exploiting a business within a certain geographical area. For example, sports arenas or public parks may have concession stands; and public services such as water supply

	may be operated as concessions.
Legal system	Legal system refers to system of rules that regulate behavior and the processes by which the laws of a country are enforced and through which redress of grievances is obtained.
Complaint	The pleading in a civil case in which the plaintiff states his claim and requests relief is called complaint. In the common law, it is a formal legal document that sets out the basic facts and legal reasons that the filing party (the plaintiffs) believes are sufficient to support a claim against another person, persons, entity or entities (the defendants) that entitles the plaintiff(s) to a remedy (either money damages or injunctive relief).
Exchange	The trade of things of value between buyer and seller so that each is better off after the trade is called the exchange.
License	A license in the sphere of Intellectual Property Rights (IPR) is a document, contract or agreement giving permission or the 'right' to a legally-definable entity to do something (such as manufacture a product or to use a service), or to apply something (such as a trademark), with the objective of achieving commercial gain.
Economic freedom	Freedom to engage in economic transactions, without government interference but with government support of the institutions necessary for that freedom, including rule of law, sound money, and open markets is referred to as economic freedom.
Nestle	Nestle is the world's biggest food and beverage company. In the 1860s, a pharmacist, developed a food for babies who were unable to be breastfed. His first success was a premature infant who could not tolerate his own mother's milk nor any of the usual substitutes. The value of the new product was quickly recognized when his new formula saved the child's life.
Points	Loan origination fees that may be deductible as interest by a buyer of property. A seller of property who pays points reduces the selling price by the amount of the points paid for the buyer.
Multinational corporations	Firms that own production facilities in two or more countries and produce and sell their products globally are referred to as multinational corporations.
Multinational corporation	An organization that manufactures and markets products in many different countries and has multinational stock ownership and multinational management is referred to as multinational corporation.
Partnership	In the common law, a partnership is a type of business entity in which partners share with each other the profits or losses of the business undertaking in which they have all invested.
Barriers to entry	In economics and especially in the theory of competition, barriers to entry are obstacles in the path of a firm which wants to enter a given market.
Microsoft	Microsoft is a multinational computer technology corporation with 2004 global annual sales of US$39.79 billion and 71,553 employees in 102 countries and regions as of July 2006. It develops, manufactures, licenses, and supports a wide range of software products for computing devices.
Remainder	A remainder in property law is a future interest created in a transferee that is capable of becoming possessory upon the natural termination of a prior estate created by the same instrument.
Turnover	Turnover in a financial context refers to the rate at which a provider of goods cycles through its average inventory. Turnover in a human resources context refers to the characteristic of a given company or industry, relative to rate at which an employer gains and loses staff.

192

Go to **Cram101.com** for the Practice Tests for this Chapter.

Bilateral agreement	A bilateral agreement is between two countries or organizations, as opposed to several countries.
Securities market	The securities market is the market for securities, where companies and the government can raise long-term funds.
Foreign exchange	In finance, foreign exchange means currencies, such as U.S. Dollars and Euros. These are traded on foreign exchange markets.
Confirmed	When the seller's bank agrees to assume liability on the letter of credit issued by the buyer's bank the transaction is confirmed. The term means that the credit is not only backed up by the issuing foreign bank, but that payment is also guaranteed by the notifying American bank.
Security	Security refers to a claim on the borrower future income that is sold by the borrower to the lender. A security is a type of transferable interest representing financial value.
Stock market	An organized marketplace in which common stocks are traded. In the United States, the largest stock market is the New York Stock Exchange, on which are traded the stocks of the largest U.S. companies.
Stock	In financial terminology, stock is the capital raized by a corporation, through the issuance and sale of shares.
Initial public offering	Firms in the process of becoming publicly traded companies will issue shares of stock using an initial public offering, which is merely the process of selling stock for the first time to interested investors.
Capital movement	Capital inflow and/or outflow is referred to as capital movement.
Rule of law	A legal system in which rules are clear, well-understood, and fairly enforced, including property rights and enforcement of contracts is called rule of law.
Reuters	Reuters is best known as a news service that provides reports from around the world to newspapers and broadcasters. Its main focus is on supplying the financial markets with information and trading products.
Real trade	Real trade refers to a shorthand term for most of the theory of international trade, which consists largely of real models. Contrasts with international finance.
Trade dispute	Trade dispute refers to any disagreement between nations involving their international trade or trade policies.
Restricted trade	Trade that is restrained in some fashion by tariffs, transport costs, or non-tariff barriers is referred to as restricted trade.
Corporate governance	Corporate governance is the set of processes, customs, policies, laws and institutions affecting the way a corporation is directed, administered or controlled.
Comprehensive	A comprehensive refers to a layout accurate in size, color, scheme, and other necessary details to show how a final ad will look. For presentation only, never for reproduction.
Red tape	Red tape is a derisive term for excessive regulations or rigid conformity to formal rules that are considered redundant or bureaucratic and hinders or prevents action or decision-making.
Management control	That aspect of management concerned with the comparison of actual versus planned performance as well as the development and implementation of procedures to correct substandard performance is called management control.
Monopoly	A monopoly is defined as a persistent market situation where there is only one provider of a kind of product or service.

Go to **Cram101.com** for the Practice Tests for this Chapter.

Quantitative restriction	Quantitative restriction refers to a restriction on trade, usually imports, limiting the quantity of the good or service that is traded; a quota is the most common example.
Direct investment	Direct investment refers to a domestic firm actually investing in and owning a foreign subsidiary or division.
Estate	An estate is the totality of the legal rights, interests, entitlements and obligations attaching to property. In the context of wills and probate, it refers to the totality of the property which the deceased owned or in which some interest was held.
Foreign direct investment	Foreign direct investment refers to the buying of permanent property and businesses in foreign nations.
Protective tariff	A tariff designed to shield domestic producers of a good or service from the competition of foreign producers is referred to as a protective tariff.
Intellectual property rights	Intellectual property rights, such as patents, copyrights, trademarks, trade secrets, trade names, and domain names are very valuable business assets. Federal and state laws protect intellectual property rights from misappropriation and infringement.
Intellectual property right	Intellectual property right refers to the right to control and derive the benefits from something one has invented, discovered, or created.
Labor law	Labor law is the body of laws, administrative rulings, and precedents which addresses the legal rights of, and restrictions on, workers and their organizations.
Bribery	When one person gives another person money, property, favors, or anything else of value for a favor in return, we have bribery. Often referred to as a payoff or 'kickback.'
Foreign corporation	Foreign corporation refers to a corporation incorporated in one state doing business in another state. A corporation doing business in a jurisdiction in which it was not formed.
Browser	A program that allows a user to connect to the World Wide Web by simply typing in a URL is a browser.
Embargo	Embargo refers to the prohibition of some category of trade. May apply to exports and/or imports, of particular products or of all trade, vis a vis the world or a particular country or countries.
Joint venture	Joint venture refers to an undertaking by two parties for a specific purpose and duration, taking any of several legal forms.
Quota	A government-imposed restriction on quantity, or sometimes on total value, used to restrict the import of something to a specific quantity is called a quota.
Market research	Market research is the process of systematic gathering, recording and analyzing of data about customers, competitors and the market. Market research can help create a business plan, launch a new product or service, fine tune existing products and services, expand into new markets etc. It can be used to determine which portion of the population will purchase the product/service, based on variables like age, gender, location and income level. It can be found out what market characteristics your target market has.
Gain	In finance, gain is a profit or an increase in value of an investment such as a stock or bond. Gain is calculated by fair market value or the proceeds from the sale of the investment minus the sum of the purchase price and all costs associated with it.
Forbes	David Churbuck founded online Forbes in 1996. The site drew attention when it uncovered Stephen Glass' journalistic fraud in The New Republic in 1998, a scoop that gave credibility to internet journalism.
Unskilled labor	Unskilled labor refers to labor with a low level of skill or human capital. Identified

empirically as labor earning a low wage, with a low level of education, or in an occupational category associated with these.

Labor force	In economics the labor force is the group of people who have a potential for being employed.
Developed country	A developed country is one that enjoys a relatively high standard of living derived through an industrialized, diversified economy. Countries with a very high Human Development Index are generally considered developed countries.
Durable good	A durable good is a good which does not quickly wear out, or more specifically, it yields services or utility over time rather than being completely used up when used once.
Nissan	Nissan is Japan's second largest car company after Toyota. Nissan is among the top three Asian rivals of the "big three" in the US.
Sustainable growth	A maximum amount of growth a firm can sustain without increasing financial leverage is called sustainable growth.
Controlling interest	A firm has a controlling interest in another business entity when it owns more than 50 percent of that entity's voting stock.
Controlling	A management function that involves determining whether or not an organization is progressing toward its goals and objectives, and taking corrective action if it is not is called controlling.
Scope	Scope of a project is the sum total of all projects products and their requirements or features.
Marketing Plan	Marketing plan refers to a road map for the marketing activities of an organization for a specified future period of time, such as one year or five years.

Go to **Cram101.com** for the Practice Tests for this Chapter.
And, **NEVER** highlight a book again!

199

North American Free Trade Agreement	A 1993 agreement establishing, over a 15-year period, a free trade zone composed of Canada, Mexico, and the United States is referred to as the North American Free Trade Agreement.
Free trade area	Free trade area refers to a group of countries that adopt free trade on trade among group members, while not necessarily changing the barriers that each member country has on trade with the countries outside the group.
Marketing mix	The marketing mix approach to marketing is a model of crafting and implementing marketing strategies. It stresses the "mixing" or blending of various factors in such a way that both organizational and consumer (target markets) objectives are attained.
Free trade	Free trade refers to a situation in which there are no artificial barriers to trade, such as tariffs and quotas. Usually used, often only implicitly, with frictionless trade, so that it implies that there are no barriers to trade of any kind.
Marketing	Promoting and selling products or services to customers, or prospective customers, is referred to as marketing.
Market	A market is, as defined in economics, a social arrangement that allows buyers and sellers to discover information and carry out a voluntary exchange of goods or services.
Union	A worker association that bargains with employers over wages and working conditions is called a union.
Economy	The income, expenditures, and resources that affect the cost of running a business and household are called an economy.
Interdependence	The extent to which departments depend on each other for resources or materials to accomplish their tasks is referred to as interdependence.
Economic interdependence	Economic interdependence describes countries/nation-states and/or supranational states such as the European Union (EU) or North American Free Trade Agreement (NAFTA) that are interdependent for any (or all) of the following: food , energy, minerals,manufactured goods, multinational/transnational corporations , financial institutions and foreign debt.
United Nations	An international organization created by multilateral treaty in 1945 to promote social and economic cooperation among nations and to protect human rights is the United Nations.
Capital	Capital generally refers to financial wealth, especially that used to start or maintain a business. In classical economics, capital is one of four factors of production, the others being land and labor and entrepreneurship.
Revenue	Revenue is a U.S. business term for the amount of money that a company receives from its activities, mostly from sales of products and/or services to customers.
Boycott	To protest by refusing to purchase from someone, or otherwise do business with them. In international trade, a boycott most often takes the form of refusal to import a country's goods.
Operation	A standardized method or technique that is performed repetitively, often on different materials resulting in different finished goods is called an operation.
Innovation	Innovation refers to the first commercially successful introduction of a new product, the use of a new method of production, or the creation of a new form of business organization.
Market opportunities	Market opportunities refer to areas where a company believes there are favorable demand trends, needs, and/or wants that are not being satisfied, and where it can compete effectively.
Single market	A single market is a customs union with common policies on product regulation, and freedom of

movement of all the four factors of production (goods, services, capital and labor).

Market system	All the product and resource markets of a market economy and the relationships among them are called a market system.
Common market	Common market refers to a group of countries that eliminate all barriers to movement of both goods and factors among themselves, and that also, on each product, agree to levy the same tariff on imports from outside the group.
Free market	A free market is a market where price is determined by the unregulated interchange of supply and demand rather than set by artificial means.
Trend	Trend refers to the long-term movement of an economic variable, such as its average rate of increase or decrease over enough years to encompass several business cycles.
Restructuring	Restructuring is the corporate management term for the act of partially dismantling and reorganizing a company for the purpose of making it more efficient and therefore more profitable.
Trade pattern	What goods a country trades, with whom, and in what direction. Explaining the trade pattern is one of the major purposes of trade theory, especially which goods a country will export and which it will import.
Tariff	A tax imposed by a nation on an imported good is called a tariff.
Social benefit	Social benefit refers to the benefit to society as a whole following an event or policy change. Includes externalities and deducts any benefits that are transfers from others.
Affiliation	A relationship with other websites in which a company can cross-promote and is credited for sales that accrue through their site is an affiliation.
Cooperative	A business owned and controlled by the people who use it, producers, consumers, or workers with similar needs who pool their resources for mutual gain is called cooperative.
International Business	International business refers to any firm that engages in international trade or investment.
Interest	In finance and economics, interest is the price paid by a borrower for the use of a lender's money. In other words, interest is the amount of paid to "rent" money for a period of time.
Association of Southeast Asian Nations	The Association of Southeast Asian Nations is a political, economic, and cultural organization of countries located in Southeast Asia.
Mercosur	Pact between Argentina, Brazil, Paraguay, and Uruguay to establish a free trade area is called mercosur.
Global competition	Global competition exists when competitive conditions across national markets are linked strongly enough to form a true international market and when leading competitors compete head to head in many different countries.
Trading bloc	Trading bloc refers to a group of countries that are somehow closely associated in international trade, usually in some sort of PTA.
Market position	Market position is a measure of the position of a company or product on a market.
Points	Loan origination fees that may be deductible as interest by a buyer of property. A seller of property who pays points reduces the selling price by the amount of the points paid for the buyer.
Economic union	A common market with the added feature that additional policies -- monetary, fiscal, welfare -- are also harmonized across the member countries is an economic union.

Sovereignty	A country or region's power and ability to rule itself and manage its own affairs. Some feel that membership in international organizations such as the WTO is a threat to their sovereignty.
Security	Security refers to a claim on the borrower future income that is sold by the borrower to the lender. A security is a type of transferable interest representing financial value.
Economic integration	Occurs when two or more nations join to form a free-trade zone are called economic integration. As economic integration increases, the barriers of trade between markets diminishes.
Integration	Economic integration refers to reducing barriers among countries to transactions and to movements of goods, capital, and labor, including harmonization of laws, regulations, and standards. Integrated markets theoretically function as a unified market.
Communism	Communism refers to an economic system in which capital is owned by private government. Contrasts with capitalism.
Shares	Shares refer to an equity security, representing a shareholder's ownership of a corporation. Shares are one of a finite number of equal portions in the capital of a company, entitling the owner to a proportion of distributed, non-reinvested profits known as dividends and to a portion of the value of the company in case of liquidation.
Economic development	Increase in the economic standard of living of a country's population, normally accomplished by increasing its stocks of physical and human capital and improving its technology is an economic development.
Customs union	Customs union refers to a group of countries that adopt free trade on trade among themselves, and that also, on each product, agree to levy the same tariff on imports from outside the group. Equivalent to an FTA plus a common external tariff.
Customs	Customs is an authority or agency in a country responsible for collecting customs duties and for controlling the flow of people, animals and goods (including personal effects and hazardous items) in and out of the country.
Domestic	From or in one's own country. A domestic producer is one that produces inside the home country. A domestic price is the price inside the home country. Opposite of 'foreign' or 'world.'.
Monetary policy	The use of the money supply and/or the interest rate to influence the level of economic activity and other policy objectives including the balance of payments or the exchange rate is called monetary policy.
Policy	Similar to a script in that a policy can be a less than completely rational decision-making method. Involves the use of a pre-existing set of decision steps for any problem that presents itself.
Regulation	Regulation refers to restrictions state and federal laws place on business with regard to the conduct of its activities.
Trade association	An industry trade group or trade association is generally a public relations organization founded and funded by corporations that operate in a specific industry. Its purpose is generally to promote that industry through PR activities such as advertizing, education, political donations, political pressure, publishing, and astroturfing.
International trade	The export of goods and services from a country and the import of goods and services into a country is referred to as the international trade.
Economics	The social science dealing with the use of scarce resources to obtain the maximum satisfaction of society's virtually unlimited economic wants is an economics.

Go to **Cram101.com** for the Practice Tests for this Chapter.

Go to **Cram101.com** for the Practice Tests for this Chapter.
And, **NEVER** highlight a book again!

205

Consideration	Consideration in contract law, a basic requirement for an enforceable agreement under traditional contract principles, defined in this text as legal value, bargained for and given in exchange for an act or promise. In corporation law, cash or property contributed to a corporation in exchange for shares, or a promise to contribute such cash or property.
Compatibility	Compatibility refers to used to describe a product characteristic, it means a good fit with other products used by the consumer or with the consumer's lifestyle. Used in a technical context, it means the ability of systems to work together.
Possession	Possession refers to respecting real property, exclusive dominion and control such as owners of like property usually exercise over it. Manual control of personal property either as owner or as one having a qualified right in it.
Journal	Book of original entry, in which transactions are recorded in a general ledger system, is referred to as a journal.
Immigration	Immigration refers to the migration of people into a country.
Regional economic integration	Agreements among countries in a geographic region to reduce and ultimately remove tariff and nontariff barriers to the free flow of goods, services, and factors of production between each other is called regional economic integration.
Wall Street Journal	Dow Jones & Company was founded in 1882 by reporters Charles Dow, Edward Jones and Charles Bergstresser. Jones converted the small Customers' Afternoon Letter into The Wall Street Journal, first published in 1889, and began delivery of the Dow Jones News Service via telegraph. The Journal featured the Jones 'Average', the first of several indexes of stock and bond prices on the New York Stock Exchange.
Euro	The common currency of a subset of the countries of the EU, adopted January 1, 1999 is called euro.
Evaluation	The consumer's appraisal of the product or brand on important attributes is called evaluation.
Federal Express	The company officially began operations on April 17, 1973, utilizing a network of 14 Dassault Falcon 20s which connected 25 U.S. cities. FedEx, the first cargo airline to use jet aircraft for its services, expanded greatly after the deregulation of the cargo airlines sector. Federal Express use of the hub-spoke distribution paradigm in air freight enabled it to become a world leader in its field.
Service	Service refers to a "non tangible product" that is not embodied in a physical good and that typically effects some change in another product, person, or institution. Contrasts with good.
License	A license in the sphere of Intellectual Property Rights (IPR) is a document, contract or agreement giving permission or the 'right' to a legally-definable entity to do something (such as manufacture a product or to use a service), or to apply something (such as a trademark), with the objective of achieving commercial gain.
Export	In economics, an export is any good or commodity, shipped or otherwise transported out of a country, province, town to another part of the world in a legitimate fashion, typically for use in trade or sale.
Rules of origin	Rules of origin refer to rules included in a FTA specifying when a good will be regarded as produced within the FTA, so as to cross between members without tariff. Typical rules of origin are based on percentage of value added or on changes in tariff heading.
Expense	In accounting, an expense represents an event in which an asset is used up or a liability is incurred. In terms of the accounting equation, expenses reduce owners' equity.

Industry	A group of firms that produce identical or similar products is an industry. It is also used specifically to refer to an area of economic production focused on manufacturing which involves large amounts of capital investment before any profit can be realized, also called "heavy industry".
Aid	Assistance provided by countries and by international institutions such as the World Bank to developing countries in the form of monetary grants, loans at low interest rates, in kind, or a combination of these is called aid. Aid can also refer to assistance of any type rendered to benefit some group or individual.
Small business	Small business refers to a business that is independently owned and operated, is not dominant in its field of operation, and meets certain standards of size in terms of employees or annual receipts.
Entrepreneur	The owner/operator. The person who organizes, manages, and assumes the risks of a firm, taking a new idea or a new product and turning it into a successful business is an entrepreneur.
Business Week	Business Week is a business magazine published by McGraw-Hill. It was first published in 1929 under the direction of Malcolm Muir, who was serving as president of the McGraw-Hill Publishing company at the time. It is considered to be the standard both in industry and among students.
Trade pact	A trade pact is a wide ranging tax, tariff and trade agreement that often includes investment guarantees. They are frequently politically contentious since they may change economic customs and deepen interdependence with trade partners.
Trade war	Trade war refers to generally, a period in which each of two countries alternate in further restricting trade from the other. More specifically, the process of tariffs and retaliation.
Pact	Pact refers to a set of principles endorsed by 21 of the largest U.S. ad agencies aimed at improving the research used in preparing and testing ads, providing a better creative product for clients, and controlling the cost of TV commercials.
Joint venture	Joint venture refers to an undertaking by two parties for a specific purpose and duration, taking any of several legal forms.
Trade barrier	An artificial disincentive to export and/or import, such as a tariff, quota, or other NTB is called a trade barrier.
Customs duty	A customs duty is a tariff or tax on the import or export of goods.
Common external tariff	When a group of countries form a customs union they must introduce a common external tariff. The same customs duties, quotas, preferences or other non-tariff barriers to trade apply to all goods entering the area, regardless of which country within the area they are entering. It is designed to end re-exportation.
Labor	People's physical and mental talents and efforts that are used to help produce goods and services are called labor.
Quota	A government-imposed restriction on quantity, or sometimes on total value, used to restrict the import of something to a specific quantity is called a quota.
Fiscal policy	Fiscal policy refers to any macroeconomic policy involving the levels of government purchases, transfers, or taxes, usually implicitly focused on domestic goods, residents, or firms.
Prohibition	Prohibition refers to denial of the right to import or export, applying to particular products and/or particular countries. Includes embargo.
Investment	Investment refers to spending for the production and accumulation of capital and additions to

Go to **Cram101.com** for the Practice Tests for this Chapter.

Go to **Cram101.com** for the Practice Tests for this Chapter.
And, **NEVER** highlight a book again!

209

inventories. In a financial sense, buying an asset with the expectation of making a return.

Welfare	Welfare refers to the economic well being of an individual, group, or economy. For individuals, it is conceptualized by a utility function. For groups, including countries and the world, it is a tricky philosophical concept, since individuals fare differently.
Cartel	Cartel refers to a group of firms that seeks to raise the price of a good by restricting its supply. The term is usually used for international groups, especially involving state-owned firms and/or governments.
Fund	Independent accounting entity with a self-balancing set of accounts segregated for the purposes of carrying on specific activities is referred to as a fund.
Wage	The payment for the service of a unit of labor, per unit time. In trade theory, it is the only payment to labor, usually unskilled labor. In empirical work, wage data may exclude other compenzation, which must be added to get the total cost of employment.
Maastricht Treaty	Treaty agreed to in 1991, but not ratified until January 1, 1994, that committed the 12 member states of the European Community to a closer economic and political union is the Maastricht Treaty.
Extension	Extension refers to an out-of-court settlement in which creditors agree to allow the firm more time to meet its financial obligations. A new repayment schedule will be developed, subject to the acceptance of creditors.
Dissolution	Dissolution is the process of admitting or removing a partner in a partnership.
Comecon	Comecon is a multilateral economic alliance of Eastern European Communist states founed in 1949 and headquarted in the former Soviet Union. Also called CEMA or CMEA, is was created to promote economic development of member states through cooperation and specialization and to counter the Marshall Plan until it disbanded in 1991
Authority	Authority in agency law, refers to an agent's ability to affect his principal's legal relations with third parties. Also used to refer to an actor's legal power or ability to do something. In addition, sometimes used to refer to a statute, case, or other legal source that justifies a particular result.
Compliance	A type of influence process where a receiver accepts the position advocated by a source to obtain favorable outcomes or to avoid punishment is the compliance.
Common currency	A situation where several countries form a monetary union with a single currency and a unified central bank is referred to as common currency.
Monetary union	An arrangement by which several nations adopt a common currency as a unit of account and medium of exchange. The European Monetary Union is scheduled to adopt the 'Euro' as the common currency in 1999.
Market potential	Market potential refers to maximum total sales of a product by all firms to a segment during a specified time period under specified environmental conditions and marketing efforts of the firms.
Globalization	The increasing world-wide integration of markets for goods, services and capital that attracted special attention in the late 1990s is called globalization.
Context	The effect of the background under which a message often takes on more and richer meaning is a context. Context is especially important in cross-cultural interactions because some cultures are said to be high context or low context.
Globalization of markets	Moving away from an economic system in which national markets are distinct entities, isolated by trade barriers and barriers of distance, time, and culture, and toward a system in which national markets are merging into one global market is globalization of markets.

Go to **Cram101.com** for the Practice Tests for this Chapter.
And, **NEVER** highlight a book again!

211

Forming	The first stage of team development, where the team is formed and the objectives for the team are set is referred to as forming.
Coalition	An informal alliance among managers who support a specific goal is called coalition.
Complete economic integration	Complete economic integration is the final stage of economic integration. After complete economic integration, the integrated units have no or negligible control of economic policy, including full monetary union and complete or near-complete fiscal policy harmonization.
Market access	The ability of firms from one country to sell in another is market access.
Excise tax	A tax levied on the production of a specific product or on the quantity of the product purchased is an excise tax.
Commercial policy	Commercial policy refers to government policies intended to influence international commerce, including international trade. Includes tariffs and quotas, as well as policies regarding exports.
Mutual recognition	The acceptance by one country of another country's certification that a satisfactory standard has been met for ability, performance, safety, etc a mutual recognition.
Harmonization	Harmonization refers to the changing of government regulations and practices, as a result of an international agreement, to make those of different countries the same or more compatible.
European Currency Unit	The European Currency Unit was a basket of the currencies of the European Community member states, used as the unit of account of the European Community before being replaced by the euro.
Exchange rate	Exchange rate refers to the price at which one country's currency trades for another, typically on the exchange market.
Exchange	The trade of things of value between buyer and seller so that each is better off after the trade is called the exchange.
Margin	A deposit by a buyer in stocks with a seller or a stockbroker, as security to cover fluctuations in the market in reference to stocks that the buyer has purchased but for which he has not paid is a margin. Commodities are also traded on margin.
Consumption	In Keynesian economics consumption refers to personal consumption expenditure, i.e., the purchase of currently produced goods and services out of income, out of savings (net worth), or from borrowed funds. It refers to that part of disposable income that does not go to saving.
Nontariff barrier	Any policy that interferes with exports or imports other than a simple tariff, prominently including quotas and vers is referred to as nontariff barrier.
Argument	The discussion by counsel for the respective parties of their contentions on the law and the facts of the case being tried in order to aid the jury in arriving at a correct and just conclusion is called argument.
Licensing	Licensing is a form of strategic alliance which involves the sale of a right to use certain proprietary knowledge (so called intellectual property) in a defined way.
Cabotage	Cabotage is the transport of goods or passengers between two points in the same country.
Gross domestic product	Gross domestic product refers to the total value of new goods and services produced in a given year within the borders of a country, regardless of by whom.
Consumer good	Products and services that are ultimately consumed rather than used in the production of another good are a consumer good.
Honda	With more than 14 million internal combustion engines built each year, Honda is the largest

Go to **Cram101.com** for the Practice Tests for this Chapter.
And, **NEVER** highlight a book again!

213

engine-maker in the world. In 2004, the company began to produce diesel motors, which were both very quiet whilst not requiring particulate filters to pass pollution standards. It is arguable, however, that the foundation of their success is the motorcycle division.

Judicial branch	Judicial branch refers to the part of the government that consists of the Supreme Court and other federal courts.
Enterprise	Enterprise refers to another name for a business organization. Other similar terms are business firm, sometimes simply business, sometimes simply firm, as well as company, and entity.
Instrument	Instrument refers to an economic variable that is controlled by policy makers and can be used to influence other variables, called targets. Examples are monetary and fiscal policies used to achieve external and internal balance.
Clinique	In 1968 Clinique was the first dermatologist-guided, allergy-tested, and fragrance-free cosmetic brand. Clinique was at that time different from most cosmetic companies in that its goal was to meet individual skin care needs by categorizing skin types.
Sexual harassment	Unwelcome sexual advances, requests for sexual favors, and other conduct of a sexual nature is called sexual harassment.
Edict	Edict refers to a command or prohibition promulgated by a sovereign and having the effect of
Grant	Grant refers to an intergovernmental transfer of funds . Since the New Deal, state and local governments have become increasingly dependent upon federal grants for an almost infinite variety of programs.
Negotiation	Negotiation is the process whereby interested parties resolve disputes, agree upon courses of action, bargain for individual or collective advantage, and/or attempt to craft outcomes which serve their mutual interests.
Openness	Openness refers to the extent to which an economy is open, often measured by the ratio of its trade to GDP.
Inflation	An increase in the overall price level of an economy, usually as measured by the CPI or by the implicit price deflator is called inflation.
Deficit	The deficit is the amount by which expenditure exceed revenue.
Political risk	Refers to the many different actions of people, subgroups, and whole countries that have the potential to affect the financial status of a firm is called political risk.
Economic growth	Economic growth refers to the increase over time in the capacity of an economy to produce goods and services and to improve the well-being of its citizens.
Short run	Short run refers to a period of time that permits an increase or decrease in current production volume with existing capacity, but one that is too short to permit enlargement of that capacity itself (eg, the building of new plants, training of additional workers, etc.).
Foundation	A Foundation is a type of philanthropic organization set up by either individuals or institutions as a legal entity (either as a corporation or trust) with the purpose of distributing grants to support causes in line with the goals of the foundation.
Financial institution	A financial institution acts as an agent that provides financial services for its clients. Financial institutions generally fall under financial regulation from a government authority.
Face value	The nominal or par value of an instrument as expressed on its face is referred to as the face value.
Hyperinflation	Hyperinflation refers to a very rapid rise in the price level; an extremely high rate of inflation.

Go to **Cram101.com** for the Practice Tests for this Chapter.
And, **NEVER** highlight a book again!

215

Conversion	Conversion refers to any distinct act of dominion wrongfully exerted over another's personal property in denial of or inconsistent with his rights therein. That tort committed by a person who deals with chattels not belonging to him in a manner that is inconsistent with the ownership of the lawful owner.
Illegal immigrant	A person who enters a country unlawfully for the purpose of residing there is called an illegal immigrant.
Applicant	In many tribunal and administrative law suits, the person who initiates the claim is called the applicant.
Firm	An organization that employs resources to produce a good or service for profit and owns and operates one or more plants is referred to as a firm.
Production	The creation of finished goods and services using the factors of production: land, labor, capital, entrepreneurship, and knowledge.
Anticipation	In finance, anticipation is where debts are paid off early, generally in order to pay less interest.
Acquisition	A company's purchase of the property and obligations of another company is an acquisition.
Merger	Merger refers to the combination of two firms into a single firm.
Complexity	The technical sophistication of the product and hence the amount of understanding required to use it is referred to as complexity. It is the opposite of simplicity.
Profit	Profit refers to the return to the resource entrepreneurial ability; total revenue minus total cost.
Economies of scale	In economics, returns to scale and economies of scale are related terms that describe what happens as the scale of production increases. They are different terms and not to be used interchangeably.
Mass production	The process of making a large number of a limited variety of products at very low cost is referred to as mass production.
Distribution	Distribution in economics, the manner in which total output and income is distributed among individuals or factors.
Competitive market	A market in which no buyer or seller has market power is called a competitive market.
Purchasing power	The amount of goods that money will buy, usually measured by the CPI is referred to as purchasing power.
Purchasing	Purchasing refers to the function in a firm that searches for quality material resources, finds the best suppliers, and negotiates the best price for goods and services.
Manufacturing	Production of goods primarily by the application of labor and capital to raw materials and other intermediate inputs, in contrast to agriculture, mining, forestry, fishing, and services a manufacturing.
Exporter	A firm that sells its product in another country is an exporter.
Gain	In finance, gain is a profit or an increase in value of an investment such as a stock or bond. Gain is calculated by fair market value or the proceeds from the sale of the investment minus the sum of the purchase price and all costs associated with it.
Protectionism	Protectionism refers to advocacy of protection. The word has a negative connotation, and few advocates of protection in particular situations will acknowledge being protectionists.
Reciprocity	An industrial buying practice in which two organizations agree to purchase each other's

products and services is called reciprocity.

Parallel import	Trade that is made possible when the owner of intellectual property causes the same product to be sold in different countries for different prices. If someone else imports the low-price good into the high-price country, it is a parallel import.
Standardization	Standardization, in the context related to technologies and industries, is the process of establishing a technical standard among competing entities in a market, where this will bring benefits without hurting competition.
Adoption	In corporation law, a corporation's acceptance of a pre-incorporation contract by action of its board of directors, by which the corporation becomes liable on the contract, is referred to as adoption.
Balance	In banking and accountancy, the outstanding balance is the amount of money owned, (or due), that remains in a deposit account (or a loan account) at a given date, after all past remittances, payments and withdrawal have been accounted for. It can be positive (then, in the balance sheet of a firm, it is an asset) or negative (a liability).
Advertising	Advertising refers to paid, nonpersonal communication through various media by organizations and individuals who are in some way identified in the advertising message.
Promotion	Promotion refers to all the techniques sellers use to motivate people to buy products or services. An attempt by marketers to inform people about products and to persuade them to participate in an exchange.
Brand	A name, symbol, or design that identifies the goods or services of one seller or group of sellers and distinguishes them from the goods and services of competitors is a brand.
Core	A core is the set of feasible allocations in an economy that cannot be improved upon by subset of the set of the economy's consumers (a coalition). In construction, when the force in an element is within a certain center section, the core, the element will only be under compression.
Distribution channel	A distribution channel is a chain of intermediaries, each passing a product down the chain to the next organization, before it finally reaches the consumer or end-user.
Channel	Channel, in communications (sometimes called communications channel), refers to the medium used to convey information from a sender (or transmitter) to a receiver.
Central planning	The guidance of the economy by direct government control over a large portion of economic activity, as contrasted with allowing markets to serve this purpose is called central planning.
Economic policy	Economic policy refers to the actions that governments take in the economic field. It covers the systems for setting interest rates and government deficit as well as the labor market, national ownership, and many other areas of government.
Market economy	A market economy is an economic system in which the production and distribution of goods and services takes place through the mechanism of free markets guided by a free price system rather than by the state in a planned economy.
Free enterprise	Free enterprise refers to a system in which economic agents are free to own property and engage in commercial transactions.
Logo	Logo refers to device or other brand name that cannot be spoken.
Nike	Because Nike creates goods for a wide range of sports, they have competition from every sports and sports fashion brand there is. Nike has no direct competitors because there is no single brand which can compete directly with their range of sports and non-sports oriented gear, except for Reebok.

Free trade zone	A free trade zone is one or more areas of a country where tariffs and quotas are eliminated and bureaucratic requirements are lowered in order to attract companies by raising the incentives for doing business there.
Peak	Peak refers to the point in the business cycle when an economic expansion reaches its highest point before turning down. Contrasts with trough.
Economic problem	Economic problem refers to how to determine the use of scarce resources among competing uses. Because resources are scarce, the economy must choose what products to produce; how these products are to be produced: and for whom.
Duty free	Duty Free is the term that is often used to describe goods bought at ports and airports that do not attract the usual government taxes and customs duties.
Slowdown	A slowdown is an industrial action in which employees perform their duties but seek to reduce productivity or efficiency in their performance of these duties. A slowdown may be used as either a prelude or an alternative to a strike, as it is seen as less disruptive as well as less risky and costly for workers and their union.
Accession	Accession refers to the process of adding a country to an international agreement, such as the GATT, WTO, EU, or NAFTA.
Bilateral trade	Bilateral trade refers to the trade between two countries; that is, the value or quantity of one country's exports to the other, or the sum of exports and imports between them.
Disparity	Disparity refers to the regional and economic differences in a country, province, state, or continent
Technology	The body of knowledge and techniques that can be used to combine economic resources to produce goods and services is called technology.
Consumer protection	Consumer protection is government regulation to protect the interests of consumers, for example by requiring businesses to disclose detailed information about products, particularly in areas where safety or public health is an issue, such as food.
Microsoft	Microsoft is a multinational computer technology corporation with 2004 global annual sales of US$39.79 billion and 71,553 employees in 102 countries and regions as of July 2006. It develops, manufactures, licenses, and supports a wide range of software products for computing devices.
General Motors	General Motors is the world's largest automaker. Founded in 1908, today it employs about 327,000 people around the world. With global headquarters in Detroit, it manufactures its cars and trucks in 33 countries.
Food and Drug Administration	The Food and Drug Administration is an agency of the United States Department of Health and Human Services and is responsible for regulating food (human and animal), dietary supplements, drugs (human and animal), cosmetics, medical devices (human and animal) and radiation emitting devices (including non-medical devices), biologics, and blood products in the United States.
Administration	Administration refers to the management and direction of the affairs of governments and institutions; a collective term for all policymaking officials of a government; the execution and implementation of public policy.
Kraft Foods	Kraft Foods is the largest food and beverage company headquartered in North America and the second largest in the world. In 1993 the Kraft Foods plant in Boston was hit with a $250,000 fine for violating the Clean Air Act of 1970.
Industrial goods	Components produced for use in the production of other products are called industrial goods.
Free rider	Free rider refers to someone who enjoys the benefits of a public good without bearing the

Go to **Cram101.com** for the Practice Tests for this Chapter.

Go to **Cram101.com** for the Practice Tests for this Chapter.
And, **NEVER** highlight a book again!

221

cost. An example, in trade policy, is that trade liberalization benefits the majority of consumers without their lobbying for it.

Customs procedure	Customs procedure refers to the practices used by customs officers to clear goods into a country and levy tariffs. Includes clearance procedures such as documentation and inspection, methods of determining a good's classification, and methods of assignment.
Verification	Verification refers to the final stage of the creative process where the validity or truthfulness of the insight is determined. The feedback portion of communication in which the receiver sends a message to the source indicating receipt of the message and the degree to which he or she understood the message.
Preference	The act of a debtor in paying or securing one or more of his creditors in a manner more favorable to them than to other creditors or to the exclusion of such other creditors is a preference. In the absence of statute, a preference is perfectly good, but to be legal it must be bona fide, and not a mere subterfuge of the debtor to secure a future benefit to himself or to prevent the application of his property to his debts.
Competitor	Other organizations in the same industry or type of business that provide a good or service to the same set of customers is referred to as a competitor.
Comprehensive	A comprehensive refers to a layout accurate in size, color, scheme, and other necessary details to show how a final ad will look. For presentation only, never for reproduction.
Trade secret	Trade secret refers to a secret formula, pattern, process, program, device, method, technique, or compilation of information that is used in its owner's business and affords that owner a competitive advantage. Trade secrets are protected by state law.
Trademark	A distinctive word, name, symbol, device, or combination thereof, which enables consumers to identify favored products or services and which may find protection under state or federal law is a trademark.
Copyright	The legal right to the proceeds from and control over the use of a created product, such a written work, audio, video, film, or software is a copyright. This right generally extends over the life of the author plus fifty years.
Patent	The legal right to the proceeds from and control over the use of an invented product or process, granted for a fixed period of time, usually 20 years. Patent is one form of intellectual property that is subject of the TRIPS agreement.
Government procurement	Government procurement refers to purchase of goods and services by government and by state-owned enterprises.
Procurement	Procurement is the acquisition of goods or services at the best possible total cost of ownership, in the right quantity, at the right time, in the right place for the direct benefit or use of the governments, corporations, or individuals generally via, but not limited to a contract.
Inception	The date and time on which coverage under an insurance policy takes effect is inception. Also refers to the date at which a stock or mutual fund was first traded.
Financial crisis	A loss of confidence in a country's currency or other financial assets causing international investors to withdraw their funds from the country is referred to as a financial crisis.
Devaluation	Lowering the value of a nation's currency relative to other currencies is called devaluation.
Management	Management characterizes the process of leading and directing all or part of an organization, often a business, through the deployment and manipulation of resources. Early twentieth-century management writer Mary Parker Follett defined management as "the art of getting things done through people."

222

Go to **Cram101.com** for the Practice Tests for this Chapter.

World Bank	The World Bank is a group of five international organizations responsible for providing finance and advice to countries for the purposes of economic development and poverty reduction, and for encouraging and safeguarding international investment.
Raw material	Raw material refers to a good that has not been transformed by production; a primary product.
Supply	Supply is the aggregate amount of any material good that can be called into being at a certain price point; it comprises one half of the equation of supply and demand. In classical economic theory, a curve representing supply is one of the factors that produce price.
Direct investment	Direct investment refers to a domestic firm actually investing in and owning a foreign subsidiary or division.
Foreign direct investment	Foreign direct investment refers to the buying of permanent property and businesses in foreign nations.
Lucent Technologies	Lucent Technologies is a company composed of what was formerly AT&T Technologies, which included Western Electric and Bell Labs. It was spun-off from AT&T on September 30, 1996. On April 2, 2006, they announced a merger with its French competitor, Alcatel. The combined company has revenues of approximately $25 billion U.S. based on 2005 calendar results.
Maquiladora	A maquiladora is a factory that imports materials and equipment on a duty-free and tariff-free basis for assembly or manufacturing and then re-exports the assembled product usually back to the originating country.
Closing	The finalization of a real estate sales transaction that passes title to the property from the seller to the buyer is referred to as a closing. Closing is a sales term which refers to the process of making a sale. It refers to reaching the final step, which may be an exchange of money or acquiring a signature.
Slump	A decline in performance, in a firm is a slump in sales or profits, or in a country is a slump in output or employment.
Bottleneck	An operation where the work to be performed approaches or exceeds the capacity available to do it is a bottleneck.
Accord	An agreement whereby the parties agree to accept something different in satisfaction of the original contract is an accord.
Intellectual property	In law, intellectual property is an umbrella term for various legal entitlements which attach to certain types of information, ideas, or other intangibles in their expressed form. The holder of this legal entitlement is generally entitled to exercise various exclusive rights in relation to its subject matter.
Convergence	The blending of various facets of marketing functions and communication technology to create more efficient and expanded synergies is a convergence.
Property	Assets defined in the broadest legal sense. Property includes the unrealized receivables of a cash basis taxpayer, but not services rendered.
Economic system	Economic system refers to a particular set of institutional arrangements and a coordinating mechanism for solving the economizing problem; a method of organizing an economy, of which the market system and the command system are the two general types.
Caribbean Community and Common Market	The Caribbean Community and Common Market was established by the Treaty of Chaguaramas which came into effect on August 1, 1973. The first four signatories were Barbados, Jamaica, Guyana and Trinidad and Tobago.
Fair trade	The Fair Trade movement promotes international labor, environmental and social standards for the production of labelled and unlabelled goods ranging from handcrafts to agricultural commodities. The movement focuses in particular on exports from developing countries to

	developed countries.
Trade bloc	Trade bloc refers to a group of nations that lower or abolish trade barriers among members. Examples include the European Union and the nations of the North American Free Trade Agreement.
Leadership	Management merely consists of leadership applied to business situations; or in other words: management forms a sub-set of the broader process of leadership.
Deregulation	The lessening or complete removal of government regulations on an industry, especially concerning the price that firms are allowed to charge and leaving price to be determined by market forces a deregulation.
Facilitation	Facilitation refers to helping a team or individual achieve a goal. Often used in meetings or with teams to help the teams achieve their objectives.
Tactic	A short-term immediate decision that, in its totality, leads to the achievement of strategic goals is called a tactic.
Trade sanction	Use of a trade policy as a sanction, most commonly an embargo imposed against a country for violating human rights is referred to as trade sanction.
Dumping	Dumping refers to a practice of charging a very low price in a foreign market for such economic purposes as putting rival suppliers out of business.
Bargaining power	Bargaining power refers to the ability to influence the setting of prices or wages, usually arising from some sort of monopoly or monopsony position
Treaties	The first source of international law, consisting of agreements or contracts between two or more nations that are formally signed by an authorized representative and ratified by the supreme power of each nation are called treaties.
Corporate Strategy	Corporate strategy is concerned with the firm's choice of business, markets and activities and thus it defines the overall scope and direction of the business.
Incentive	An incentive is any factor (financial or non-financial) that provides a motive for a particular course of action, or counts as a reason for preferring one choice to the alternatives.
Asset	An item of property, such as land, capital, money, a share in ownership, or a claim on others for future payment, such as a bond or a bank deposit is an asset.
Configuration	An organization's shape, which reflects the division of labor and the means of coordinating the divided tasks is configuration.
Trade liberalization	Reduction of tariffs and removal or relaxation of NTBs is referred to as trade liberalization.
Collaboration	Collaboration occurs when the interaction between groups is very important to goal attainment and the goals are compatible. Wherein people work together —applying both to the work of individuals as well as larger collectives and societies.
Objection	In the trial of a case the formal remonstrance made by counsel to something that has been said or done, in order to obtain the court's ruling thereon is an objection.
Market development	Selling existing products to new markets is called market development.
Market share	That fraction of an industry's output accounted for by an individual firm or group of firms is called market share.
Economic	Economic infrastructure refers to a country's communications, transportation, financial, and

Go to **Cram101.com** for the Practice Tests for this Chapter.

infrastructure	distribution systems.
Insurance	Insurance refers to a system by which individuals can reduce their exposure to risk of large losses by spreading the risks among a large number of persons.
Labor force	In economics the labor force is the group of people who have a potential for being employed.
Emerging markets	The term emerging markets is commonly used to describe business and market activity in industrializing or emerging regions of the world. It is sometimes loosely used as a replacement for emerging economies, but really signifies a business phenomenon that is not fully described by or constrained to geography or economic strength; such countries are considered to be in a transitional phase between developing and developed status.
Emerging market	The term emerging market is commonly used to describe business and market activity in industrializing or emerging regions of the world.
Speculation	The purchase or sale of an asset in hopes that its price will rise or fall respectively, in order to make a profit is called speculation.
Developed country	A developed country is one that enjoys a relatively high standard of living derived through an industrialized, diversified economy. Countries with a very high Human Development Index are generally considered developed countries.
Developing country	Developing country refers to a country whose per capita income is low by world standards. Same as LDC. As usually used, it does not necessarily connote that the country's income is rising.
Production efficiency	A situation in which the economy cannot produce more of one good without producing less of some other good is referred to as production efficiency.
Factors of production	Economic resources: land, capital, labor, and entrepreneurial ability are called factors of production.
Marketing strategy	Marketing strategy refers to the means by which a marketing goal is to be achieved, usually characterized by a specified target market and a marketing program to reach it.
Positioning	The art and science of fitting the product or service to one or more segments of the market in such a way as to set it meaningfully apart from competition is called positioning.

Go to **Cram101.com** for the Practice Tests for this Chapter.
And, **NEVER** highlight a book again!

Joint venture	Joint venture refers to an undertaking by two parties for a specific purpose and duration, taking any of several legal forms.
Service	Service refers to a "non tangible product" that is not embodied in a physical good and that typically effects some change in another product, person, or institution. Contrasts with good.
Points	Loan origination fees that may be deductible as interest by a buyer of property. A seller of property who pays points reduces the selling price by the amount of the points paid for the buyer.
Users	Users refer to people in the organization who actually use the product or service purchased by the buying center.
Yahoo	Yahoo is an American computer services company. It operates an Internet portal, the Yahoo Directory and a host of other services including the popular Yahoo Mail. Yahoo is the most visited website on the Internet today with more than 400 million unique users. The global network of Yahoo! websites received 3.4 billion page views per day on average as of October 2005.
Corporation	A legal entity chartered by a state or the Federal government that is distinct and separate from the individuals who own it is a corporation. This separation gives the corporation unique powers which other legal entities lack.
Competitor	Other organizations in the same industry or type of business that provide a good or service to the same set of customers is referred to as a competitor.
Forming	The first stage of team development, where the team is formed and the objectives for the team are set is referred to as forming.
Wall Street Journal	Dow Jones & Company was founded in 1882 by reporters Charles Dow, Edward Jones and Charles Bergstresser. Jones converted the small Customers' Afternoon Letter into The Wall Street Journal, first published in 1889, and began delivery of the Dow Jones News Service via telegraph. The Journal featured the Jones 'Average', the first of several indexes of stock and bond prices on the New York Stock Exchange.
Journal	Book of original entry, in which transactions are recorded in a general ledger system, is referred to as a journal.
Marketing	Promoting and selling products or services to customers, or prospective customers, is referred to as marketing.
Marketing strategy	Marketing strategy refers to the means by which a marketing goal is to be achieved, usually characterized by a specified target market and a marketing program to reach it.
Global marketing	A strategy of using a common marketing plan and program for all countries in which a company operates, thus selling the product or services the same way everywhere in the world is called global marketing.
Global marketing strategy	The practice of standardizing marketing activities when there are cultural similarities and adapting them when cultures differ is referred to as global marketing strategy.
Global competition	Global competition exists when competitive conditions across national markets are linked strongly enough to form a true international market and when leading competitors compete head to head in many different countries.
Market	A market is, as defined in economics, a social arrangement that allows buyers and sellers to discover information and carry out a voluntary exchange of goods or services.
Organizational	Organizational structure is the way in which the interrelated groups of an organization are

Go to **Cram101.com** for the Practice Tests for this Chapter.
And, **NEVER** highlight a book again!

structure	constructed. From a managerial point of view the main concerns are ensuring effective communication and coordination.
Competitiveness	Competitiveness usually refers to characteristics that permit a firm to compete effectively with other firms due to low cost or superior technology, perhaps internationally.
Positioning	The art and science of fitting the product or service to one or more segments of the market in such a way as to set it meaningfully apart from competition is called positioning.
Firm	An organization that employs resources to produce a good or service for profit and owns and operates one or more plants is referred to as a firm.
Operation	A standardized method or technique that is performed repetitively, often on different materials resulting in different finished goods is called an operation.
Scope	Scope of a project is the sum total of all projects products and their requirements or features.
Marketing management	Marketing management refers to the process of planning and executing the conception, pricing, promotion, and distribution of ideas, goods, and services to create mutually beneficial exchanges.
Standardization	Standardization, in the context related to technologies and industries, is the process of establishing a technical standard among competing entities in a market, where this will bring benefits without hurting competition.
Management	Management characterizes the process of leading and directing all or part of an organization, often a business, through the deployment and manipulation of resources. Early twentieth-century management writer Mary Parker Follett defined management as "the art of getting things done through people."
Argument	The discussion by counsel for the respective parties of their contentions on the law and the facts of the case being tried in order to aid the jury in arriving at a correct and just conclusion is called argument.
Localization	As an element of wireless marketing strategy, transmitting messages that are relevant to the user's current geographical location are referred to as localization.
Integration	Economic integration refers to reducing barriers among countries to transactions and to movements of goods, capital, and labor, including harmonization of laws, regulations, and standards. Integrated markets theoretically function as a unified market.
Marketing mix	The marketing mix approach to marketing is a model of crafting and implementing marketing strategies. It stresses the "mixing" or blending of various factors in such a way that both organizational and consumer (target markets) objectives are attained.
Ford	Ford is an American company that manufactures and sells automobiles worldwide. Ford introduced methods for large-scale manufacturing of cars, and large-scale management of an industrial workforce, especially elaborately engineered manufacturing sequences typified by the moving assembly lines.
Manufacturing	Production of goods primarily by the application of labor and capital to raw materials and other intermediate inputs, in contrast to agriculture, mining, forestry, fishing, and services a manufacturing.
Flexible manufacturing	Flexible manufacturing refers to designing machines to do multiple tasks so that they can produce a variety of products.
Trend	Trend refers to the long-term movement of an economic variable, such as its average rate of increase or decrease over enough years to encompass several business cycles.

International Business	International business refers to any firm that engages in international trade or investment.
Advertising Age	Advertising Age is the world's leading source of news, analysis, information and data on advertising, marketing and media. The magazine was started as a broadsheet newspaper in Chicago in 1930.
Advertising	Advertising refers to paid, nonpersonal communication through various media by organizations and individuals who are in some way identified in the advertising message.
Marketing communication	The communication components of marketing, which include public relations, advertising, personal selling, and sales promotion is a marketing communication.
Brand	A name, symbol, or design that identifies the goods or services of one seller or group of sellers and distinguishes them from the goods and services of competitors is a brand.
Industry	A group of firms that produce identical or similar products is an industry. It is also used specifically to refer to an area of economic production focused on manufacturing which involves large amounts of capital investment before any profit can be realized, also called "heavy industry".
Disney	Disney is one of the largest media and entertainment corporations in the world. Founded on October 16, 1923 by brothers Walt and Roy Disney as a small animation studio, today it is one of the largest Hollywood studios and also owns nine theme parks and several television networks, including the American Broadcasting Company (ABC).
Economies of scale	In economics, returns to scale and economies of scale are related terms that describe what happens as the scale of production increases. They are different terms and not to be used interchangeably.
Economy	The income, expenditures, and resources that affect the cost of running a business and household are called an economy.
Customer satisfaction	Customer satisfaction is a business term which is used to capture the idea of measuring how satisfied an enterprise's customers are with the organization's efforts in a marketplace.
Proactive	To be proactive is to act before a situation becomes a source of confrontation or crisis. It is the opposite of "retroactive," which refers to actions taken after an event.
Variable	A variable is something measured by a number; it is used to analyze what happens to other things when the size of that number changes.
Interest	In finance and economics, interest is the price paid by a borrower for the use of a lender's money. In other words, interest is the amount of paid to "rent" money for a period of time.
Viacom	Viacom is an American-based media conglomerate with various worldwide interests in cable and satellite television networks (MTV Networks and BET), video gaming (part of Sega of America), and movie production and distribution (the Paramount Pictures movie studio and DreamWorks).
Business strategy	Business strategy, which refers to the aggregated operational strategies of single business firm or that of an SBU in a diversified corporation refers to the way in which a firm competes in its chosen arenas.
Nestle	Nestle is the world's biggest food and beverage company. In the 1860s, a pharmacist, developed a food for babies who were unable to be breastfed. His first success was a premature infant who could not tolerate his own mother's milk nor any of the usual substitutes. The value of the new product was quickly recognized when his new formula saved the child's life.
Exporting	Selling products to another country is called exporting.

Go to **Cram101.com** for the Practice Tests for this Chapter.
And, **NEVER** highlight a book again!

235

Agent	A person who makes economic decisions for another economic actor. A hired manager operates as an agent for a firm's owner.
Bid	A bid price is a price offered by a buyer when he/she buys a good. In the context of stock trading on a stock exchange, the bid price is the highest price a buyer of a stock is willing to pay for a share of that given stock.
Supply	Supply is the aggregate amount of any material good that can be called into being at a certain price point; it comprises one half of the equation of supply and demand. In classical economic theory, a curve representing supply is one of the factors that produce price.
Trademark	A distinctive word, name, symbol, device, or combination thereof, which enables consumers to identify favored products or services and which may find protection under state or federal law is a trademark.
Retailing	All activities involved in selling, renting, and providing goods and services to ultimate consumers for personal, family, or household use is referred to as retailing.
Foundation	A Foundation is a type of philanthropic organization set up by either individuals or institutions as a legal entity (either as a corporation or trust) with the purpose of distributing grants to support causes in line with the goals of the foundation.
Distribution center	Designed to facilitate the timely movement of goods and represent a very important part of a supply chain is a distribution center.
Distribution	Distribution in economics, the manner in which total output and income is distributed among individuals or factors.
Warehouse	Warehouse refers to a location, often decentralized, that a firm uses to store, consolidate, age, or mix stock; house product-recall programs; or ease tax burdens.
Corporate culture	The whole collection of beliefs, values, and behaviors of a firm that send messages to those within and outside the company about how business is done is the corporate culture.
Competitive advantage	A business is said to have a competitive advantage when its unique strengths, often based on cost, quality, time, and innovation, offer consumers a greater percieved value and there by differtiating it from its competitors.
Market segments	Market segments refer to the groups that result from the process of market segmentation; these groups ideally have common needs and will respond similarly to a marketing action.
Production	The creation of finished goods and services using the factors of production: land, labor, capital, entrepreneurship, and knowledge.
Product development	In business and engineering, new product development is the complete process of bringing a new product to market. There are two parallel aspects to this process : one involves product engineering ; the other marketing analysis. Marketers see new product development as the first stage in product life cycle management, engineers as part of Product Lifecycle Management.
Purchasing	Purchasing refers to the function in a firm that searches for quality material resources, finds the best suppliers, and negotiates the best price for goods and services.
Subsidiary	A company that is controlled by another company or corporation is a subsidiary.
Alcoa	Alcoa (NYSE: AA) is the world's leading producer of alumina, primary and fabricated aluminum, with operations in 43 countries. (It is followed in this by a former subsidiary, Alcan, the second-leading producer.)
Portfolio	In finance, a portfolio is a collection of investments held by an institution or a private individual. Holding but not always a portfolio is part of an investment and risk-limiting

236

Go to **Cram101.com** for the Practice Tests for this Chapter.

Go to **Cram101.com** for the Practice Tests for this Chapter.
And, **NEVER** highlight a book again!

237

strategy called diversification. By owning several assets, certain types of risk (in particular specific risk) can be reduced.

Revenue	Revenue is a U.S. business term for the amount of money that a company receives from its activities, mostly from sales of products and/or services to customers.
Downturn	A decline in a stock market or economic cycle is a downturn.
Market share	That fraction of an industry's output accounted for by an individual firm or group of firms is called market share.
Margin	A deposit by a buyer in stocks with a seller or a stockbroker, as security to cover fluctuations in the market in reference to stocks that the buyer has purchased but for which he has not paid is a margin. Commodities are also traded on margin.
Personnel	A collective term for all of the employees of an organization. Personnel is also commonly used to refer to the personnel management function or the organizational unit responsible for administering personnel programs.
Homogeneous	In the context of procurement/purchasing, homogeneous is used to describe goods that do not vary in their essential characteristic irrespective of the source of supply.
Global strategy	Global strategy refers to strategy focusing on increasing profitability by reaping cost reductions from experience curve and location economies.
Advertising campaign	A comprehensive advertising plan that consists of a series of messages in a variety of media that center on a single theme or idea is referred to as an advertising campaign.
Global advertising	Global advertising refers to the use of the same basic advertising message in all international markets.
Logo	Logo refers to device or other brand name that cannot be spoken.
Advertisement	Advertisement is the promotion of goods, services, companies and ideas, usually by an identified sponsor. Marketers see advertising as part of an overall promotional strategy.
Profit	Profit refers to the return to the resource entrepreneurial ability; total revenue minus total cost.
General manager	A manager who is responsible for several departments that perform different functions is called general manager.
License	A license in the sphere of Intellectual Property Rights (IPR) is a document, contract or agreement giving permission or the 'right' to a legally-definable entity to do something (such as manufacture a product or to use a service), or to apply something (such as a trademark), with the objective of achieving commercial gain.
Specialist	A specialist is a trader who makes a market in one or several stocks and holds the limit order book for those stocks.
Technology	The body of knowledge and techniques that can be used to combine economic resources to produce goods and services is called technology.
Export	In economics, an export is any good or commodity, shipped or otherwise transported out of a country, province, town to another part of the world in a legitimate fashion, typically for use in trade or sale.
Lucent Technologies	Lucent Technologies is a company composed of what was formerly AT&T Technologies, which included Western Electric and Bell Labs. It was spun-off from AT&T on September 30, 1996. On April 2, 2006, they announced a merger with its French competitor, Alcatel. The combined company has revenues of approximately $25 billion U.S. based on 2005 calendar results.

238

Go to **Cram101.com** for the Practice Tests for this Chapter.

Go to **Cram101.com** for the Practice Tests for this Chapter.
And, **NEVER** highlight a book again!

Bottleneck	An operation where the work to be performed approaches or exceeds the capacity available to do it is a bottleneck.
Strategic plan	The formal document that presents the ways and means by which a strategic goal will be achieved is a strategic plan. A long-term flexible plan that does not regulate activities but rather outlines the means to achieve certain results, and provides the means to alter the course of action should the desired ends change.
Enterprise	Enterprise refers to another name for a business organization. Other similar terms are business firm, sometimes simply business, sometimes simply firm, as well as company, and entity.
Strategic planning	The process of determining the major goals of the organization and the policies and strategies for obtaining and using resources to achieve those goals is called strategic planning.
Capital	Capital generally refers to financial wealth, especially that used to start or maintain a business. In classical economics, capital is one of four factors of production, the others being land and labor and entrepreneurship.
Multinational corporation	An organization that manufactures and markets products in many different countries and has multinational stock ownership and multinational management is referred to as multinational corporation.
Evaluation	The consumer's appraisal of the product or brand on important attributes is called evaluation.
Parent company	Parent company refers to the entity that has a controlling influence over another company. It may have its own operations, or it may have been set up solely for the purpose of owning the Subject Company.
International division	Division responsible for a firm's international activities is an international division.
Domestic	From or in one's own country. A domestic producer is one that produces inside the home country. A domestic price is the price inside the home country. Opposite of 'foreign' or 'world.'.
Policy	Similar to a script in that a policy can be a less than completely rational decision-making method. Involves the use of a pre-existing set of decision steps for any problem that presents itself.
Market opportunities	Market opportunities refer to areas where a company believes there are favorable demand trends, needs, and/or wants that are not being satisfied, and where it can compete effectively.
International firm	International firm refers to those firms who have responded to stiff competition domestically by expanding their sales abroad. They may start a production facility overseas and send some of their managers, who report to a global division, to that country.
Investment	Investment refers to spending for the production and accumulation of capital and additions to inventories. In a financial sense, buying an asset with the expectation of making a return.
Channel	Channel, in communications (sometimes called communications channel), refers to the medium used to convey information from a sender (or transmitter) to a receiver.
Marketing Plan	Marketing plan refers to a road map for the marketing activities of an organization for a specified future period of time, such as one year or five years.
Senior management	Senior management is generally a team of individuals at the highest level of organizational management who have the day-to-day responsibilities of managing a corporation.

Go to **Cram101.com** for the Practice Tests for this Chapter.

Screening	Screening in economics refers to a strategy of combating adverse selection, one of the potential decision-making complications in cases of asymmetric information.
Market potential	Market potential refers to maximum total sales of a product by all firms to a segment during a specified time period under specified environmental conditions and marketing efforts of the firms.
Consideration	Consideration in contract law, a basic requirement for an enforceable agreement under traditional contract principles, defined in this text as legal value, bargained for and given in exchange for an act or promise. In corporation law, cash or property contributed to a corporation in exchange for shares, or a promise to contribute such cash or property.
Distribution channel	A distribution channel is a chain of intermediaries, each passing a product down the chain to the next organization, before it finally reaches the consumer or end-user.
Emerging markets	The term emerging markets is commonly used to describe business and market activity in industrializing or emerging regions of the world. It is sometimes loosely used as a replacement for emerging economies, but really signifies a business phenomenon that is not fully described by or constrained to geography or economic strength; such countries are considered to be in a transitional phase between developing and developed status.
Emerging market	The term emerging market is commonly used to describe business and market activity in industrializing or emerging regions of the world.
Action plan	Action plan refers to a written document that includes the steps the trainee and manager will take to ensure that training transfers to the job.
Mistake	In contract law a mistake is incorrect understanding by one or more parties to a contract and may be used as grounds to invalidate the agreement. Common law has identified three different types of mistake in contract: unilateral mistake, mutual mistake, and common mistake.
Promotion	Promotion refers to all the techniques sellers use to motivate people to buy products or services. An attempt by marketers to inform people about products and to persuade them to participate in an exchange.
Closing	The finalization of a real estate sales transaction that passes title to the property from the seller to the buyer is referred to as a closing. Closing is a sales term which refers to the process of making a sale. It refers to reaching the final step, which may be an exchange of money or acquiring a signature.
Target market	One or more specific groups of potential consumers toward which an organization directs its marketing program are a target market.
Product manager	Product manager refers to a person who plans, implements, and controls the annual and long-range plans for the products for which he or she is responsible.
Exporter	A firm that sells its product in another country is an exporter.
Tactic	A short-term immediate decision that, in its totality, leads to the achievement of strategic goals is called a tactic.
Situation analysis	Taking stock of where the fine or product has been recently, where it is now, and where it is headed in terms of the organization's plans and the external factors and trends affecting it is a situation analysis.
Budget	Budget refers to an account, usually for a year, of the planned expenditures and the expected receipts of an entity. For a government, the receipts are tax revenues.
Control system	A control system is a device or set of devices that manage the behavior of other devices. Some devices or systems are not controllable.A control system is an interconnection of components connected or related in such a manner as to command, direct, or regulate itself or

Go to **Cram101.com** for the Practice Tests for this Chapter.

	another system.
Controlling	A management function that involves determining whether or not an organization is progressing toward its goals and objectives, and taking corrective action if it is not is called controlling.
Complexity	The technical sophistication of the product and hence the amount of understanding required to use it is referred to as complexity. It is the opposite of simplicity.
Marketing research	Marketing research refers to the analysis of markets to determine opportunities and challenges, and to find the information needed to make good decisions.
Indirect exporting	A firm selling its domestically produced goods in a foreign country through an intermediary is referred to as indirect exporting.
Market development	Selling existing products to new markets is called market development.
Economic problem	Economic problem refers to how to determine the use of scarce resources among competing uses. Because resources are scarce, the economy must choose what products to produce; how these products are to be produced: and for whom.
Strategic alliance	Strategic alliance refers to a long-term partnership between two or more companies established to help each company build competitive market advantages.
Equity	Equity is the name given to the set of legal principles, in countries following the English common law tradition, which supplement strict rules of law where their application would operate harshly, so as to achieve what is sometimes referred to as "natural justice."
Timing of entry	Entry is early when a firm enters a foreign market before other foreign firms and late when a firm enters after other international businesses have established themselves is referred to as timing of entry.
Buyer	A buyer refers to a role in the buying center with formal authority and responsibility to select the supplier and negotiate the terms of the contract.
Wholesale	According to the United Nations Statistics Division Wholesale is the resale of new and used goods to retailers, to industrial, commercial, institutional or professional users, or to other wholesalers, or involves acting as an agent or broker in buying merchandise for, or selling merchandise, to such persons or companies.
Sears	Before the Sears catalog, farmers typically bought supplies (often at very high prices) from local general stores. Sears took advantage of this by publishing his catalog with clearly stated prices, so that consumers could know what he was selling and at what price, and order and obtain them conveniently. The catalog business soon grew quickly.
Gain	In finance, gain is a profit or an increase in value of an investment such as a stock or bond. Gain is calculated by fair market value or the proceeds from the sale of the investment minus the sum of the purchase price and all costs associated with it.
Media plan	A document consisting of objectives, strategies, and tactics for reaching a target audience through various media vehicles is a media plan.
Dell Computer	Dell Computer, formerly PC's Limited, was founded on the principle that by selling personal computer systems directly to customers, PC's Limited could best understand their needs and provide the most effective computing solutions to meet those needs.
Venue	A requirement distinct from jurisdiction that the court be geographically situated so that it is the most appropriate and convenient court to try the case is the venue.
Federal Express	The company officially began operations on April 17, 1973, utilizing a network of 14 Dassault

Go to **Cram101.com** for the Practice Tests for this Chapter.

Go to **Cram101.com** for the Practice Tests for this Chapter.
And, **NEVER** highlight a book again!

245

	Falcon 20s which connected 25 U.S. cities. FedEx, the first cargo airline to use jet aircraft for its services, expanded greatly after the deregulation of the cargo airlines sector. Federal Express use of the hub-spoke distribution paradigm in air freight enabled it to become a world leader in its field.
Credit	Credit refers to a recording as positive in the balance of payments, any transaction that gives rise to a payment into the country, such as an export, the sale of an asset, or borrowing from abroad.
Direct sale	A direct sale is a sale to customers through distributors or self-employed sales people rather than through shops. Includes both personal contact with consumers in their homes (and other nonstore locations such as offices) and phone solicitations initiated by a retailer.
Sales management	Planning the selling program and implementing and controlling the personal selling effort of the firm is called sales management.
Licensing	Licensing is a form of strategic alliance which involves the sale of a right to use certain proprietary knowledge (so called intellectual property) in a defined way.
Patent	The legal right to the proceeds from and control over the use of an invented product or process, granted for a fixed period of time, usually 20 years. Patent is one form of intellectual property that is subject of the TRIPS agreement.
Foreign ownership	Foreign ownership refers to the complete or majority ownership/control of businesses or resources in a country, by individuals who are not citizens of that country, or by companies whose headquarters are not in that country.
Contract	A contract is a "promise" or an "agreement" that is enforced or recognized by the law. In the civil law, a contract is considered to be part of the general law of obligations.
Direct investment	Direct investment refers to a domestic firm actually investing in and owning a foreign subsidiary or division.
Intellectual property	In law, intellectual property is an umbrella term for various legal entitlements which attach to certain types of information, ideas, or other intangibles in their expressed form. The holder of this legal entitlement is generally entitled to exercise various exclusive rights in relation to its subject matter.
Property	Assets defined in the broadest legal sense. Property includes the unrealized receivables of a cash basis taxpayer, but not services rendered.
Trade name	A commercial legal name under which a company does business is referred to as the trade name.
Licensee	A person lawfully on land in possession of another for purposes unconnected with the business interests of the possessor is referred to as the licensee.
Franchising	Franchising is a method of doing business wherein a franchisor licenses trademarks and tried and proven methods of doing business to a franchisee in exchange for a recurring payment, and usually a percentage piece of gross sales or gross profits as well as the annual fees. The term " franchising " is used to describe a wide variety of business systems which may or may not fall into the legal definition provided above.
Franchisor	A company that develops a product concept and sells others the rights to make and sell the products is referred to as a franchisor.
Vertical market	A vertical market, or niche market, is a group of similar businesses and customers which engage in trade based on specific and specialized needs. Often times, participants in a vertical market are very limited to a subset of a larger industry.
Decentralization	Decentralization is the process of redistributing decision-making closer to the point of service or action. This gives freedom to managers at lower levels of the organization to make

Go to **Cram101.com** for the Practice Tests for this Chapter.

Go to **Cram101.com** for the Practice Tests for this Chapter.
And, **NEVER** highlight a book again!

	decisions.
Centralization	A structural policy in which decision-making authority is concentrated at the top of the organizational hierarchy is referred to as centralization.
Franchise	A contractual right to sell certain products or services, use certain trademarks, or perform activities in a geographical region is called a franchise.
Asset protection	Asset protection refers to a set of legal techniques for protecting one's belongings against lawsuits and judgments.
Asset	An item of property, such as land, capital, money, a share in ownership, or a claim on others for future payment, such as a bond or a bank deposit is an asset.
Pizza Hut	Pizza Hut is the world's largest pizza restaurant chain with nearly 34,000 restaurants, delivery-carry out units, and kiosks in 100 countries
International franchising	International franchising refers to a contractual agreement whereby a company permits another company to market its trademarked goods or services in a foriegn nation.
Market economy	A market economy is an economic system in which the production and distribution of goods and services takes place through the mechanism of free markets guided by a free price system rather than by the state in a planned economy.
Regulation	Regulation refers to restrictions state and federal laws place on business with regard to the conduct of its activities.
Franchise agreement	An arrangement whereby someone with a good idea for a business sells the rights to use the business name and sell a product or service to others in a given territory is a franchise agreement.
Authority	Authority in agency law, refers to an agent's ability to affect his principal's legal relations with third parties. Also used to refer to an actor's legal power or ability to do something. In addition, sometimes used to refer to a statute, case, or other legal source that justifies a particular result.
Entrepreneur	The owner/operator. The person who organizes, manages, and assumes the risks of a firm, taking a new idea or a new product and turning it into a successful business is an entrepreneur.
Royalties	Remuneration paid to the owners of technology, patents, or trade names for the use of same name are called royalties.
Vendor	A person who sells property to a vendee is a vendor. The words vendor and vendee are more commonly applied to the seller and purchaser of real estate, and the words seller and buyer are more commonly applied to the seller and purchaser of personal property.
Dealer	People who link buyers with sellers by buying and selling securities at stated prices are referred to as a dealer.
Competitive Strategy	An outline of how a business intends to compete with other firms in the same industry is called competitive strategy.
Marketing cost	Marketing cost refers to the cost incurred in selling goods or services. Includes order-getting costs and order-filling or distribution costs.
Strategic partnership	Strategic partnership refers to an association between two firms by which they agree to work together to achieve a strategic goal. This is often associated with long-term supplier-customer relationships.
Partnership	In the common law, a partnership is a type of business entity in which partners share with each other the profits or losses of the business undertaking in which they have all invested.

Go to **Cram101.com** for the Practice Tests for this Chapter.

American Airlines	American Airlines developed from a conglomeration of about 82 small airlines through a series of corporate acquisitions and reorganizations: initially, the name American Airways was used as a common brand by a number of independent air carriers. American Airlines is the largest airline in the world in terms of total passengers transported and fleet size, and the second-largest airline in the world.
Lufthansa	Lufthansa is a founding member of Star Alliance, the largest airline alliance in the world. The Lufthansa Group operates more than 400 aircraft and employs nearly 100,000 people world-wide.
Contribution	In business organization law, the cash or property contributed to a business by its owners is referred to as contribution.
Labor intensive	Describing an industry or sector of the economy that relies relatively heavily on inputs of labor, usually relative to capital but sometimes to human capital or skilled labor, compared to other industries or sectors is labor intensive.
Labor	People's physical and mental talents and efforts that are used to help produce goods and services are called labor.
General Mills	In 2001, the General Mills purchased Pillsbury, although it was officially described as a "merger." While many of the Pillsbury-branded products are still manufactured by General Mills, some products had to be sold off to allow the merger since the new company would have held a very strong monopoly position.
Raw material	Raw material refers to a good that has not been transformed by production; a primary product.
Commodity	Could refer to any good, but in trade a commodity is usually a raw material or primary product that enters into international trade, such as metals or basic agricultural products.
Proprietary	Proprietary indicates that a party, or proprietor, exercises private ownership, control or use over an item of property, usually to the exclusion of other parties. Where a party, holds or claims proprietary interests in relation to certain types of property (eg. a creative literary work, or software), that property may also be the subject of intellectual property law (eg. copyright or patents).
Economic risk	The likelihood that events, including economic mismanagement, will cause drastic changes in a country's business environment that adversely affects the profit and other goals of a particular business enterprise is referred to as economic risk.
Acquisition	A company's purchase of the property and obligations of another company is an acquisition.
Holding	The holding is a court's determination of a matter of law based on the issue presented in the particular case. In other words: under this law, with these facts, this result.
Legal entity	A legal entity is a legal construct through which the law allows a group of natural persons to act as if it were an individual for certain purposes. The most common purposes are lawsuits, property ownership, and contracts.
Conference Board	The Conference Board is the world's preeminent business membership and research organization, best known for the Consumer Confidence Index and the index of leading indicators. For 90 years, The Conference Board has equipped the world's leading corporations with practical knowledge through issues-oriented research and senior executive peer-to-peer meetings.
Tariff	A tax imposed by a nation on an imported good is called a tariff.
Quota	A government-imposed restriction on quantity, or sometimes on total value, used to restrict the import of something to a specific quantity is called a quota.
Consortia	B2B marketplaces sponsored by a group of otherwise competitive enterprises in a specific industry like automobile manufacturing or airline operations are called a consortia.

Go to **Cram101.com** for the Practice Tests for this Chapter.
And, **NEVER** highlight a book again!

251

Trust	An arrangement in which shareholders of independent firms agree to give up their stock in exchange for trust certificates that entitle them to a share of the trust's common profits.
Airbus	In 2003, for the first time in its 33-year history, Airbus delivered more jet-powered airliners than Boeing. Boeing states that the Boeing 777 has outsold its Airbus counterparts, which include the A340 family as well as the A330-300. The smaller A330-200 competes with the 767, outselling its Boeing counterpart.
Boeing	Boeing is the world's largest aircraft manufacturer by revenue. Headquartered in Chicago, Illinois, Boeing is the second-largest defense contractor in the world. In 2005, the company was the world's largest civil aircraft manufacturer in terms of value.
Initial public offering	Firms in the process of becoming publicly traded companies will issue shares of stock using an initial public offering, which is merely the process of selling stock for the first time to interested investors.
Euro	The common currency of a subset of the countries of the EU, adopted January 1, 1999 is called euro.
Air France	Air France took over the Dutch company KLM in May 2004, resulting in the creation of Air France -KLM. Air France -KLM is the largest airline company in the world in terms of operating revenues, and the third-largest in the world in terms of passengers-kilometers.
Monopoly	A monopoly is defined as a persistent market situation where there is only one provider of a kind of product or service.
Consolidation	The combination of two or more firms, generally of equal size and market power, to form an entirely new entity is a consolidation.
Business Week	Business Week is a business magazine published by McGraw-Hill. It was first published in 1929 under the direction of Malcolm Muir, who was serving as president of the McGraw-Hill Publishing company at the time. It is considered to be the standard both in industry and among students.
DaimlerChrysler	In 2002, the merged company, DaimlerChrysler, appeared to run two independent product lines, with few signs of corporate integration. In 2003, however, it was alleged by the Detroit News that the "merger of equals" was, in fact, a takeover.
Aerospatiale	Aerospatiale was a French aerospace manufacturer that primarily built both civilian and military aircraft and rockets. The company was created in 1970 from the state-owned companies Sud Aviation, Nord Aviation and Société d'études et de réalization d'engins balistiques (SÉREB).
BAE Systems	BAE Systems was formed on 30th November 1999 with the merger of British Aerospace and Marconi Electronic Systems, the defence arm of The General Electric Company. By the combination of the two, BAE systems is the successor to many of the most famous British aircraft, defence electronics and warship manufacturers.
Intel	Intel Corporation, founded in 1968 and based in Santa Clara, California, USA, is the world's largest semiconductor company. Intel is best known for its PC microprocessors, where it maintains roughly 80% market share.
Instrument	Instrument refers to an economic variable that is controlled by policy makers and can be used to influence other variables, called targets. Examples are monetary and fiscal policies used to achieve external and internal balance.
Motorola	The Six Sigma quality system was developed at Motorola even though it became most well known because of its use by General Electric. It was created by engineer Bill Smith, under the direction of Bob Galvin (son of founder Paul Galvin) when he was running the company.

Investment portfolio	An investment portfolio is an aggregate of investments, such as stocks, bonds, real estate, arts or even fine wines. What distinguishes an investment portfolio from net worth is that some asset classes are not considered investments.
Nissan	Nissan is Japan's second largest car company after Toyota. Nissan is among the top three Asian rivals of the "big three" in the US.
General Motors	General Motors is the world's largest automaker. Founded in 1908, today it employs about 327,000 people around the world. With global headquarters in Detroit, it manufactures its cars and trucks in 33 countries.
Shareholder	A shareholder is an individual or company (including a corporation) that legally owns one or more shares of stock in a joined stock company.
Oppression	The officers, directors, or controlling shareholder's isolation of one group of shareholders for disadvantageous treatment to the benefit of another group of shareholders is oppression.
Petition	A petition is a request to an authority, most commonly a government official or public entity. In the colloquial sense, a petition is a document addressed to some official and signed by numerous individuals.
Restructuring	Restructuring is the corporate management term for the act of partially dismantling and reorganizing a company for the purpose of making it more efficient and therefore more profitable.
Free trade area	Free trade area refers to a group of countries that adopt free trade on trade among group members, while not necessarily changing the barriers that each member country has on trade with the countries outside the group.
Free trade	Free trade refers to a situation in which there are no artificial barriers to trade, such as tariffs and quotas. Usually used, often only implicitly, with frictionless trade, so that it implies that there are no barriers to trade of any kind.
Samsung	On November 30, 2005 Samsung pleaded guilty to a charge it participated in a worldwide DRAM price fixing conspiracy during 1999-2002 that damaged competition and raized PC prices.
Chain of command	An unbroken line of authority that links all individuals in the organization and specifies who reports to whom is a chain of command. The concept of chain of command also implies that higher rank alone does not entitle a person to give commands.
Devise	In a will, a gift of real property is called a devise.
Diversification	Investing in a collection of assets whose returns do not always move together, with the result that overall risk is lower than for individual assets is referred to as diversification.
Foreign direct investment	Foreign direct investment refers to the buying of permanent property and businesses in foreign nations.
Matrix organization	Matrix organization refers to an organization in which specialists from different parts of the organization are brought together to work on specific projects but still remain part of a traditional line-and-staff structure.
Product management	Product management is a function within a company dealing with the day-to-day management and welfare of a product or family of products at all stages of the product lifecycle. The product management function is responsible for defining the products in the marketing mix.
Product line	A group of products that are physically similar or are intended for a similar market are called the product line.
Matrix structure	An organizational structure which typically crosses a functional approach with a product or

254

Go to **Cram101.com** for the Practice Tests for this Chapter.

	service-based design, often resulting in employees having two bosses is the matrix structure.
Business unit	The lowest level of the company which contains the set of functions that carry a product through its life span from concept through manufacture, distribution, sales and service is a business unit.
Core	A core is the set of feasible allocations in an economy that cannot be improved upon by subset of the set of the economy's consumers (a coalition). In construction, when the force in an element is within a certain center section, the core, the element will only be under compression.
Foreign subsidiary	A company owned in a foreign country by another company is referred to as foreign subsidiary.
Committee	A long-lasting, sometimes permanent team in the organization structure created to deal with tasks that recur regularly is the committee.
Line organization	An organization that has direct two-way lines of responsibility, authority, and communication running from the top to the bottom of the organization, with all people reporting to only one supervisor is referred to as line organization.
Organizational strategy	The process of positioning the Organization in the competitive environment and implementing actions to compete successfully is an organizational strategy.
Informal organization	Informal organization refers to the system of relationships and lines of authority that develops spontaneously as employees meet and form power centers; that is, the human side of the organization that does not appear on any organization chart.
Competitive market	A market in which no buyer or seller has market power is called a competitive market.
Product life cycle	Product life cycle refers to a series of phases in a product's sales and cash flows over time; these phases, in order of occurrence, are introductory, growth, maturity, and decline.

Disney	Disney is one of the largest media and entertainment corporations in the world. Founded on October 16, 1923 by brothers Walt and Roy Disney as a small animation studio, today it is one of the largest Hollywood studios and also owns nine theme parks and several television networks, including the American Broadcasting Company (ABC).
Investment	Investment refers to spending for the production and accumulation of capital and additions to inventories. In a financial sense, buying an asset with the expectation of making a return.
Joint venture	Joint venture refers to an undertaking by two parties for a specific purpose and duration, taking any of several legal forms.
Service	Service refers to a "non tangible product" that is not embodied in a physical good and that typically effects some change in another product, person, or institution. Contrasts with good.
Licensing	Licensing is a form of strategic alliance which involves the sale of a right to use certain proprietary knowledge (so called intellectual property) in a defined way.
Profit	Profit refers to the return to the resource entrepreneurial ability; total revenue minus total cost.
Assault	An intentional tort that prohibits any attempt or offer to cause harmful or offensive contact with another if it results in a well-grounded apprehension of imminent battery in the mind of the threatened person is called assault.
Mistake	In contract law a mistake is incorrect understanding by one or more parties to a contract and may be used as grounds to invalidate the agreement. Common law has identified three different types of mistake in contract: unilateral mistake, mutual mistake, and common mistake.
Consideration	Consideration in contract law, a basic requirement for an enforceable agreement under traditional contract principles, defined in this text as legal value, bargained for and given in exchange for an act or promise. In corporation law, cash or property contributed to a corporation in exchange for shares, or a promise to contribute such cash or property.
Closing	The finalization of a real estate sales transaction that passes title to the property from the seller to the buyer is referred to as a closing. Closing is a sales term which refers to the process of making a sale. It refers to reaching the final step, which may be an exchange of money or acquiring a signature.
Marketing strategy	Marketing strategy refers to the means by which a marketing goal is to be achieved, usually characterized by a specified target market and a marketing program to reach it.
Global marketing	A strategy of using a common marketing plan and program for all countries in which a company operates, thus selling the product or services the same way everywhere in the world is called global marketing.
Consumer good	Products and services that are ultimately consumed rather than used in the production of another good are a consumer good.
Marketing	Promoting and selling products or services to customers, or prospective customers, is referred to as marketing.
Global marketing strategy	The practice of standardizing marketing activities when there are cultural similarities and adapting them when cultures differ is referred to as global marketing strategy.
Emerging markets	The term emerging markets is commonly used to describe business and market activity in industrializing or emerging regions of the world. It is sometimes loosely used as a replacement for emerging economies, but really signifies a business phenomenon that is not fully described by or constrained to geography or economic strength; such countries are

Go to **Cram101.com** for the Practice Tests for this Chapter.

Go to **Cram101.com** for the Practice Tests for this Chapter.
And, **NEVER** highlight a book again!

	considered to be in a transitional phase between developing and developed status.
Emerging market	The term emerging market is commonly used to describe business and market activity in industrializing or emerging regions of the world.
Market	A market is, as defined in economics, a social arrangement that allows buyers and sellers to discover information and carry out a voluntary exchange of goods or services.
Purchasing power	The amount of goods that money will buy, usually measured by the CPI is referred to as purchasing power.
Purchasing	Purchasing refers to the function in a firm that searches for quality material resources, finds the best suppliers, and negotiates the best price for goods and services.
Domestic	From or in one's own country. A domestic producer is one that produces inside the home country. A domestic price is the price inside the home country. Opposite of 'foreign' or 'world.'.
Trend	Trend refers to the long-term movement of an economic variable, such as its average rate of increase or decrease over enough years to encompass several business cycles.
Firm	An organization that employs resources to produce a good or service for profit and owns and operates one or more plants is referred to as a firm.
Preference	The act of a debtor in paying or securing one or more of his creditors in a manner more favorable to them than to other creditors or to the exclusion of such other creditors is a preference. In the absence of statute, a preference is perfectly good, but to be legal it must be bona fide, and not a mere subterfuge of the debtor to secure a future benefit to himself or to prevent the application of his property to his debts.
Global competition	Global competition exists when competitive conditions across national markets are linked strongly enough to form a true international market and when leading competitors compete head to head in many different countries.
Product life cycle	Product life cycle refers to a series of phases in a product's sales and cash flows over time; these phases, in order of occurrence, are introductory, growth, maturity, and decline.
Marketing management	Marketing management refers to the process of planning and executing the conception, pricing, promotion, and distribution of ideas, goods, and services to create mutually beneficial exchanges.
Prentice Hall	Prentice Hall is a leading educational publisher. It is an imprint of the Pearson Education Company, based in New Jersey, USA.
Management	Management characterizes the process of leading and directing all or part of an organization, often a business, through the deployment and manipulation of resources. Early twentieth-century management writer Mary Parker Follett defined management as "the art of getting things done through people."
Points	Loan origination fees that may be deductible as interest by a buyer of property. A seller of property who pays points reduces the selling price by the amount of the points paid for the buyer.
Customer satisfaction	Customer satisfaction is a business term which is used to capture the idea of measuring how satisfied an enterprise's customers are with the organization's efforts in a marketplace.
Conformance	A dimension of quality that refers to the extent to which a product lies within an allowable range of deviation from its specification is called the conformance.
Consumption	In Keynesian economics consumption refers to personal consumption expenditure, i.e., the purchase of currently produced goods and services out of income, out of savings (net worth),

Go to **Cram101.com** for the Practice Tests for this Chapter.

	or from borrowed funds. It refers to that part of disposable income that does not go to saving.
Expense	In accounting, an expense represents an event in which an asset is used up or a liability is incurred. In terms of the accounting equation, expenses reduce owners' equity.
Gilt	A gilt is a bond issued by the governments of the United Kingdom, South Africa, or Ireland. The term is of British origin, and refers to the debt securities issued by the Bank of England, which had a gilt (or gilded) edge.
Wall Street Journal	Dow Jones & Company was founded in 1882 by reporters Charles Dow, Edward Jones and Charles Bergstresser. Jones converted the small Customers' Afternoon Letter into The Wall Street Journal, first published in 1889, and began delivery of the Dow Jones News Service via telegraph. The Journal featured the Jones 'Average', the first of several indexes of stock and bond prices on the New York Stock Exchange.
Journal	Book of original entry, in which transactions are recorded in a general ledger system, is referred to as a journal.
Brand	A name, symbol, or design that identifies the goods or services of one seller or group of sellers and distinguishes them from the goods and services of competitors is a brand.
Industry	A group of firms that produce identical or similar products is an industry. It is also used specifically to refer to an area of economic production focused on manufacturing which involves large amounts of capital investment before any profit can be realized, also called "heavy industry".
Commerce	Commerce is the exchange of something of value between two entities. It is the central mechanism from which capitalism is derived.
Distribution	Distribution in economics, the manner in which total output and income is distributed among individuals or factors.
Product mix	The combination of product lines offered by a manufacturer is referred to as product mix.
Quality improvement	Quality is inversely proportional to variability thus quality Improvement is the reduction of variability in products and processes.
Marketing research	Marketing research refers to the analysis of markets to determine opportunities and challenges, and to find the information needed to make good decisions.
Portfolio	In finance, a portfolio is a collection of investments held by an institution or a private individual. Holding but not always a portfolio is part of an investment and risk-limiting strategy called diversification. By owning several assets, certain types of risk (in particular specific risk) can be reduced.
Yield	The interest rate that equates a future value or an annuity to a given present value is a yield.
Core	A core is the set of feasible allocations in an economy that cannot be improved upon by subset of the set of the economy's consumers (a coalition). In construction, when the force in an element is within a certain center section, the core, the element will only be under compression.
Technology	The body of knowledge and techniques that can be used to combine economic resources to produce goods and services is called technology.
Gain	In finance, gain is a profit or an increase in value of an investment such as a stock or bond. Gain is calculated by fair market value or the proceeds from the sale of the investment minus the sum of the purchase price and all costs associated with it.

Go to **Cram101.com** for the Practice Tests for this Chapter.

Go to **Cram101.com** for the Practice Tests for this Chapter.
And, **NEVER** highlight a book again!

263

Union	A worker association that bargains with employers over wages and working conditions is called a union.
Euro	The common currency of a subset of the countries of the EU, adopted January 1, 1999 is called euro.
World Health Organization	The World Health Organization is a specialized agency of the United Nations, acting as a coordinating authority on international public health, headquartered in Geneva, Switzerland. It's constitution states that its mission "is the attainment by all peoples of the highest possible level of health". Its major task is to combat disease, especially key infectious diseases, and to promote the general health of the peoples of the world.
PepsiCo	In many ways, PepsiCo differs from its main competitor, having three times as many employees, larger revenues, but a smaller net profit.
General Motors	General Motors is the world's largest automaker. Founded in 1908, today it employs about 327,000 people around the world. With global headquarters in Detroit, it manufactures its cars and trucks in 33 countries.
Consumer behavior	Consumer behavior refers to the actions a person takes in purchasing and using products and services, including the mental and social processes that precede and follow these actions.
Developing country	Developing country refers to a country whose per capita income is low by world standards. Same as LDC. As usually used, it does not necessarily connote that the country's income is rising.
Green marketing	Green marketing refers to marketing efforts to produce, promote, and reclaim environmentally sensitive products.
Product development	In business and engineering, new product development is the complete process of bringing a new product to market. There are two parallel aspects to this process : one involves product engineering ; the other marketing analysis. Marketers see new product development as the first stage in product life cycle management, engineers as part of Product Lifecycle Management.
Consumer demand	Consumer demand or consumption is also known as personal consumption expenditure. It is the largest part of aggregate demand or effective demand at the macroeconomic level.There are two variants of consumption in the aggregate demand model, including induced consumption and autonomous consumption.
Manufacturing	Production of goods primarily by the application of labor and capital to raw materials and other intermediate inputs, in contrast to agriculture, mining, forestry, fishing, and services a manufacturing.
Compliance	A type of influence process where a receiver accepts the position advocated by a source to obtain favorable outcomes or to avoid punishment is the compliance.
Incentive	An incentive is any factor (financial or non-financial) that provides a motive for a particular course of action, or counts as a reason for preferring one choice to the alternatives.
Operation	A standardized method or technique that is performed repetitively, often on different materials resulting in different finished goods is called an operation.
Market share	That fraction of an industry's output accounted for by an individual firm or group of firms is called market share.
Complexity	The technical sophistication of the product and hence the amount of understanding required to use it is referred to as complexity. It is the opposite of simplicity.
Utility	Utility refers to the want-satisfying power of a good or service; the satisfaction or

Go to Cram101.com for the Practice Tests for this Chapter.

pleasure a consumer obtains from the consumption of a good or service.

Buyer	A buyer refers to a role in the buying center with formal authority and responsibility to select the supplier and negotiate the terms of the contract.
Customs	Customs is an authority or agency in a country responsible for collecting customs duties and for controlling the flow of people, animals and goods (including personal effects and hazardous items) in and out of the country.
Competitor	Other organizations in the same industry or type of business that provide a good or service to the same set of customers is referred to as a competitor.
Product concept	The verbal and perhaps pictorial description of the benefits and features of a proposed product; also the early stage of the product development process in which only the product concept exists.
Adoption	In corporation law, a corporation's acceptance of a pre-incorporation contract by action of its board of directors, by which the corporation becomes liable on the contract, is referred to as adoption.
Usury	Usury refers to the taking of more than the law allows on a loan or for forbearance of a debt. Illegal interest.
Probable cause	The reasonable inference from the available facts and circumstances that the suspect committed the crime is referred to as the probable cause.
Resistance to change	Resistance to change refers to an attitude or behavior that shows unwillingness to make or support a change.
Acquisition	A company's purchase of the property and obligations of another company is an acquisition.
Decline stage	The fourth and last stage of the product life cycle when sales and profits begin to drop is called the decline stage.
Innovation	Innovation refers to the first commercially successful introduction of a new product, the use of a new method of production, or the creation of a new form of business organization.
Maturity	Maturity refers to the final payment date of a loan or other financial instrument, after which point no further interest or principal need be paid.
Product strategy	Decisions on the management of products or services based on the conditions of a given market is product strategy. Two general strategies that are well known in the marketing discipline are marketing mix and relational marketing.
Diffusion	Diffusion is the process by which a new idea or new product is accepted by the market. The rate of diffusion is the speed that the new idea spreads from one consumer to the next.
Sony	Sony is a multinational corporation and one of the world's largest media conglomerates founded in Tokyo, Japan. One of its divisions Sony Electronics is one of the leading manufacturers of electronics, video, communications, and information technology products for the consumer and professional markets.
Target market	One or more specific groups of potential consumers toward which an organization directs its marketing program are a target market.
Product innovations	Innovations that introduce new goods or services to better meet customer needs are product innovations.
Product innovation	The development and sale of a new or improved product is a product innovation. Production of a new product on a commercial basis.
Variable	A variable is something measured by a number; it is used to analyze what happens to other

Go to **Cram101.com** for the Practice Tests for this Chapter.
And, **NEVER** highlight a book again!

	things when the size of that number changes.
Compatibility	Compatibility refers to used to describe a product characteristic, it means a good fit with other products used by the consumer or with the consumer's lifestyle. Used in a technical context, it means the ability of systems to work together.
Evaluation	The consumer's appraisal of the product or brand on important attributes is called evaluation.
Analyst	Analyst refers to a person or tool with a primary function of information analysis, generally with a more limited, practical and short term set of goals than a researcher.
Brand management	Brand management is the application of marketing techniques to a specific product, product line, or brand. It seeks to increase the product's perceived value to the customer and thereby increase brand franchise and brand equity.
Diffusion of innovation	Diffusion of innovation is a concept suggesting that customers first enter a market at different times, depending on their attitude to innovation and new products, and their willingness to take risks. Customers can thus be classified as innovators, early adopters, early majority, late majority and laggards.
Cultural values	The values that employees need to have and act on for the organization to act on the strategic values are called cultural values.
Production	The creation of finished goods and services using the factors of production: land, labor, capital, entrepreneurship, and knowledge.
Users	Users refer to people in the organization who actually use the product or service purchased by the buying center.
Economy	The income, expenditures, and resources that affect the cost of running a business and household are called an economy.
New product development	New product development is the complete process of bringing a new product to market. There are two parallel aspects to this process : one involves product engineering ; the other marketing analysis.
Vertical integration	Vertical integration refers to production of different stages of processing of a product within the same firm.
Conglomerate	A conglomerate is a large company that consists of divisions of often seemingly unrelated businesses.
Integration	Economic integration refers to reducing barriers among countries to transactions and to movements of goods, capital, and labor, including harmonization of laws, regulations, and standards. Integrated markets theoretically function as a unified market.
Product development teams	Combinations of work teams and problem-solving teams that create new designs for products or services that will satisfy customer needs are product development teams.
Samsung	On November 30, 2005 Samsung pleaded guilty to a charge it participated in a worldwide DRAM price fixing conspiracy during 1999-2002 that damaged competition and raized PC prices.
Tying	Tying is the practice of making the sale of one good (the tying good) to the de facto or de jure customer conditional on the purchase of a second distinctive good.
Business Week	Business Week is a business magazine published by McGraw-Hill. It was first published in 1929 under the direction of Malcolm Muir, who was serving as president of the McGraw-Hill Publishing company at the time. It is considered to be the standard both in industry and among students.

268

Capital	Capital generally refers to financial wealth, especially that used to start or maintain a business. In classical economics, capital is one of four factors of production, the others being land and labor and entrepreneurship.
Nestle	Nestle is the world's biggest food and beverage company. In the 1860s, a pharmacist, developed a food for babies who were unable to be breastfed. His first success was a premature infant who could not tolerate his own mother's milk nor any of the usual substitutes. The value of the new product was quickly recognized when his new formula saved the child's life.
Household	An economic unit that provides the economy with resources and uses the income received to purchase goods and services that satisfy economic wants is called household.
Trademark	A distinctive word, name, symbol, device, or combination thereof, which enables consumers to identify favored products or services and which may find protection under state or federal law is a trademark.
Apple Computer	Apple Computer has been a major player in the evolution of personal computing since its founding in 1976. The Apple II microcomputer, introduced in 1977, was a hit with home users.
Personnel	A collective term for all of the employees of an organization. Personnel is also commonly used to refer to the personnel management function or the organizational unit responsible for administering personnel programs.
Ford	Ford is an American company that manufactures and sells automobiles worldwide. Ford introduced methods for large-scale manufacturing of cars, and large-scale management of an industrial workforce, especially elaborately engineered manufacturing sequences typified by the moving assembly lines.
Shelf life	Shelf life is the length of time that corresponds to a tolerable loss in quality of a processed food and other perishable items.
Contribution	In business organization law, the cash or property contributed to a business by its owners is referred to as contribution.
Boycott	To protest by refusing to purchase from someone, or otherwise do business with them. In international trade, a boycott most often takes the form of refusal to import a country's goods.
Warranty	An obligation of a company to replace defective goods or correct any deficiencies in performance or quality of a product is called a warranty.
Option	A contract that gives the purchaser the option to buy or sell the underlying financial instrument at a specified price, called the exercise price or strike price, within a specific period of time.
Developed country	A developed country is one that enjoys a relatively high standard of living derived through an industrialized, diversified economy. Countries with a very high Human Development Index are generally considered developed countries.
Preventive maintenance	Maintaining scheduled upkeep and improvement to equipment so equipment can actually improve with age is called the preventive maintenance.
Customer service	The ability of logistics management to satisfy users in terms of time, dependability, communication, and convenience is called the customer service.
General Electric	In 1876, Thomas Alva Edison opened a new laboratory in Menlo Park, New Jersey. Out of the laboratory was to come perhaps the most famous invention of all—a successful development of the incandescent electric lamp. By 1890, Edison had organized his various businesses into the Edison General Electric Company.

Go to **Cram101.com** for the Practice Tests for this Chapter.

Frequency	Frequency refers to the speed of the up and down movements of a fluctuating economic variable; that is, the number of times per unit of time that the variable completes a cycle of up and down movement.
Microsoft	Microsoft is a multinational computer technology corporation with 2004 global annual sales of US$39.79 billion and 71,553 employees in 102 countries and regions as of July 2006. It develops, manufactures, licenses, and supports a wide range of software products for computing devices.
General manager	A manager who is responsible for several departments that perform different functions is called general manager.
Advertising	Advertising refers to paid, nonpersonal communication through various media by organizations and individuals who are in some way identified in the advertising message.
Tangible	Having a physical existence is referred to as the tangible. Personal property other than real estate, such as cars, boats, stocks, or other assets.
Intrinsic value	Intrinsic value refers to as applied to a warrant, this represents the market value of common stock minus the exercise price. The difference is then multiplied by the number of shares each warrant entitles the holder to purchase.
Accommodation	Accommodation is a term used to describe a delivery of nonconforming goods meant as a partial performance of a contract for the sale of goods, where a full performance is not possible.
Insurance	Insurance refers to a system by which individuals can reduce their exposure to risk of large losses by spreading the risks among a large number of persons.
Quality assurance	Those activities associated with assuring the quality of a product or service is called quality assurance.
Anticipation	In finance, anticipation is where debts are paid off early, generally in order to pay less interest.
Export	In economics, an export is any good or commodity, shipped or otherwise transported out of a country, province, town to another part of the world in a legitimate fashion, typically for use in trade or sale.
Supply	Supply is the aggregate amount of any material good that can be called into being at a certain price point; it comprises one half of the equation of supply and demand. In classical economic theory, a curve representing supply is one of the factors that produce price.
Boeing	Boeing is the world's largest aircraft manufacturer by revenue. Headquartered in Chicago, Illinois, Boeing is the second-largest defense contractor in the world. In 2005, the company was the world's largest civil aircraft manufacturer in terms of value.
United Nations	An international organization created by multilateral treaty in 1945 to promote social and economic cooperation among nations and to protect human rights is the United Nations.
Budget	Budget refers to an account, usually for a year, of the planned expenditures and the expected receipts of an entity. For a government, the receipts are tax revenues.
National Cash Register	In 1884 John Henry Patterson and his brother Frank Jefferson Patterson bought the National Manufacturing Company which they renamed the National Cash Register Company. They turned the firm into one of the first modern American companies, introducing new, aggressive sales methods and business techniques. They established the first sales training school in 1893, and introduced a comprehensive social welfare program for factory workers.
Gap	In December of 1995, Gap became the first major North American retailer to accept independent monitoring of the working conditions in a contract factory producing its garments. Gap is the largest specialty retailer in the United States.

Go to **Cram101.com** for the Practice Tests for this Chapter.

Go to **Cram101.com** for the Practice Tests for this Chapter.
And, **NEVER** highlight a book again!

Merrill Lynch	Merrill Lynch through its subsidiaries and affiliates, provides capital markets services, investment banking and advisory services, wealth management, asset management, insurance, banking and related products and services on a global basis. It is best known for its Global Private Client services and its strong sales force.
Broker	In commerce, a broker is a party that mediates between a buyer and a seller. A broker who also acts as a seller or as a buyer becomes a principal party to the deal.
Wireless communication	Wireless communication refers to a method of communication that uses low-powered radio waves to transmit data between devices. The term refers to communication without cables or cords, chiefly using radio frequency and infrared waves. Common uses include the various communications defined by the IrDA, the wireless networking of computers and cellular mobile phones.
Gallup Poll	The Gallup Poll has existed since the 1930s. Historically, it has measured and tracked the public's attitudes concerning virtually every political, social, and economic issue of the day, including highly sensitive or controversial subjects. Typically it uses a simple random sampling method in order to keep the level of bias to a minimum.
Exporting	Selling products to another country is called exporting.
Direct investment	Direct investment refers to a domestic firm actually investing in and owning a foreign subsidiary or division.
Franchising	Franchising is a method of doing business wherein a franchisor licenses trademarks and tried and proven methods of doing business to a franchisee in exchange for a recurring payment, and usually a percentage piece of gross sales or gross profits as well as the annual fees. The term " franchising " is used to describe a wide variety of business systems which may or may not fall into the legal definition provided above.
Intellectual property	In law, intellectual property is an umbrella term for various legal entitlements which attach to certain types of information, ideas, or other intangibles in their expressed form. The holder of this legal entitlement is generally entitled to exercise various exclusive rights in relation to its subject matter.
Protectionism	Protectionism refers to advocacy of protection. The word has a negative connotation, and few advocates of protection in particular situations will acknowledge being protectionists.
Property	Assets defined in the broadest legal sense. Property includes the unrealized receivables of a cash basis taxpayer, but not services rendered.
Single market	A single market is a customs union with common policies on product regulation, and freedom of movement of all the four factors of production (goods, services, capital and labor).
Harmonization	Harmonization refers to the changing of government regulations and practices, as a result of an international agreement, to make those of different countries the same or more compatible.
Reciprocity	An industrial buying practice in which two organizations agree to purchase each other's products and services is called reciprocity.
Quota	A government-imposed restriction on quantity, or sometimes on total value, used to restrict the import of something to a specific quantity is called a quota.
Instrument	Instrument refers to an economic variable that is controlled by policy makers and can be used to influence other variables, called targets. Examples are monetary and fiscal policies used to achieve external and internal balance.
Public policy	Decision making by government. Governments are constantly concerned about what they should or should not do. And whatever they do or do not do is public policy. public program All those activities designed to implement a public policy; often this calls for the creation of

274

Go to **Cram101.com** for the Practice Tests for this Chapter.

Go to **Cram101.com** for the Practice Tests for this Chapter.
And, **NEVER** highlight a book again!

275

	organizations, public agencies, and bureaus.
Policy	Similar to a script in that a policy can be a less than completely rational decision-making method. Involves the use of a pre-existing set of decision steps for any problem that presents itself.
Revenue	Revenue is a U.S. business term for the amount of money that a company receives from its activities, mostly from sales of products and/or services to customers.
Data processing	Data processing refers to a name for business technology in the 1970s; included technology that supported an existing business and was primarily used to improve the flow of financial information.
Copyright	The legal right to the proceeds from and control over the use of a created product, such a written work, audio, video, film, or software is a copyright. This right generally extends over the life of the author plus fifty years.
Patent	The legal right to the proceeds from and control over the use of an invented product or process, granted for a fixed period of time, usually 20 years. Patent is one form of intellectual property that is subject of the TRIPS agreement.
Intellectual property rights	Intellectual property rights, such as patents, copyrights, trademarks, trade secrets, trade names, and domain names are very valuable business assets. Federal and state laws protect intellectual property rights from misappropriation and infringement.
Intellectual property right	Intellectual property right refers to the right to control and derive the benefits from something one has invented, discovered, or created.
Property rights	Bundle of legal rights over the use to which a resource is put and over the use made of any income that may be derived from that resource are referred to as property rights.
Human capital	Human capital refers to the stock of knowledge and skill, embodied in an individual as a result of education, training, and experience that makes them more productive. The stock of knowledge and skill embodied in the population of an economy.
Complaint	The pleading in a civil case in which the plaintiff states his claim and requests relief is called complaint. In the common law, it is a formal legal document that sets out the basic facts and legal reasons that the filing party (the plaintiffs) believes are sufficient to support a claim against another person, persons, entity or entities (the defendants) that entitles the plaintiff(s) to a remedy (either money damages or injunctive relief).
Layout	Layout refers to the physical arrangement of the various parts of an advertisement including the headline, subheads, illustrations, body copy, and any identifying marks.
Host country	The country in which the parent-country organization seeks to locate or has already located a facility is a host country.
Trade in services	Trade in services refers to the provision of a service to buyers within or from one country by a firm in or from another country.
Credit	Credit refers to a recording as positive in the balance of payments, any transaction that gives rise to a payment into the country, such as an export, the sale of an asset, or borrowing from abroad.
Trust	An arrangement in which shareholders of independent firms agree to give up their stock in exchange for trust certificates that entitle them to a share of the trust's common profits.
Brand image	The advertising metric that measures the type and favorability of consumer perceptions of the brand is referred to as the brand image.
Context	The effect of the background under which a message often takes on more and richer meaning is

Go to **Cram101.com** for the Practice Tests for this Chapter.

Go to **Cram101.com** for the Practice Tests for this Chapter.
And, **NEVER** highlight a book again!

	a context. Context is especially important in cross-cultural interactions because some cultures are said to be high context or low context.
Jack Welch	In 1986, GE acquired NBC. During the 90s, Jack Welch helped to modernize GE by emphasizing a shift from manufacturing to services. He also made hundreds of acquisitions and made a push to dominate markets abroad. Welch adopted the Six Sigma quality program in late 1995.
Merchandising	Merchandising refers to the business of acquiring finished goods for resale, either in a wholesale or a retail operation.
Extension	Extension refers to an out-of-court settlement in which creditors agree to allow the firm more time to meet its financial obligations. A new repayment schedule will be developed, subject to the acceptance of creditors.
Appeal	Appeal refers to the act of asking an appellate court to overturn a decision after the trial court's final judgment has been entered.
Enron	Enron Corportaion's global reputation was undermined by persistent rumours of bribery and political pressure to secure contracts in Central America, South America, Africa, and the Philippines. Especially controversial was its $3 billion contract with the Maharashtra State Electricity Board in India, where it is alleged that Enron officials used political connections within the Clinton and Bush administrations to exert pressure on the board.
Commodity	Could refer to any good, but in trade a commodity is usually a raw material or primary product that enters into international trade, such as metals or basic agricultural products.
Compaq	Compaq was founded in February 1982 by Rod Canion, Jim Harris and Bill Murto, three senior managers from semiconductor manufacturer Texas Instruments. Each invested $1,000 to form the company. Their first venture capital came from Ben Rosen and Sevin-Rosen partners. It is often told that the architecture of the original PC was first sketched out on a placemat by the founders while dining in the Houston restaurant, House of Pies.
Merger	Merger refers to the combination of two firms into a single firm.
Corporation	A legal entity chartered by a state or the Federal government that is distinct and separate from the individuals who own it is a corporation. This separation gives the corporation unique powers which other legal entities lack.
Premium	Premium refers to the fee charged by an insurance company for an insurance policy. The rate of losses must be relatively predictable: In order to set the premium (prices) insurers must be able to estimate them accurately.
Profit margin	Profit margin is a measure of profitability. It is calculated using a formula and written as a percentage or a number. Profit margin = Net income before tax and interest / Revenue.
Margin	A deposit by a buyer in stocks with a seller or a stockbroker, as security to cover fluctuations in the market in reference to stocks that the buyer has purchased but for which he has not paid is a margin. Commodities are also traded on margin.
BMW	BMW is an independent German company and manufacturer of automobiles and motorcycles. BMW is the world's largest premium carmaker and is the parent company of the BMW MINI and Rolls-Royce car brands, and, formerly, Rover.
Toyota	Toyota is a Japanese multinational corporation that manufactures automobiles, trucks and buses. Toyota is the world's second largest automaker by sales. Toyota also provides financial services through its subsidiary, Toyota Financial Services, and participates in other lines of business.
Globalization	The increasing world-wide integration of markets for goods, services and capital that attracted special attention in the late 1990s is called globalization.

Go to **Cram101.com** for the Practice Tests for this Chapter.

Brand architecture	Brand architecture is the structure of brands within an organizational entity. It is the way in which the brands within a company's portfolio are related to, and differentiated from, one another. The architecture should define the different leagues of branding within the organization; how the corporate brand and sub-brands relate to and support each other; and how the sub-brands reflect or reinforce the core purpose of the corporate brand to which they belong.
Caterpillar	Caterpillar is a United States based corporation headquartered in Peoria, Illinois. Caterpillar is "the world's largest manufacturer of construction and mining equipment, diesel and natural gas engines, and industrial gas turbines."
Gillette	On October 1, 2005, Gillette finalized its purchase by Procter & Gamble. As a result of this merger, the Gillette Company no longer exists. Its last day of market trading - symbol G on the New York Stock Exchange - was September 30, 2005. The merger created the world's largest personal care and household products company.
Balance	In banking and accountancy, the outstanding balance is the amount of money owned, (or due), that remains in a deposit account (or a loan account) at a given date, after all past remittances, payments and withdrawal have been accounted for. It can be positive (then, in the balance sheet of a firm, it is an asset) or negative (a liability).
Global strategy	Global strategy refers to strategy focusing on increasing profitability by reaping cost reductions from experience curve and location economies.
Product line	A group of products that are physically similar or are intended for a similar market are called the product line.
International strategy	Trying to create value by transferring core competencies to foreign markets where indigenous competitors lack those competencies is called international strategy.
Harvard Business Review	Harvard Business Review is a research-based magazine written for business practitioners, it claims a high ranking business readership and enjoys the reverence of academics, executives, and management consultants. It has been the frequent publishing home for well known scholars and management thinkers.
Argument	The discussion by counsel for the respective parties of their contentions on the law and the facts of the case being tried in order to aid the jury in arriving at a correct and just conclusion is called argument.
Standardization	Standardization, in the context related to technologies and industries, is the process of establishing a technical standard among competing entities in a market, where this will bring benefits without hurting competition.
Promotion	Promotion refers to all the techniques sellers use to motivate people to buy products or services. An attempt by marketers to inform people about products and to persuade them to participate in an exchange.
Versace	The first Versace boutique was opened in Milan's Via della Spiga in 1978, and its popularity was immediate. Today, Versace is one of the world's leading international fashion houses. Versace designs, markets and distributes luxury clothing, accessories, fragrances, makeup and home furnishings under the various brands of the Versace Group.
Gucci	Gucci, or the House of Gucci, is an Italian fashion and leather goods label. It was founded by Guccio Gucci (1881-1953) in Florence in 1921. In the late 1980s made Gucci one of the world's most influential fashion houses and a highly profitable business operation. In October of 1995 Gucci decided to go public and had its first initial public offering on the AEX and NYSE for $22 per share..
Ethnocentrism	Ironically, ethnocentrism may be something that all cultures have in common. People often

Go to **Cram101.com** for the Practice Tests for this Chapter.

feel this occurring during what some call culture shock. Ethnocentrism often entails the belief that one's own race or ethnic group is the most important and/or that some or all aspects of its culture are superior to those of other groups.

International Business

International business refers to any firm that engages in international trade or investment.

Honda

With more than 14 million internal combustion engines built each year, Honda is the largest engine-maker in the world. In 2004, the company began to produce diesel motors, which were both very quiet whilst not requiring particulate filters to pass pollution standards. It is arguable, however, that the foundation of their success is the motorcycle division.

Advertisement

Advertisement is the promotion of goods, services, companies and ideas, usually by an identified sponsor. Marketers see advertising as part of an overall promotional strategy.

Loyalty

Marketers tend to define customer loyalty as making repeat purchases. Some argue that it should be defined attitudinally as a strongly positive feeling about the brand.

Polaroid

The Polaroid Corporation was founded in 1937 by Edwin H. Land. It is most famous for its instant film cameras, which reached the market in 1948, and continue to be the company's flagship product line.

Newly industrializing country

Refers to a group of countries previously regarded as LDCs that have recently achieved high rates and levels of economic growth are newly industrializing country.

Hypermarket

A large retail store offering a mix of food products and general merchandise products under one roof is called a hypermarket.

BlackBerry

The BlackBerry is a wireless handheld device introduced in 1999 which supports push e-mail, mobile telephone, text messaging, internet faxing, web browsing and other wireless information services. It was developed by Research In Motion (RIM) and delivers information over the wireless data networks of cellular telephone companies.

Operating profit

Operating profit is a measure of a company's earning power from ongoing operations, equal to earnings before the deduction of interest payments and income taxes.

Go to **Cram101.com** for the Practice Tests for this Chapter.
And, **NEVER** highlight a book again!

Revenue	Revenue is a U.S. business term for the amount of money that a company receives from its activities, mostly from sales of products and/or services to customers.
A share	In finance the term A share has two distinct meanings, both relating to securities. The first is a designation for a 'class' of common or preferred stock. A share of common or preferred stock typically has enhanced voting rights or other benefits compared to the other forms of shares that may have been created. The equity structure, or how many types of shares are offered, is determined by the corporate charter.
Layoff	A layoff is the termination of an employee or (more commonly) a group of employees for business reasons, such as the decision that certain positions are no longer necessary.
Stock	In financial terminology, stock is the capital raized by a corporation, through the issuance and sale of shares.
Intel	Intel Corporation, founded in 1968 and based in Santa Clara, California, USA, is the world's largest semiconductor company. Intel is best known for its PC microprocessors, where it maintains roughly 80% market share.
Economy	The income, expenditures, and resources that affect the cost of running a business and household are called an economy.
Profit	Profit refers to the return to the resource entrepreneurial ability; total revenue minus total cost.
Market	A market is, as defined in economics, a social arrangement that allows buyers and sellers to discover information and carry out a voluntary exchange of goods or services.
Firm	An organization that employs resources to produce a good or service for profit and owns and operates one or more plants is referred to as a firm.
Business Week	Business Week is a business magazine published by McGraw-Hill. It was first published in 1929 under the direction of Malcolm Muir, who was serving as president of the McGraw-Hill Publishing company at the time. It is considered to be the standard both in industry and among students.
Marketing strategy	Marketing strategy refers to the means by which a marketing goal is to be achieved, usually characterized by a specified target market and a marketing program to reach it.
Global marketing	A strategy of using a common marketing plan and program for all countries in which a company operates, thus selling the product or services the same way everywhere in the world is called global marketing.
Consumer good	Products and services that are ultimately consumed rather than used in the production of another good are a consumer good.
Advertising	Advertising refers to paid, nonpersonal communication through various media by organizations and individuals who are in some way identified in the advertising message.
Accounting	A system that collects and processes financial information about an organization and reports that information to decision makers is referred to as accounting.
Insurance	Insurance refers to a system by which individuals can reduce their exposure to risk of large losses by spreading the risks among a large number of persons.
Marketing	Promoting and selling products or services to customers, or prospective customers, is referred to as marketing.
Service	Service refers to a "non tangible product" that is not embodied in a physical good and that typically effects some change in another product, person, or institution. Contrasts with good.

Go to **Cram101.com** for the Practice Tests for this Chapter.
And, **NEVER** highlight a book again!

Capital	Capital generally refers to financial wealth, especially that used to start or maintain a business. In classical economics, capital is one of four factors of production, the others being land and labor and entrepreneurship.
Export	In economics, an export is any good or commodity, shipped or otherwise transported out of a country, province, town to another part of the world in a legitimate fashion, typically for use in trade or sale.
Supply	Supply is the aggregate amount of any material good that can be called into being at a certain price point; it comprises one half of the equation of supply and demand. In classical economic theory, a curve representing supply is one of the factors that produce price.
Global marketing strategy	The practice of standardizing marketing activities when there are cultural similarities and adapting them when cultures differ is referred to as global marketing strategy.
Commerce	Commerce is the exchange of something of value between two entities. It is the central mechanism from which capitalism is derived.
Industrial goods	Components produced for use in the production of other products are called industrial goods.
International trade	The export of goods and services from a country and the import of goods and services into a country is referred to as the international trade.
Balance of trade	Balance of trade refers to the sum of the money gained by a given economy by selling exports, minus the cost of buying imports. They form part of the balance of payments, which also includes other transactions such as the international investment position.
Contribution	In business organization law, the cash or property contributed to a business by its owners is referred to as contribution.
Balance	In banking and accountancy, the outstanding balance is the amount of money owned, (or due), that remains in a deposit account (or a loan account) at a given date, after all past remittances, payments and withdrawal have been accounted for. It can be positive (then, in the balance sheet of a firm, it is an asset) or negative (a liability).
Lucent Technologies	Lucent Technologies is a company composed of what was formerly AT&T Technologies, which included Western Electric and Bell Labs. It was spun-off from AT&T on September 30, 1996. On April 2, 2006, they announced a merger with its French competitor, Alcatel. The combined company has revenues of approximately $25 billion U.S. based on 2005 calendar results.
Technology	The body of knowledge and techniques that can be used to combine economic resources to produce goods and services is called technology.
BellSouth	BellSouth is currently the only "Baby Bell" that does not operate pay telephones. By 2003, the payphone operation was discontinued because it had become too unprofitable, most likely due to the increased availability of cell phones. Cincinnati Bell has taken their place for payphones in northern BellSouth territory; independents have set in further south.
Siemens	Siemens is the world's largest conglomerate company. Worldwide, Siemens and its subsidiaries employs 461,000 people (2005) in 190 countries and reported global sales of €75.4 billion in fiscal year 2005.
Management	Management characterizes the process of leading and directing all or part of an organization, often a business, through the deployment and manipulation of resources. Early twentieth-century management writer Mary Parker Follett defined management as "the art of getting things done through people."
Consumer market	All the individuals or households that want goods and services for personal consumption or use are a consumer market.

Go to **Cram101.com** for the Practice Tests for this Chapter.

Consideration	Consideration in contract law, a basic requirement for an enforceable agreement under traditional contract principles, defined in this text as legal value, bargained for and given in exchange for an act or promise. In corporation law, cash or property contributed to a corporation in exchange for shares, or a promise to contribute such cash or property.
Intangibility	A unique element of services-services cannot be held, touched, or seen before the purchase decision which is referred to as intangibility.
Protectionism	Protectionism refers to advocacy of protection. The word has a negative connotation, and few advocates of protection in particular situations will acknowledge being protectionists.
Joint venture	Joint venture refers to an undertaking by two parties for a specific purpose and duration, taking any of several legal forms.
Prototype	A prototype is built to test the function of a new design before starting production of a product.
Volatility	Volatility refers to the extent to which an economic variable, such as a price or an exchange rate, moves up and down over time.
Microsoft	Microsoft is a multinational computer technology corporation with 2004 global annual sales of US$39.79 billion and 71,553 employees in 102 countries and regions as of July 2006. It develops, manufactures, licenses, and supports a wide range of software products for computing devices.
Budget	Budget refers to an account, usually for a year, of the planned expenditures and the expected receipts of an entity. For a government, the receipts are tax revenues.
Corporation	A legal entity chartered by a state or the Federal government that is distinct and separate from the individuals who own it is a corporation. This separation gives the corporation unique powers which other legal entities lack.
Derived demand	Derived demand refers to demand that arises or is defined indirectly from some other demand or underlying behavior.
Buyer	A buyer refers to a role in the buying center with formal authority and responsibility to select the supplier and negotiate the terms of the contract.
Purchasing	Purchasing refers to the function in a firm that searches for quality material resources, finds the best suppliers, and negotiates the best price for goods and services.
Samsung	On November 30, 2005 Samsung pleaded guilty to a charge it participated in a worldwide DRAM price fixing conspiracy during 1999-2002 that damaged competition and raized PC prices.
Toshiba	Toshiba is a Japanese high technology electrical and electronics manufacturing firm, headquartered in Tokyo, Japan. It is the 7th largest integrated manufacturer of electric and electronic equipment in the world.
Cemex	Although it is not a monopoly, Cemex, along with Holcim-Apasco, controls the Mexican cement market. This has given rise to allegations that because of the oligopolistic structure in the Mexican cement market (as in many other markets in Mexico) consumers pay a higher price for cement than in other countries. However given the peculiarities of the Mexican cement market, the fact that it is sold mostly in bags, and the fact that cement is not an easily transported commodity make this accuzation difficult, if not impossible to prove.
Agent	A person who makes economic decisions for another economic actor. A hired manager operates as an agent for a firm's owner.
Acer	Acer is one of the world's top five branded PC vendors. It owns the largest computer retail chain in Taiwan. Acer's product offering includes desktop and mobile PCs, servers and storage, displays, peripherals, and e-business solutions for business, government, education,

Go to Cram101.com for the Practice Tests for this Chapter.

	and home users.
Electronic business	Electronic business is any business process that is empowered by an information system. Today, this is mostly done with Web-based technologies.
Consumer demand	Consumer demand or consumption is also known as personal consumption expenditure. It is the largest part of aggregate demand or effective demand at the macroeconomic level.There are two variants of consumption in the aggregate demand model, including induced consumption and autonomous consumption.
Industry	A group of firms that produce identical or similar products is an industry. It is also used specifically to refer to an area of economic production focused on manufacturing which involves large amounts of capital investment before any profit can be realized, also called "heavy industry".
Strategic goal	A strategic goal is a broad statement of where an organization wants to be in the future; pertains to the organization as a whole rather than to specific divisions or departments.
Product line	A group of products that are physically similar or are intended for a similar market are called the product line.
Market share	That fraction of an industry's output accounted for by an individual firm or group of firms is called market share.
Competitor	Other organizations in the same industry or type of business that provide a good or service to the same set of customers is referred to as a competitor.
Wall Street Journal	Dow Jones & Company was founded in 1882 by reporters Charles Dow, Edward Jones and Charles Bergstresser. Jones converted the small Customers' Afternoon Letter into The Wall Street Journal, first published in 1889, and began delivery of the Dow Jones News Service via telegraph. The Journal featured the Jones 'Average', the first of several indexes of stock and bond prices on the New York Stock Exchange.
Southwest airlines	Southwest Airlines is a low-fare airline in the United States. It is the third-largest airline in the world, by number of passengers carried, and the largest in the United States by number of passengers carried domestically.
General Electric	In 1876, Thomas Alva Edison opened a new laboratory in Menlo Park, New Jersey. Out of the laboratory was to come perhaps the most famous invention of all—a successful development of the incandescent electric lamp. By 1890, Edison had organized his various businesses into the Edison General Electric Company.
Portfolio	In finance, a portfolio is a collection of investments held by an institution or a private individual. Holding but not always a portfolio is part of an investment and risk-limiting strategy called diversification. By owning several assets, certain types of risk (in particular specific risk) can be reduced.
Journal	Book of original entry, in which transactions are recorded in a general ledger system, is referred to as a journal.
Globalization	The increasing world-wide integration of markets for goods, services and capital that attracted special attention in the late 1990s is called globalization.
Globalization of markets	Moving away from an economic system in which national markets are distinct entities, isolated by trade barriers and barriers of distance, time, and culture, and toward a system in which national markets are merging into one global market is globalization of markets.
Marketing mix	The marketing mix approach to marketing is a model of crafting and implementing marketing strategies. It stresses the "mixing" or blending of various factors in such a way that both organizational and consumer (target markets) objectives are attained.

Go to **Cram101.com** for the Practice Tests for this Chapter.
And, **NEVER** highlight a book again!

Economic development	Increase in the economic standard of living of a country's population, normally accomplished by increasing its stocks of physical and human capital and improving its technology is an economic development.
Manufacturing	Production of goods primarily by the application of labor and capital to raw materials and other intermediate inputs, in contrast to agriculture, mining, forestry, fishing, and services a manufacturing.
Maturity	Maturity refers to the final payment date of a loan or other financial instrument, after which point no further interest or principal need be paid.
Consumption	In Keynesian economics consumption refers to personal consumption expenditure, i.e., the purchase of currently produced goods and services out of income, out of savings (net worth), or from borrowed funds. It refers to that part of disposable income that does not go to saving.
Leverage	Leverage is using given resources in such a way that the potential positive or negative outcome is magnified. In finance, this generally refers to borrowing.
International Business	International business refers to any firm that engages in international trade or investment.
Per capita	Per capita refers to per person. Usually used to indicate the average per person of any given statistic, commonly income.
Economic growth	Economic growth refers to the increase over time in the capacity of an economy to produce goods and services and to improve the well-being of its citizens.
Control system	A control system is a device or set of devices that manage the behavior of other devices. Some devices or systems are not controllable.A control system is an interconnection of components connected or related in such a manner as to command, direct, or regulate itself or another system.
Raw material	Raw material refers to a good that has not been transformed by production; a primary product.
Labor	People's physical and mental talents and efforts that are used to help produce goods and services are called labor.
Information technology	Information technology refers to technology that helps companies change business by allowing them to use new methods.
Competitiveness	Competitiveness usually refers to characteristics that permit a firm to compete effectively with other firms due to low cost or superior technology, perhaps internationally.
Disintegration	Disintegration is an organization of production in which different stages of production are divided among different suppliers that are located in different countries.
Privatization	A process in which investment bankers take companies that were previously owned by the government to the public markets is referred to as privatization.
Trend	Trend refers to the long-term movement of an economic variable, such as its average rate of increase or decrease over enough years to encompass several business cycles.
Exporter	A firm that sells its product in another country is an exporter.
Communism	Communism refers to an economic system in which capital is owned by private government. Contrasts with capitalism.
Compliance	A type of influence process where a receiver accepts the position advocated by a source to obtain favorable outcomes or to avoid punishment is the compliance.
Evaluation	The consumer's appraisal of the product or brand on important attributes is called

	evaluation.
Distribution	Distribution in economics, the manner in which total output and income is distributed among individuals or factors.
Variable	A variable is something measured by a number; it is used to analyze what happens to other things when the size of that number changes.
Marketing management	Marketing management refers to the process of planning and executing the conception, pricing, promotion, and distribution of ideas, goods, and services to create mutually beneficial exchanges.
Operation	A standardized method or technique that is performed repetitively, often on different materials resulting in different finished goods is called an operation.
Committee	A long-lasting, sometimes permanent team in the organization structure created to deal with tasks that recur regularly is the committee.
Domestic	From or in one's own country. A domestic producer is one that produces inside the home country. A domestic price is the price inside the home country. Opposite of 'foreign' or 'world.'.
Writ	Writ refers to a commandment of a court given for the purpose of compelling certain action from the defendant, and usually executed by a sheriff or other judicial officer.
Enabling	Enabling refers to giving workers the education and tools they need to assume their new decision-making powers.
Union	A worker association that bargains with employers over wages and working conditions is called a union.
Complaint	The pleading in a civil case in which the plaintiff states his claim and requests relief is called complaint. In the common law, it is a formal legal document that sets out the basic facts and legal reasons that the filing party (the plaintiffs) believes are sufficient to support a claim against another person, persons, entity or entities (the defendants) that entitles the plaintiff(s) to a remedy (either money damages or injunctive relief).
Bearer	A person in possession of a negotiable instrument that is payable to him, his order, or to whoever is in possession of the instrument is referred to as bearer.
Product development	In business and engineering, new product development is the complete process of bringing a new product to market. There are two parallel aspects to this process : one involves product engineering ; the other marketing analysis. Marketers see new product development as the first stage in product life cycle management, engineers as part of Product Lifecycle Management.
Quality management	Quality management is a method for ensuring that all the activities necessary to design, develop and implement a product or service are effective and efficient with respect to the system and its performance.
Total quality management	The broad set of management and control processes designed to focus an entire organization and all of its employees on providing products or services that do the best possible job of satisfying the customer is called total quality management.
Eastman Kodak	Eastman Kodak Company is an American multinational public company producing photographic materials and equipment. Long known for its wide range of photographic film products, it has focused in recent years on three main businesses: digital photography, health imaging, and printing. This company remains the largest supplier of films in the world, both for the amateur and professional markets.
Scope	Scope of a project is the sum total of all projects products and their requirements or

features.

Prime minister	The Prime Minister of the United Kingdom of Great Britain and Northern Ireland is the head of government and so exercises many of the executive functions nominally vested in the Sovereign, who is head of state. According to custom, the Prime Minister and the Cabinet (which he or she heads) are accountable for their actions to Parliament, of which they are members by (modern) convention.
Quality control	The measurement of products and services against set standards is referred to as quality control.
Wireless communication	Wireless communication refers to a method of communication that uses low-powered radio waves to transmit data between devices. The term refers to communication without cables or cords, chiefly using radio frequency and infrared waves. Common uses include the various communications defined by the IrDA, the wireless networking of computers and cellular mobile phones.
Harmonization	Harmonization refers to the changing of government regulations and practices, as a result of an international agreement, to make those of different countries the same or more compatible.
Task force	A temporary team or committee formed to solve a specific short-term problem involving several departments is the task force.
Negotiation	Negotiation is the process whereby interested parties resolve disputes, agree upon courses of action, bargain for individual or collective advantage, and/or attempt to craft outcomes which serve their mutual interests.
Compatibility	Compatibility refers to used to describe a product characteristic, it means a good fit with other products used by the consumer or with the consumer's lifestyle. Used in a technical context, it means the ability of systems to work together.
Conversion	Conversion refers to any distinct act of dominion wrongfully exerted over another's personal property in denial of or inconsistent with his rights therein. That tort committed by a person who deals with chattels not belonging to him in a manner that is inconsistent with the ownership of the lawful owner.
Economic expansion	The upward phase of the business cycle, in which GDP is rising and unemployment is falling over time is called economic expansion.
National Aeronautics and Space Administration	The National Aeronautics and Space Administration is an agency of the United States Government, responsible for the nation's public space program. Its annual funding amounts to $16 billion and is widely regarded as the forefront leader of space agencies worldwide.In addition to the space program, it is also responsible for long-term civilian and military aerospace research.
Administration	Administration refers to the management and direction of the affairs of governments and institutions; a collective term for all policymaking officials of a government; the execution and implementation of public policy.
Edict	Edict refers to a command or prohibition promulgated by a sovereign and having the effect of
Production	The creation of finished goods and services using the factors of production: land, labor, capital, entrepreneurship, and knowledge.
Integration	Economic integration refers to reducing barriers among countries to transactions and to movements of goods, capital, and labor, including harmonization of laws, regulations, and standards. Integrated markets theoretically function as a unified market.
Global competition	Global competition exists when competitive conditions across national markets are linked strongly enough to form a true international market and when leading competitors compete head

Go to **Cram101.com** for the Practice Tests for this Chapter.

Go to **Cram101.com** for the Practice Tests for this Chapter.
And, **NEVER** highlight a book again!

297

to head in many different countries.

Conformance
A dimension of quality that refers to the extent to which a product lies within an allowable range of deviation from its specification is called the conformance.

ISO 9000
ISO 9000 is a family of ISO standards for Quality Management Systems. It does not guarantee the quality of end products and services; rather, it certifies that consistent business processes are being applied.

International Organization for Standardization
The International Organization for Standardization is an international standard-setting body composed of representatives from national standards bodies. Founded on February 23, 1947, the organization produces world-wide industrial and commercial standards.

Quality assurance
Those activities associated with assuring the quality of a product or service is called quality assurance.

Standardization
Standardization, in the context related to technologies and industries, is the process of establishing a technical standard among competing entities in a market, where this will bring benefits without hurting competition.

Iso 9000 standards
International quality-control standards issued by the International Standards Organization are ISO 9000 standards. The standards do not specify a quality target level (99%, etc.), but stress the ability of a company to prove via third-party audit that they are complying with their defined procedures.

Assessment
Collecting information and providing feedback to employees about their behavior, communication style, or skills is an assessment.

Audit
An examination of the financial reports to ensure that they represent what they claim and conform with generally accepted accounting principles is referred to as audit.

Assessor
An assessor is an expert who calculates the value of property. The value calculated by the assessor is then used as the basis for determining the amounts to be paid or assessed for tax or insurance purposes.

Comprehensive
A comprehensive refers to a layout accurate in size, color, scheme, and other necessary details to show how a final ad will look. For presentation only, never for reproduction.

Product liability
Part of tort law that holds businesses liable for harm that results from the production, design, sale, or use of products they market is referred to as product liability.

Liability
A liability is a present obligation of the enterprise arizing from past events, the settlement of which is expected to result in an outflow from the enterprise of resources embodying economic benefits.

Negligence
The omission to do something that a reasonable person, guided by those considerations that ordinarily regulate human affairs, would do, or doing something that a prudent and reasonable person would not do is negligence.

Regulation
Regulation refers to restrictions state and federal laws place on business with regard to the conduct of its activities.

Interest
In finance and economics, interest is the price paid by a borrower for the use of a lender's money. In other words, interest is the amount of paid to "rent" money for a period of time.

Contract
A contract is a "promise" or an "agreement" that is enforced or recognized by the law. In the civil law, a contract is considered to be part of the general law of obligations.

Subsidiary
A company that is controlled by another company or corporation is a subsidiary.

Euro
The common currency of a subset of the countries of the EU, adopted January 1, 1999 is called

Go to Cram101.com for the Practice Tests for this Chapter.

	euro.
Acquisition	A company's purchase of the property and obligations of another company is an acquisition.
Government procurement	Government procurement refers to purchase of goods and services by government and by state-owned enterprises.
Procurement	Procurement is the acquisition of goods or services at the best possible total cost of ownership, in the right quantity, at the right time, in the right place for the direct benefit or use of the governments, corporations, or individuals generally via, but not limited to a contract.
Customer satisfaction	Customer satisfaction is a business term which is used to capture the idea of measuring how satisfied an enterprise's customers are with the organization's efforts in a marketplace.
Appeal	Appeal refers to the act of asking an appellate court to overturn a decision after the trial court's final judgment has been entered.
Users	Users refer to people in the organization who actually use the product or service purchased by the buying center.
Quality improvement	Quality is inversely proportional to variability thus quality Improvement is the reduction of variability in products and processes.
Gain	In finance, gain is a profit or an increase in value of an investment such as a stock or bond. Gain is calculated by fair market value or the proceeds from the sale of the investment minus the sum of the purchase price and all costs associated with it.
Product design	Product Design is defined as the idea generation, concept development, testing and manufacturing or implementation of a physical object or service. It is possibly the evolution of former discipline name - Industrial Design.
Marketing research	Marketing research refers to the analysis of markets to determine opportunities and challenges, and to find the information needed to make good decisions.
Personnel	A collective term for all of the employees of an organization. Personnel is also commonly used to refer to the personnel management function or the organizational unit responsible for administering personnel programs.
Cisco Systems	While Cisco Systems was not the first company to develop and sell a router (a device that forwards computer traffic from one network to another), it did create the first commercially successful multi-protocol router to allow previously incompatible computers to communicate using different network protocols.
Exporting	Selling products to another country is called exporting.
Aftermarket	The market for a new security offering immediately after it is sold to the public is referred to as aftermarket.
Customer service	The ability of logistics management to satisfy users in terms of time, dependability, communication, and convenience is called the customer service.
Inventory	Tangible property held for sale in the normal course of business or used in producing goods or services for sale is an inventory.
Premium	Premium refers to the fee charged by an insurance company for an insurance policy. The rate of losses must be relatively predictable: In order to set the premium (prices) insurers must be able to estimate them accurately.
Customer loyalty	Marketers tend to define customer loyalty as making repeat purchases. Some argue that it should be defined attitudinally as a strongly positive feeling about the brand.

Go to **Cram101.com** for the Practice Tests for this Chapter.

Go to **Cram101.com** for the Practice Tests for this Chapter.
And, **NEVER** highlight a book again!

Affiliation	A relationship with other websites in which a company can cross-promote and is credited for sales that accrue through their site is an affiliation.
Consultant	A professional that provides expert advice in a particular field or area in which customers occassionaly require this type of knowledge is a consultant.
Infant industry	Infant industry refers to a young industry that may need temporary protection from competition from the established industries of other countries to develop an acquired comparative advantage.
Security	Security refers to a claim on the borrower future income that is sold by the borrower to the lender. A security is a type of transferable interest representing financial value.
Trade in services	Trade in services refers to the provision of a service to buyers within or from one country by a firm in or from another country.
Open business	Open business is in general the concept of doing business in a transparent way by intimately integrating an ecosystem of stake holders and abiding by a model of transparency.
Controlling	A management function that involves determining whether or not an organization is progressing toward its goals and objectives, and taking corrective action if it is not is called controlling.
Tariff	A tax imposed by a nation on an imported good is called a tariff.
Trade show	A type of exhibition or forum where manufacturers can display their products to current as well as prospective buyers is referred to as trade show.
Brand awareness	How quickly or easily a given brand name comes to mind when a product category is mentioned is brand awareness.
Brand	A name, symbol, or design that identifies the goods or services of one seller or group of sellers and distinguishes them from the goods and services of competitors is a brand.
Sponsorship	When the advertiser assumes responsibility for the production and usually the content of a television program as well as the advertising that appears within it, we have sponsorship.
Promotion	Promotion refers to all the techniques sellers use to motivate people to buy products or services. An attempt by marketers to inform people about products and to persuade them to participate in an exchange.
Target market	One or more specific groups of potential consumers toward which an organization directs its marketing program are a target market.
Administrator	Administrator refers to the personal representative appointed by a probate court to settle the estate of a deceased person who died.
Franchising	Franchising is a method of doing business wherein a franchisor licenses trademarks and tried and proven methods of doing business to a franchisee in exchange for a recurring payment, and usually a percentage piece of gross sales or gross profits as well as the annual fees. The term " franchising " is used to describe a wide variety of business systems which may or may not fall into the legal definition provided above.
Promoter	A person who incorporates a business, organizes its initial management, and raises its initial capital is a promoter.
Accommodation	Accommodation is a term used to describe a delivery of nonconforming goods meant as a partial performance of a contract for the sale of goods, where a full performance is not possible.
Expense	In accounting, an expense represents an event in which an asset is used up or a liability is incurred. In terms of the accounting equation, expenses reduce owners' equity.

Go to **Cram101.com** for the Practice Tests for this Chapter.

Go to **Cram101.com** for the Practice Tests for this Chapter.
And, **NEVER** highlight a book again!

303

Entrepreneur	The owner/operator. The person who organizes, manages, and assumes the risks of a firm, taking a new idea or a new product and turning it into a successful business is an entrepreneur.
Boeing	Boeing is the world's largest aircraft manufacturer by revenue. Headquartered in Chicago, Illinois, Boeing is the second-largest defense contractor in the world. In 2005, the company was the world's largest civil aircraft manufacturer in terms of value.
Policy	Similar to a script in that a policy can be a less than completely rational decision-making method. Involves the use of a pre-existing set of decision steps for any problem that presents itself.
Relationship marketing	Marketing whose goal is to keep individual customers over time by offering them products that exactly meet their requirements is called relationship marketing.
Context	The effect of the background under which a message often takes on more and richer meaning is a context. Context is especially important in cross-cultural interactions because some cultures are said to be high context or low context.
Trust	An arrangement in which shareholders of independent firms agree to give up their stock in exchange for trust certificates that entitle them to a share of the trust's common profits.
Relationship management	A method for developing long-term associations with customers is referred to as relationship management.
Warehouse	Warehouse refers to a location, often decentralized, that a firm uses to store, consolidate, age, or mix stock; house product-recall programs; or ease tax burdens.
Relational marketing	The business marketing strategy in which emphasis is on retaining, upgrading, and cross-selling customers, often using targeted marketing media is relational marketing.
Conflict management	Conflict management refers to the long-term management of intractable conflicts. It is the label for the variety of ways by which people handle grievances -- standing up for what they consider to be right and against what they consider to be wrong.
Parent corporation	Parent corporation refers to a corporation that owns a controlling interest of another corporation, called a subsidiary corporation.
Caterpillar	Caterpillar is a United States based corporation headquartered in Peoria, Illinois. Caterpillar is "the world's largest manufacturer of construction and mining equipment, diesel and natural gas engines, and industrial gas turbines."
Customer contact	Customer contact refers to a characteristic of services that notes that customers tend to be more involved in the production of services than they are in manufactured goods.
Sales engineer	A salesperson who specializes in identifying, analyzing, and solving customer problems and who brings know-how and technical expertise to the selling situations, but does not actually sell goods and services is a sales engineer.
Vendor	A person who sells property to a vendee is a vendor. The words vendor and vendee are more commonly applied to the seller and purchaser of real estate, and the words seller and buyer are more commonly applied to the seller and purchaser of personal property.
Personal selling	Personal selling is interpersonal communication, often face to face, between a sales representative and an individual or group, usually with the objective of making a sale.
Project manager	Project manager refers to a manager responsible for a temporary work project that involves the participation of other people from various functions and levels of the organization.
Quality audit	Quality audit means a systematic, independent examination of a quality system. A quality audit is typically performed at defined intervals and ensures that the institution has

Go to **Cram101.com** for the Practice Tests for this Chapter.
And, **NEVER** highlight a book again!

clearly-defined internal quality monitoring procedures linked to effective action. The checking determines if the quality system complies with applicable regulations or standards The process involves assessing the standard operating procedures (SOP's) for compliance to the regulations, and also assessing the actual process and results against what is stated in the SOP.

Liaison

An individual who serves as a bridge between groups, tying groups together and facilitating the communication flow needed to integrate group activities is a liaison.

Affiliates

Local television stations that are associated with a major network are called affiliates. Affiliates agree to preempt time during specified hours for programming provided by the network and carry the advertising contained in the program.

Shell

One of the original Seven Sisters, Royal Dutch/Shell is the world's third-largest oil company by revenue, and a major player in the petrochemical industry and the solar energy business. Shell has six core businesses: Exploration and Production, Gas and Power, Downstream, Chemicals, Renewables, and Trading/Shipping, and operates in more than 140 countries.

Invoice

The itemized bill for a transaction, stating the nature of the transaction and its cost. In international trade, the invoice price is often the preferred basis for levying an ad valorem tariff.

306

Go to **Cram101.com** for the Practice Tests for this Chapter.

Developing country	Developing country refers to a country whose per capita income is low by world standards. Same as LDC. As usually used, it does not necessarily connote that the country's income is rising.
Distribution	Distribution in economics, the manner in which total output and income is distributed among individuals or factors.
Market	A market is, as defined in economics, a social arrangement that allows buyers and sellers to discover information and carry out a voluntary exchange of goods or services.
Word of mouth	People influencing each other during their face-to-face converzations is called word of mouth.
Incentive	An incentive is any factor (financial or non-financial) that provides a motive for a particular course of action, or counts as a reason for preferring one choice to the alternatives.
Brand	A name, symbol, or design that identifies the goods or services of one seller or group of sellers and distinguishes them from the goods and services of competitors is a brand.
Point of Sale	Point of sale can mean a retail shop, a checkout counter in a shop, or a variable location where a transaction occurs.
Bleed	Printed matter that runs over the edges of an outdoor board or of a page, leaving no margin is called a bleed.
Customs	Customs is an authority or agency in a country responsible for collecting customs duties and for controlling the flow of people, animals and goods (including personal effects and hazardous items) in and out of the country.
Firm	An organization that employs resources to produce a good or service for profit and owns and operates one or more plants is referred to as a firm.
Warehouse	Warehouse refers to a location, often decentralized, that a firm uses to store, consolidate, age, or mix stock; house product-recall programs; or ease tax burdens.
Buyer	A buyer refers to a role in the buying center with formal authority and responsibility to select the supplier and negotiate the terms of the contract.
Wholesale	According to the United Nations Statistics Division Wholesale is the resale of new and used goods to retailers, to industrial, commercial, institutional or professional users, or to other wholesalers, or involves acting as an agent or broker in buying merchandise for, or selling merchandise, to such persons or companies.
Competitor	Other organizations in the same industry or type of business that provide a good or service to the same set of customers is referred to as a competitor.
Stock	In financial terminology, stock is the capital raized by a corporation, through the issuance and sale of shares.
International Business	International business refers to any firm that engages in international trade or investment.
Margin	A deposit by a buyer in stocks with a seller or a stockbroker, as security to cover fluctuations in the market in reference to stocks that the buyer has purchased but for which he has not paid is a margin. Commodities are also traded on margin.
Market share	That fraction of an industry's output accounted for by an individual firm or group of firms is called market share.
Marketing strategy	Marketing strategy refers to the means by which a marketing goal is to be achieved, usually characterized by a specified target market and a marketing program to reach it.

Go to Cram101.com for the Practice Tests for this Chapter.

Global marketing	A strategy of using a common marketing plan and program for all countries in which a company operates, thus selling the product or services the same way everywhere in the world is called global marketing.
Target market	One or more specific groups of potential consumers toward which an organization directs its marketing program are a target market.
Business Week	Business Week is a business magazine published by McGraw-Hill. It was first published in 1929 under the direction of Malcolm Muir, who was serving as president of the McGraw-Hill Publishing company at the time. It is considered to be the standard both in industry and among students.
Marketing	Promoting and selling products or services to customers, or prospective customers, is referred to as marketing.
Journal	Book of original entry, in which transactions are recorded in a general ledger system, is referred to as a journal.
Channel	Channel, in communications (sometimes called communications channel), refers to the medium used to convey information from a sender (or transmitter) to a receiver.
Global marketing strategy	The practice of standardizing marketing activities when there are cultural similarities and adapting them when cultures differ is referred to as global marketing strategy.
Channel of distribution	A whole set of marketing intermediaries, such as wholesalers and retailers, who join together to transport and store goods in their path from producers to consumers is referred to as channel of distribution.
Competitive advantage	A business is said to have a competitive advantage when its unique strengths, often based on cost, quality, time, and innovation, offer consumers a greater percieved value and there by differtiating it from its competitors.
Negotiation	Negotiation is the process whereby interested parties resolve disputes, agree upon courses of action, bargain for individual or collective advantage, and/or attempt to craft outcomes which serve their mutual interests.
Policy	Similar to a script in that a policy can be a less than completely rational decision-making method. Involves the use of a pre-existing set of decision steps for any problem that presents itself.
Economic development	Increase in the economic standard of living of a country's population, normally accomplished by increasing its stocks of physical and human capital and improving its technology is an economic development.
Service	Service refers to a "non tangible product" that is not embodied in a physical good and that typically effects some change in another product, person, or institution. Contrasts with good.
Emerging markets	The term emerging markets is commonly used to describe business and market activity in industrializing or emerging regions of the world. It is sometimes loosely used as a replacement for emerging economies, but really signifies a business phenomenon that is not fully described by or constrained to geography or economic strength; such countries are considered to be in a transitional phase between developing and developed status.
Emerging market	The term emerging market is commonly used to describe business and market activity in industrializing or emerging regions of the world.
Manufactured good	A manufactured good refers to goods that have been processed in any way.

Economy	The income, expenditures, and resources that affect the cost of running a business and household are called an economy.
Supply	Supply is the aggregate amount of any material good that can be called into being at a certain price point; it comprises one half of the equation of supply and demand. In classical economic theory, a curve representing supply is one of the factors that produce price.
Market penetration	A strategy of increasing sales of present products in their existing markets is called market penetration.
Technology	The body of knowledge and techniques that can be used to combine economic resources to produce goods and services is called technology.
Scope	Scope of a project is the sum total of all projects products and their requirements or features.
Ford	Ford is an American company that manufactures and sells automobiles worldwide. Ford introduced methods for large-scale manufacturing of cars, and large-scale management of an industrial workforce, especially elaborately engineered manufacturing sequences typified by the moving assembly lines.
Internationa-ization	Internationalization refers to another term for fragmentation. Used by Grossman and Helpman.
Marketing research	Marketing research refers to the analysis of markets to determine opportunities and challenges, and to find the information needed to make good decisions.
Intermediaries	Intermediaries specialize in information either to bring together two parties to a transaction or to buy in order to sell again.
Advertising	Advertising refers to paid, nonpersonal communication through various media by organizations and individuals who are in some way identified in the advertising message.
Consumption	In Keynesian economics consumption refers to personal consumption expenditure, i.e., the purchase of currently produced goods and services out of income, out of savings (net worth), or from borrowed funds. It refers to that part of disposable income that does not go to saving.
Profit maximization	Search by a firm for the product quantity, quality, and price that gives that firm the highest possible profit is profit maximization.
Production	The creation of finished goods and services using the factors of production: land, labor, capital, entrepreneurship, and knowledge.
Profit	Profit refers to the return to the resource entrepreneurial ability; total revenue minus total cost.
Market system	All the product and resource markets of a market economy and the relationships among them are called a market system.
Nontariff barrier	Any policy that interferes with exports or imports other than a simple tariff, prominently including quotas and vers is referred to as nontariff barrier.
Case study	A case study is a particular method of qualitative research. Rather than using large samples and following a rigid protocol to examine a limited number of variables, case study methods involve an in-depth, longitudinal examination of a single instance or event: a case. They provide a systematic way of looking at events, collecting data, analyzing information, and reporting the results.
Operation	A standardized method or technique that is performed repetitively, often on different materials resulting in different finished goods is called an operation.

Go to Cram101.com for the Practice Tests for this Chapter.

Business philosophy	A business philosophy is any of a range of approaches to accounting, marketing, public relations, operations, training, labor relations, executive time management, investment, and/or corporate governance claimed to improve business performance in some measurable or otherwise provable way.
Foundation	A Foundation is a type of philanthropic organization set up by either individuals or institutions as a legal entity (either as a corporation or trust) with the purpose of distributing grants to support causes in line with the goals of the foundation.
Inventory	Tangible property held for sale in the normal course of business or used in producing goods or services for sale is an inventory.
Developed country	A developed country is one that enjoys a relatively high standard of living derived through an industrialized, diversified economy. Countries with a very high Human Development Index are generally considered developed countries.
Management	Management characterizes the process of leading and directing all or part of an organization, often a business, through the deployment and manipulation of resources. Early twentieth-century management writer Mary Parker Follett defined management as "the art of getting things done through people."
Marketing channel	Individuals and firms involved in the process of making a product or service available for use or consumption by consumers or industrial users is a marketing channel.
Free market	A free market is a market where price is determined by the unregulated interchange of supply and demand rather than set by artificial means.
Retail sale	The sale of goods and services to consumers for their own use is a retail sale.
Discount	The difference between the face value of a bond and its selling price, when a bond is sold for less than its face value it's referred to as a discount.
Promotion	Promotion refers to all the techniques sellers use to motivate people to buy products or services. An attempt by marketers to inform people about products and to persuade them to participate in an exchange.
Agent	A person who makes economic decisions for another economic actor. A hired manager operates as an agent for a firm's owner.
Consignment	Consignment refers to a bailment for sale. The consignee does not undertake the absolute obligation to sell or pay for the goods.
Credit	Credit refers to a recording as positive in the balance of payments, any transaction that gives rise to a payment into the country, such as an export, the sale of an asset, or borrowing from abroad.
Sales promotion	Sales promotion refers to the promotional tool that stimulates consumer purchasing and dealer interest by means of short-term activities.
Rebate	Rebate refers to a sales promotion in which money is returned to the consumer based on proof of purchase.
Dealer	People who link buyers with sellers by buying and selling securities at stated prices are referred to as a dealer.
Aid	Assistance provided by countries and by international institutions such as the World Bank to developing countries in the form of monetary grants, loans at low interest rates, in kind, or a combination of these is called aid. Aid can also refer to assistance of any type rendered to benefit some group or individual.
Distribution	A distribution channel is a chain of intermediaries, each passing a product down the chain to

Go to **Cram101.com** for the Practice Tests for this Chapter.
And, **NEVER** highlight a book again!

channel	the next organization, before it finally reaches the consumer or end-user.
Loyalty	Marketers tend to define customer loyalty as making repeat purchases. Some argue that it should be defined attitudinally as a strongly positive feeling about the brand.
Price competition	Price competition is where a company tries to distinguish its product or service from competing products on the basis of low price.
Consumer good	Products and services that are ultimately consumed rather than used in the production of another good are a consumer good.
Retailing	All activities involved in selling, renting, and providing goods and services to ultimate consumers for personal, family, or household use is referred to as retailing.
Ministry of International Trade and Industry	The Ministry of International Trade and Industry was the single most powerful agency in the Japanese government. At the height of its influence, it ran Japan as a centrally-managed economy, funding research and directing investment. in 2001, its role was taken over by the newly created Ministry of Economy, Trade, and Industry.
International trade	The export of goods and services from a country and the import of goods and services into a country is referred to as the international trade.
Industry	A group of firms that produce identical or similar products is an industry. It is also used specifically to refer to an area of economic production focused on manufacturing which involves large amounts of capital investment before any profit can be realized, also called "heavy industry".
Domestic	From or in one's own country. A domestic producer is one that produces inside the home country. A domestic price is the price inside the home country. Opposite of 'foreign' or 'world.'.
Regulation	Regulation refers to restrictions state and federal laws place on business with regard to the conduct of its activities.
Licensing	Licensing is a form of strategic alliance which involves the sale of a right to use certain proprietary knowledge (so called intellectual property) in a defined way.
License	A license in the sphere of Intellectual Property Rights (IPR) is a document, contract or agreement giving permission or the 'right' to a legally-definable entity to do something (such as manufacture a product or to use a service), or to apply something (such as a trademark), with the objective of achieving commercial gain.
Standard of living	Standard of living refers to the level of consumption that people enjoy, on the average, and is measured by average income per person.
Wall Street Journal	Dow Jones & Company was founded in 1882 by reporters Charles Dow, Edward Jones and Charles Bergstresser. Jones converted the small Customers' Afternoon Letter into The Wall Street Journal, first published in 1889, and began delivery of the Dow Jones News Service via telegraph. The Journal featured the Jones 'Average', the first of several indexes of stock and bond prices on the New York Stock Exchange.
Keiretsu	Keiretsu is a set of companies with interlocking business relationships and shareholdings. It is a type of business group.
Enterprise	Enterprise refers to another name for a business organization. Other similar terms are business firm, sometimes simply business, sometimes simply firm, as well as company, and entity.
Exchange	The trade of things of value between buyer and seller so that each is better off after the trade is called the exchange.

Sales tax	A sales tax is a tax on consumption. It is normally a certain percentage that is added onto the price of a good or service that is purchased.
Trend	Trend refers to the long-term movement of an economic variable, such as its average rate of increase or decrease over enough years to encompass several business cycles.
Purchasing	Purchasing refers to the function in a firm that searches for quality material resources, finds the best suppliers, and negotiates the best price for goods and services.
Gap	In December of 1995, Gap became the first major North American retailer to accept independent monitoring of the working conditions in a contract factory producing its garments. Gap is the largest specialty retailer in the United States.
Deregulation	The lessening or complete removal of government regulations on an industry, especially concerning the price that firms are allowed to charge and leaving price to be determined by market forces a deregulation.
Merchant	Under the Uniform Commercial Code, one who regularly deals in goods of the kind sold in the contract at issue, or holds himself out as having special knowledge or skill relevant to such goods, or who makes the sale through an agent who regularly deals in such goods or claims such knowledge or skill is referred to as merchant.
Entrepreneur	The owner/operator. The person who organizes, manages, and assumes the risks of a firm, taking a new idea or a new product and turning it into a successful business is an entrepreneur.
General Electric	In 1876, Thomas Alva Edison opened a new laboratory in Menlo Park, New Jersey. Out of the laboratory was to come perhaps the most famous invention of all—a successful development of the incandescent electric lamp. By 1890, Edison had organized his various businesses into the Edison General Electric Company.
Joint venture	Joint venture refers to an undertaking by two parties for a specific purpose and duration, taking any of several legal forms.
Market segments	Market segments refer to the groups that result from the process of market segmentation; these groups ideally have common needs and will respond similarly to a marketing action.
Direct marketing	Promotional element that uses direct communication with consumers to generate a response in the form of an order, a request for further information, or a visit to a retail outlet is direct marketing.
Hypermarket	A large retail store offering a mix of food products and general merchandise products under one roof is called a hypermarket.
Disparity	Disparity refers to the regional and economic differences in a country, province, state, or continent
Amway	Amway is a multi-level marketing company founded in 1959 by Jay Van Andel and Rich DeVos. The company's name is a portmanteau of "American Way." .
Avon	Avon is an American cosmetics, perfume and toy seller with markets in over 135 countries across the world and a sales of $7.74 billion worldwide.
Merchandising	Merchandising refers to the business of acquiring finished goods for resale, either in a wholesale or a retail operation.
Buying power	The dollar amount available to purchase securities on margin is buying power. The amount is calculated by adding the cash held in the brokerage accounts and the amount that could be spent if securities were fully margined to their limit. If an investor uses their buying power, they are purchasing securities on credit.

Go to **Cram101.com** for the Practice Tests for this Chapter.
And, **NEVER** highlight a book again!

Growth strategy	A strategy based on investing in companies and sectors which are growing faster than their peers is a growth strategy. The benefits are usually in the form of capital gains rather than dividends.
Value chain	The sequence of business functions in which usefulness is added to the products or services of a company is a value chain.
Minimum wage	The lowest wage employers may legally pay for an hour of work is the minimum wage.
Wage	The payment for the service of a unit of labor, per unit time. In trade theory, it is the only payment to labor, usually unskilled labor. In empirical work, wage data may exclude other compenzation, which must be added to get the total cost of employment.
Sam Walton	I guess in all my years, what I heard more often than anything was: a town of less than 50,000 population cannot support a discount store for very long. Sam Walton was the founder of two American retailers, Wal-Mart and Sam's Club.
Closing	The finalization of a real estate sales transaction that passes title to the property from the seller to the buyer is referred to as a closing. Closing is a sales term which refers to the process of making a sale. It refers to reaching the final step, which may be an exchange of money or acquiring a signature.
Binder	Binder, also called a binding slip, refers to a brief memorandum or agreement issued by an insurer as a temporary policy for the convenience of all the parties, constituting a present insurance in the amount specified, to continue in force until the execution of a formal policy.
Starbucks	Although it has endured much criticism for its purported monopoly on the global coffee-bean market, Starbucks purchases only 3% of the coffee beans grown worldwide. In 2000 the company introduced a line of fair trade products and now offers three options for socially conscious coffee drinkers. According to Starbucks, they purchased 4.8 million pounds of Certified Fair Trade coffee in fiscal year 2004 and 11.5 million pounds in 2005.
Consumer Reports	Consumer Reports is known for publishing reviews and comparisons of consumer products and services based on reporting and results from its in-house testing laboratory. Consumer Reports does not accept advertizing nor permit the commercial use of its reviews for selling products.
Euro	The common currency of a subset of the countries of the EU, adopted January 1, 1999 is called euro.
Gross margin	Gross margin is an ambiguous phrase that expresses the relationship between gross profit and sales revenue as Gross Margin = Revenue - costs of good sold.
Costco	Costco focuses on selling products at low prices, often at very high volume. These goods are usually bulk-packaged and marketed primarily to large families and small businesses. As a warehouse club, Costco is only open to members and their guests, except for purchases of liquor, gasoline and prescription drugs in some U.S. states due to state law and liquor license restrictions.
Browser	A program that allows a user to connect to the World Wide Web by simply typing in a URL is a browser.
Auction	A preexisting business model that operates successfully on the Internet by announcing an item for sale and permitting multiple purchasers to bid on them under specified rules and condition is an auction.
Extension	Extension refers to an out-of-court settlement in which creditors agree to allow the firm more time to meet its financial obligations. A new repayment schedule will be developed, subject to the acceptance of creditors.

Corporation	A legal entity chartered by a state or the Federal government that is distinct and separate from the individuals who own it is a corporation. This separation gives the corporation unique powers which other legal entities lack.
Exporting	Selling products to another country is called exporting.
International firm	International firm refers to those firms who have responded to stiff competition domestically by expanding their sales abroad. They may start a production facility overseas and send some of their managers, who report to a global division, to that country.
Complexity	The technical sophistication of the product and hence the amount of understanding required to use it is referred to as complexity. It is the opposite of simplicity.
Specialist	A specialist is a trader who makes a market in one or several stocks and holds the limit order book for those stocks.
Purchasing power	The amount of goods that money will buy, usually measured by the CPI is referred to as purchasing power.
Turnover	Turnover in a financial context refers to the rate at which a provider of goods cycles through its average inventory. Turnover in a human resources context refers to the characteristic of a given company or industry, relative to rate at which an employer gains and loses staff.
Monopoly	A monopoly is defined as a persistent market situation where there is only one provider of a kind of product or service.
Capital	Capital generally refers to financial wealth, especially that used to start or maintain a business. In classical economics, capital is one of four factors of production, the others being land and labor and entrepreneurship.
Gain	In finance, gain is a profit or an increase in value of an investment such as a stock or bond. Gain is calculated by fair market value or the proceeds from the sale of the investment minus the sum of the purchase price and all costs associated with it.
Correlation	A correlation is the measure of the extent to which two economic or statistical variables move together, normalized so that its values range from -1 to +1. It is defined as the covariance of the two variables divided by the square root of the product of their variances.
Industrial goods	Components produced for use in the production of other products are called industrial goods.
Inverse relationship	The relationship between two variables that change in opposite directions, for example, product price and quantity demanded is an inverse relationship.
Channel length	The number of intermediaries that a product has to go through before it reaches the final consumer is called channel length.
Trade association	An industry trade group or trade association is generally a public relations organization founded and funded by corporations that operate in a specific industry. Its purpose is generally to promote that industry through PR activities such as advertizing, education, political donations, political pressure, publishing, and astroturfing.
Cartel	Cartel refers to a group of firms that seeks to raise the price of a good by restricting its supply. The term is usually used for international groups, especially involving state-owned firms and/or governments.
Inflation	An increase in the overall price level of an economy, usually as measured by the CPI or by the implicit price deflator is called inflation.
BMW	BMW is an independent German company and manufacturer of automobiles and motorcycles. BMW is the world's largest premium carmaker and is the parent company of the BMW MINI and Rolls-

Go to **Cram101.com** for the Practice Tests for this Chapter.
And, **NEVER** highlight a book again!

Royce car brands, and, formerly, Rover.

Wholesaling	Wholesaling consists of the sale of goods/merchandise to retailers, to industrial, commercial, institutional, or other professional business users or to other wholesalers and related subordinated services.
Patronage	The power of elected and appointed officials to make partisan appointments to office or to confer contracts, honors, or other benefits on their political supporters. Patronage has always been one of the major tools by which political executives consolidate their power and attempt to control a bureaucracy.
Logistics Management	Logistics management refers to the practice of organizing the cost-effective flow of raw materials, in-process inventory, finished goods, and related information from point of origin to point of consumption to satisfy customer requirements.
Logistics	Those activities that focus on getting the right amount of the right products to the right place at the right time at the lowest possible cost is referred to as logistics.
Investment	Investment refers to spending for the production and accumulation of capital and additions to inventories. In a financial sense, buying an asset with the expectation of making a return.
Market makers	Market makers refer to financial service companies that connect investors and borrowers, either directly or indirectly.
Direct sale	A direct sale is a sale to customers through distributors or self-employed sales people rather than through shops. Includes both personal contact with consumers in their homes (and other nonstore locations such as offices) and phone solicitations initiated by a retailer.
Trade barrier	An artificial disincentive to export and/or import, such as a tariff, quota, or other NTB is called a trade barrier.
Complaint	The pleading in a civil case in which the plaintiff states his claim and requests relief is called complaint. In the common law, it is a formal legal document that sets out the basic facts and legal reasons that the filing party (the plaintiffs) believes are sufficient to support a claim against another person, persons, entity or entities (the defendants) that entitles the plaintiff(s) to a remedy (either money damages or injunctive relief).
Restructuring	Restructuring is the corporate management term for the act of partially dismantling and reorganizing a company for the purpose of making it more efficient and therefore more profitable.
Subsidiary	A company that is controlled by another company or corporation is a subsidiary.
End user	End user refers to the ultimate user of a product or service.
Option	A contract that gives the purchaser the option to buy or sell the underlying financial instrument at a specified price, called the exercise price or strike price, within a specific period of time.
Principal	In agency law, one under whose direction an agent acts and for whose benefit that agent acts is a principal.
Export	In economics, an export is any good or commodity, shipped or otherwise transported out of a country, province, town to another part of the world in a legitimate fashion, typically for use in trade or sale.
Profit margin	Profit margin is a measure of profitability. It is calculated using a formula and written as a percentage or a number. Profit margin = Net income before tax and interest / Revenue.
Interest	In finance and economics, interest is the price paid by a borrower for the use of a lender's money. In other words, interest is the amount of paid to "rent" money for a period of time.

Brand loyalty	The degree to which customers are satisfied, like the brand, and are committed to further purchase is referred to as brand loyalty.
Franchise	A contractual right to sell certain products or services, use certain trademarks, or perform activities in a geographical region is called a franchise.
Credit risk	The risk of loss due to a counterparty defaulting on a contract, or more generally the risk of loss due to some "credit event" is called credit risk.
Exporter	A firm that sells its product in another country is an exporter.
Brief	Brief refers to a statement of a party's case or legal arguments, usually prepared by an attorney. Also used to make legal arguments before appellate courts.
Benetton	Benetton has been known in the United States for producing a long-running series of controversial, sometimes offensive, advertisements that have caused a number of media critics to accuse the company of deliberately creating controversy in order to sell its products. This publicity campaign originated when photographer Oliviero Toscani was given carte blanche by the Benetton management.
Disney	Disney is one of the largest media and entertainment corporations in the world. Founded on October 16, 1923 by brothers Walt and Roy Disney as a small animation studio, today it is one of the largest Hollywood studios and also owns nine theme parks and several television networks, including the American Broadcasting Company (ABC).
Sears	Before the Sears catalog, farmers typically bought supplies (often at very high prices) from local general stores. Sears took advantage of this by publishing his catalog with clearly stated prices, so that consumers could know what he was selling and at what price, and order and obtain them conveniently. The catalog business soon grew quickly.
Distribution center	Designed to facilitate the timely movement of goods and represent a very important part of a supply chain is a distribution center.
Nike	Because Nike creates goods for a wide range of sports, they have competition from every sports and sports fashion brand there is. Nike has no direct competitors because there is no single brand which can compete directly with their range of sports and non-sports oriented gear, except for Reebok.
Export management company	Export management company refers to export specialists who act as an export-marketing department for client firms.
Personnel	A collective term for all of the employees of an organization. Personnel is also commonly used to refer to the personnel management function or the organizational unit responsible for administering personnel programs.
Level of service	The degree of service provided to the customer by self, limited, and full-service retailers is referred to as the level of service.
Commerce	Commerce is the exchange of something of value between two entities. It is the central mechanism from which capitalism is derived.
Trade show	A type of exhibition or forum where manufacturers can display their products to current as well as prospective buyers is referred to as trade show.
Insurance	Insurance refers to a system by which individuals can reduce their exposure to risk of large losses by spreading the risks among a large number of persons.
Trademark	A distinctive word, name, symbol, device, or combination thereof, which enables consumers to identify favored products or services and which may find protection under state or federal law is a trademark.

Patent	The legal right to the proceeds from and control over the use of an invented product or process, granted for a fixed period of time, usually 20 years. Patent is one form of intellectual property that is subject of the TRIPS agreement.
Short run	Short run refers to a period of time that permits an increase or decrease in current production volume with existing capacity, but one that is too short to permit enlargement of that capacity itself (eg, the building of new plants, training of additional workers, etc.).
Raw material	Raw material refers to a good that has not been transformed by production; a primary product.
Sogo shosha	Sogo shosha refers to Japanese trading companies; a key part of the keiretsu, the large Japanese industrial groups.
Antitrust	Government intervention to alter market structure or prevent abuse of market power is called antitrust.
Economies of scale	In economics, returns to scale and economies of scale are related terms that describe what happens as the scale of production increases. They are different terms and not to be used interchangeably.
Bank holding company	A bank holding company, in the banking law of the United States, is any entity that owns 10% or more of a bank.
Holding company	A corporation whose purpose or function is to own or otherwise hold the shares of other corporations either for investment or control is called holding company.
Holding	The holding is a court's determination of a matter of law based on the issue presented in the particular case. In other words: under this law, with these facts, this result.
Kmart	Kmart is an international chain of discount department stores in the United States, Australia, and New Zealand. Kmart merged with Sears in early 2005, creating the Sears Holdings Corporation.
Product line	A group of products that are physically similar or are intended for a similar market are called the product line.
World price	The price of a good on the 'world market,' meaning the price outside of any country's borders and therefore exclusive of any trade taxes or subsidies is the world price.
Broker	In commerce, a broker is a party that mediates between a buyer and a seller. A broker who also acts as a seller or as a buyer becomes a principal party to the deal.
Commodity	Could refer to any good, but in trade a commodity is usually a raw material or primary product that enters into international trade, such as metals or basic agricultural products.
Sherman Antitrust Act	The Sherman Antitrust Act, formally known as the Act of July 2, 1890 was the first United States federal government action to limit monopolies.
Corporate tax	Corporate tax refers to a direct tax levied by various jurisdictions on the profits made by companies or associations. As a general principle, this varies substantially between jurisdictions.
Possession	Possession refers to respecting real property, exclusive dominion and control such as owners of like property usually exercise over it. Manual control of personal property either as owner or as one having a qualified right in it.
Property	Assets defined in the broadest legal sense. Property includes the unrealized receivables of a cash basis taxpayer, but not services rendered.
Lease	A contract for the possession and use of land or other property, including goods, on one side, and a recompense of rent or other income on the other is the lease.

Manufacturing	Production of goods primarily by the application of labor and capital to raw materials and other intermediate inputs, in contrast to agriculture, mining, forestry, fishing, and services a manufacturing.
Trade dispute	Trade dispute refers to any disagreement between nations involving their international trade or trade policies.
Union	A worker association that bargains with employers over wages and working conditions is called a union.
Markup	Markup is a term used in marketing to indicate how much the price of a product is above the cost of producing and distributing the product.
Market structure	Market structure refers to the way that suppliers and demanders in an industry interact to determine price and quantity. Market structures range from perfect competition to monopoly.
Brokerage firm	A company that conducts various aspects of securities trading, analysis and advisory services is a brokerage firm.
Parent company	Parent company refers to the entity that has a controlling influence over another company. It may have its own operations, or it may have been set up solely for the purpose of owning the Subject Company.
Contract	A contract is a "promise" or an "agreement" that is enforced or recognized by the law. In the civil law, a contract is considered to be part of the general law of obligations.
Margin requirement	Margin requirement refers to a rule that specifies the amount of cash or equity that must be deposited with a brokerage firm or bank, with the balance of funds eligible for borrowing. Margin is set by the Board of Governors of the Federal Reserve Board.
Points	Loan origination fees that may be deductible as interest by a buyer of property. A seller of property who pays points reduces the selling price by the amount of the points paid for the buyer.
Strategic goal	A strategic goal is a broad statement of where an organization wants to be in the future; pertains to the organization as a whole rather than to specific divisions or departments.
Long run	In economic models, the long run time frame assumes no fixed factors of production. Firms can enter or leave the marketplace, and the cost (and availability) of land, labor, raw materials, and capital goods can be assumed to vary.
Marketing cost	Marketing cost refers to the cost incurred in selling goods or services. Includes order-getting costs and order-filling or distribution costs.
Breaking bulk	The division or separation of the contents of a package or container is breaking bulk.
Capital requirement	The capital requirement is a bank regulation, which sets a framework on how banks and depository institutions must handle their capital. The categorization of assets and capital is highly standardized so that it can be risk weighted.
Management control	That aspect of management concerned with the comparison of actual versus planned performance as well as the development and implementation of procedures to correct substandard performance is called management control.
Optimum	Optimum refers to the best. Usually refers to a most preferred choice by consumers subject to a budget constraint or a profit maximizing choice by firms or industry subject to a technological constraint.
Nokia	Nokia Corporation is the world's largest manufacturer of mobile telephones (as of June 2006), with a global market share of approximately 34% in Q2 of 2006. It produces mobile phones for every major market and protocol, including GSM, CDMA, and W-CDMA (UMTS).

Marketing mix	The marketing mix approach to marketing is a model of crafting and implementing marketing strategies. It stresses the "mixing" or blending of various factors in such a way that both organizational and consumer (target markets) objectives are attained.
Merchant wholesaler	Independently owned firms that take title to the goods they handle is a merchant wholesaler.
Mass marketing	Mass marketing or mass merchandizing refers to developing products and promotions to please large groups of people.
Conglomerate	A conglomerate is a large company that consists of divisions of often seemingly unrelated businesses.
Scrambled merchandising	The addition of unrelated products and product lines in a single retail store is referred to as scrambled merchandising.
Continuity	A media scheduling strategy where a continuous pattern of advertising is used over the time span of the advertising campaign is continuity.
Vendor	A person who sells property to a vendee is a vendor. The words vendor and vendee are more commonly applied to the seller and purchaser of real estate, and the words seller and buyer are more commonly applied to the seller and purchaser of personal property.
Selling agent	Selling agent refers to enterprises or individuals who receive a commission for selling the products of a producer or manufacturer, and they usually do not take ownership of the product.
Productivity	Productivity refers to the total output of goods and services in a given period of time divided by work hours.
Termination	The ending of a corporation that occurs only after the winding-up of the corporation's affairs, the liquidation of its assets, and the distribution of the proceeds to the claimants are referred to as a termination.
Evaluation	The consumer's appraisal of the product or brand on important attributes is called evaluation.
Publicity	Publicity refers to any information about an individual, product, or organization that's distributed to the public through the media and that's not paid for or controlled by the seller.
Final settlement	Final settlement occurs when the payor bank pays the check in cash, settles for the check without having a right to revoke the settlement, or fails to dishonor the check within certain statutory time periods.
Inventory turnover ratio	Inventory turnover ratio refers to a ratio that measures the number of times on average the inventory sold during the period; computed by dividing cost of goods sold by the average inventory during the period.
Parallel import	Trade that is made possible when the owner of intellectual property causes the same product to be sold in different countries for different prices. If someone else imports the low-price good into the high-price country, it is a parallel import.
Quota	A government-imposed restriction on quantity, or sometimes on total value, used to restrict the import of something to a specific quantity is called a quota.
Direct selling	The direct personal presentation, demonstration, and sale of products and services to consumers usually in their homes or at their jobs is referred to as direct selling.
Price point	A price point is a price for which demand is relatively high.
Supply chain	Supply chain refers to the flow of goods, services, and information from the initial sources

of materials and services to the delivery of products to consumers.

Users

Users refer to people in the organization who actually use the product or service purchased by the buying center.

Inputs

The inputs used by a firm or an economy are the labor, raw materials, electricity and other resources it uses to produce its outputs.

Inventory management

The planning, coordinating, and controlling activities related to the flow of inventory into, through, and out of an organization is referred to as inventory management.

Quality control

The measurement of products and services against set standards is referred to as quality control.

Outsourcing

Outsourcing refers to a production activity that was previously done inside a firm or plant that is now conducted outside that firm or plant.

Accounting

A system that collects and processes financial information about an organization and reports that information to decision makers is referred to as accounting.

Average cost

Average cost is equal to total cost divided by the number of goods produced (Quantity-Q). It is also equal to the sum of average variable costs (total variable costs divided by Q) plus average fixed costs (total fixed costs divided by Q).

Direct cost

A direct cost is a cost that can be identified specifically with a particular sponsored project, an instructional activity, or any other institutional activity, or that can be directly assigned to such activities relatively easily with a high degree of accuracy.

DaimlerChrysler

In 2002, the merged company, DaimlerChrysler, appeared to run two independent product lines, with few signs of corporate integration. In 2003, however, it was alleged by the Detroit News that the "merger of equals" was, in fact, a takeover.

Inventory control

Inventory control, in the field of loss prevention, are systems designed to introduce technical barriers to shoplifting.

Control system

A control system is a device or set of devices that manage the behavior of other devices. Some devices or systems are not controllable.A control system is an interconnection of components connected or related in such a manner as to command, direct, or regulate itself or another system.

Total cost

The sum of fixed cost and variable cost is referred to as total cost.

Consultant

A professional that provides expert advice in a particular field or area in which customers occassionaly require this type of knowledge is a consultant.

Socialism

An economic system under which the state owns the resources and makes the economic decisions is called socialism.

Bid

A bid price is a price offered by a buyer when he/she buys a good. In the context of stock trading on a stock exchange, the bid price is the highest price a buyer of a stock is willing to pay for a share of that given stock.

Customer service

The ability of logistics management to satisfy users in terms of time, dependability, communication, and convenience is called the customer service.

Press release

A written public news announcement normally distributed to major news services is referred to as press release.

Logo

Logo refers to device or other brand name that cannot be spoken.

Structural impediments

A 1990 agreement between the United States and Japan to decrease nontariff barriers restricting imports into Japan is referred to as the structural impediments initiative.

Go to **Cram101.com** for the Practice Tests for this Chapter.

initiative	
Globalization	The increasing world-wide integration of markets for goods, services and capital that attracted special attention in the late 1990s is called globalization.
Globalization of markets	Moving away from an economic system in which national markets are distinct entities, isolated by trade barriers and barriers of distance, time, and culture, and toward a system in which national markets are merging into one global market is globalization of markets.
Variable	A variable is something measured by a number; it is used to analyze what happens to other things when the size of that number changes.

Go to **Cram101.com** for the Practice Tests for this Chapter.

101

337

Trade show	A type of exhibition or forum where manufacturers can display their products to current as well as prospective buyers is referred to as trade show.
Market	A market is, as defined in economics, a social arrangement that allows buyers and sellers to discover information and carry out a voluntary exchange of goods or services.
Agent	A person who makes economic decisions for another economic actor. A hired manager operates as an agent for a firm's owner.
Letter of credit	An instrument containing a request to pay to the bearer or person named money, or sell him or her some commodity on credit or give something of value and look to the drawer of the letter for recompense is called letter of credit.
Credit	Credit refers to a recording as positive in the balance of payments, any transaction that gives rise to a payment into the country, such as an export, the sale of an asset, or borrowing from abroad.
Pledge	In law a pledge (also pawn) is a bailment of personal property as a security for some debt or engagement.
License	A license in the sphere of Intellectual Property Rights (IPR) is a document, contract or agreement giving permission or the 'right' to a legally-definable entity to do something (such as manufacture a product or to use a service), or to apply something (such as a trademark), with the objective of achieving commercial gain.
Controller	Controller refers to the financial executive primarily responsible for management accounting and financial accounting. Also called chief accounting officer.
Insurance	Insurance refers to a system by which individuals can reduce their exposure to risk of large losses by spreading the risks among a large number of persons.
Confirmed	When the seller's bank agrees to assume liability on the letter of credit issued by the buyer's bank the transaction is confirmed. The term means that the credit is not only backed up by the issuing foreign bank, but that payment is also guaranteed by the notifying American bank.
Export	In economics, an export is any good or commodity, shipped or otherwise transported out of a country, province, town to another part of the world in a legitimate fashion, typically for use in trade or sale.
Freight forwarder	An organization that puts many small shipments together to create a single large shipment that can be transported cost-effectively to the final destination is called freight forwarder.
Production	The creation of finished goods and services using the factors of production: land, labor, capital, entrepreneurship, and knowledge.
Production line	A production line is a set of sequential operations established in a factory whereby materials are put through a refining process to produce an end-product that is suitable for onward consumption; or components are assembled to make a finished article.
Integration	Economic integration refers to reducing barriers among countries to transactions and to movements of goods, capital, and labor, including harmonization of laws, regulations, and standards. Integrated markets theoretically function as a unified market.
Option	A contract that gives the purchaser the option to buy or sell the underlying financial instrument at a specified price, called the exercise price or strike price, within a specific period of time.
Marketing strategy	Marketing strategy refers to the means by which a marketing goal is to be achieved, usually characterized by a specified target market and a marketing program to reach it.

Go to **Cram101.com** for the Practice Tests for this Chapter.

Global marketing	A strategy of using a common marketing plan and program for all countries in which a company operates, thus selling the product or services the same way everywhere in the world is called global marketing.
Marketing	Promoting and selling products or services to customers, or prospective customers, is referred to as marketing.
Global marketing strategy	The practice of standardizing marketing activities when there are cultural similarities and adapting them when cultures differ is referred to as global marketing strategy.
Fund	Independent accounting entity with a self-balancing set of accounts segregated for the purposes of carrying on specific activities is referred to as a fund.
Exporting	Selling products to another country is called exporting.
Exporter	A firm that sells its product in another country is an exporter.
Regulation	Regulation refers to restrictions state and federal laws place on business with regard to the conduct of its activities.
Target market	One or more specific groups of potential consumers toward which an organization directs its marketing program are a target market.
Distribution	Distribution in economics, the manner in which total output and income is distributed among individuals or factors.
Sovereignty	A country or region's power and ability to rule itself and manage its own affairs. Some feel that membership in international organizations such as the WTO is a threat to their sovereignty.
Tariff	A tax imposed by a nation on an imported good is called a tariff.
Quota	A government-imposed restriction on quantity, or sometimes on total value, used to restrict the import of something to a specific quantity is called a quota.
Distribution channel	A distribution channel is a chain of intermediaries, each passing a product down the chain to the next organization, before it finally reaches the consumer or end-user.
Channel	Channel, in communications (sometimes called communications channel), refers to the medium used to convey information from a sender (or transmitter) to a receiver.
Firm	An organization that employs resources to produce a good or service for profit and owns and operates one or more plants is referred to as a firm.
Consumption	In Keynesian economics consumption refers to personal consumption expenditure, i.e., the purchase of currently produced goods and services out of income, out of savings (net worth), or from borrowed funds. It refers to that part of disposable income that does not go to saving.
Foreign exchange	In finance, foreign exchange means currencies, such as U.S. Dollars and Euros. These are traded on foreign exchange markets.
Exchange	The trade of things of value between buyer and seller so that each is better off after the trade is called the exchange.
Industry	A group of firms that produce identical or similar products is an industry. It is also used specifically to refer to an area of economic production focused on manufacturing which involves large amounts of capital investment before any profit can be realized, also called "heavy industry".
Revenue	Revenue is a U.S. business term for the amount of money that a company receives from its

340

Go to **Cram101.com** for the Practice Tests for this Chapter.

	activities, mostly from sales of products and/or services to customers.
Licensing	Licensing is a form of strategic alliance which involves the sale of a right to use certain proprietary knowledge (so called intellectual property) in a defined way.
Commodity	Could refer to any good, but in trade a commodity is usually a raw material or primary product that enters into international trade, such as metals or basic agricultural products.
Commerce	Commerce is the exchange of something of value between two entities. It is the central mechanism from which capitalism is derived.
Security	Security refers to a claim on the borrower future income that is sold by the borrower to the lender. A security is a type of transferable interest representing financial value.
Administration	Administration refers to the management and direction of the affairs of governments and institutions; a collective term for all policymaking officials of a government; the execution and implementation of public policy.
Adverse impact	Adverse impact refers to the rejection for employment, placement, or promotion of a significantly higher percentage of a protected class, when compared with a non-protected class.
Interest	In finance and economics, interest is the price paid by a borrower for the use of a lender's money. In other words, interest is the amount of paid to "rent" money for a period of time.
Supply	Supply is the aggregate amount of any material good that can be called into being at a certain price point; it comprises one half of the equation of supply and demand. In classical economic theory, a curve representing supply is one of the factors that produce price.
Policy	Similar to a script in that a policy can be a less than completely rational decision-making method. Involves the use of a pre-existing set of decision steps for any problem that presents itself.
Buyer	A buyer refers to a role in the buying center with formal authority and responsibility to select the supplier and negotiate the terms of the contract.
End user	End user refers to the ultimate user of a product or service.
Shell	One of the original Seven Sisters, Royal Dutch/Shell is the world's third-largest oil company by revenue, and a major player in the petrochemical industry and the solar energy business. Shell has six core businesses: Exploration and Production, Gas and Power, Downstream, Chemicals, Renewables, and Trading/Shipping, and operates in more than 140 countries.
Privilege	Generally, a legal right to engage in conduct that would otherwise result in legal liability is a privilege. Privileges are commonly classified as absolute or conditional. Occasionally, privilege is also used to denote a legal right to refrain from particular behavior.
Sun Microsystems	Sun Microsystems is most well known for its Unix systems, which have a reputation for system stability and a consistent design philosophy.
Negotiation	Negotiation is the process whereby interested parties resolve disputes, agree upon courses of action, bargain for individual or collective advantage, and/or attempt to craft outcomes which serve their mutual interests.
Technology	The body of knowledge and techniques that can be used to combine economic resources to produce goods and services is called technology.
Purchasing	Purchasing refers to the function in a firm that searches for quality material resources, finds the best suppliers, and negotiates the best price for goods and services.
Service	Service refers to a "non tangible product" that is not embodied in a physical good and that typically effects some change in another product, person, or institution. Contrasts with

	good.
Domestic	From or in one's own country. A domestic producer is one that produces inside the home country. A domestic price is the price inside the home country. Opposite of 'foreign' or 'world.'.
Reexport	Reexport refers to the export without further processing or transformation of a good that has been imported.
Department of Justice	The United States Department of Justice is a Cabinet department in the United States government designed to enforce the law and defend the interests of the United States according to the law and to ensure fair and impartial administration of justice for all Americans. This department is administered by the United States Attorney General, one of the original members of the cabinet.
Corporation	A legal entity chartered by a state or the Federal government that is distinct and separate from the individuals who own it is a corporation. This separation gives the corporation unique powers which other legal entities lack.
Expense	In accounting, an expense represents an event in which an asset is used up or a liability is incurred. In terms of the accounting equation, expenses reduce owners' equity.
Boycott	To protest by refusing to purchase from someone, or otherwise do business with them. In international trade, a boycott most often takes the form of refusal to import a country's goods.
Plea	A plea is an answer to a declaration or complaint or any material allegation of fact therein that, if untrue, would defeat the action. In criminal procedure, a plea is the matter that the accused, on his arraignment, alleges in answer to the charge against him.
Users	Users refer to people in the organization who actually use the product or service purchased by the buying center.
Applicant	In many tribunal and administrative law suits, the person who initiates the claim is called the applicant.
Authority	Authority in agency law, refers to an agent's ability to affect his principal's legal relations with third parties. Also used to refer to an actor's legal power or ability to do something. In addition, sometimes used to refer to a statute, case, or other legal source that justifies a particular result.
Bureaucracy	Bureaucracy refers to an organization with many layers of managers who set rules and regulations and oversee all decisions.
Single market	A single market is a customs union with common policies on product regulation, and freedom of movement of all the four factors of production (goods, services, capital and labor).
Nontariff barrier	Any policy that interferes with exports or imports other than a simple tariff, prominently including quotas and vers is referred to as nontariff barrier.
Customs duty	A customs duty is a tariff or tax on the import or export of goods.
Customs	Customs is an authority or agency in a country responsible for collecting customs duties and for controlling the flow of people, animals and goods (including personal effects and hazardous items) in and out of the country.
Trade barrier	An artificial disincentive to export and/or import, such as a tariff, quota, or other NTB is called a trade barrier.
Safeway	On April 18, 2005, Safeway began a 100 million dollar brand re-positioning campaign labeled "Ingredients for life". This was done in an attempt to differentiate itself from its

Go to **Cram101.com** for the Practice Tests for this Chapter.

	competitors, and to increase brand involvement. Steve Burd described it as "branding the shopping experience".
Journal	Book of original entry, in which transactions are recorded in a general ledger system, is referred to as a journal.
Dumping	Dumping refers to a practice of charging a very low price in a foreign market for such economic purposes as putting rival suppliers out of business.
Balance	In banking and accountancy, the outstanding balance is the amount of money owned, (or due), that remains in a deposit account (or a loan account) at a given date, after all past remittances, payments and withdrawal have been accounted for. It can be positive (then, in the balance sheet of a firm, it is an asset) or negative (a liability).
Exchange control	Rationing of foreign exchange, typically used when the exchange rate is fixed and the central bank is unable or unwilling to enforce the rate by exchange-market intervention is an exchange control.
Exchange rate	Exchange rate refers to the price at which one country's currency trades for another, typically on the exchange market.
Rate of exchange	Rate of exchange refers to the price paid in one's own money to acquire 1 unit of a foreign currency; the rate at which the money of one nation is exchanged for the money of another nation.
Favorable exchange rate	An exchange rate different from the market or official rate, provided by the government on a transaction as an indirect way of providing a subsidy is a favorable exchange rate.
Standing	Standing refers to the legal requirement that anyone seeking to challenge a particular action in court must demonstrate that such action substantially affects his legitimate interests before he will be entitled to bring suit.
Derivative	A derivative is a generic term for specific types of investments from which payoffs over time are derived from the performance of assets (such as commodities, shares or bonds), interest rates, exchange rates, or indices (such as a stock market index, consumer price index (CPI) or an index of weather conditions).
International trade	The export of goods and services from a country and the import of goods and services into a country is referred to as the international trade.
Precedent	A previously decided court decision that is recognized as authority for the disposition of future decisions is a precedent.
Appeal	Appeal refers to the act of asking an appellate court to overturn a decision after the trial court's final judgment has been entered.
Countertrade	Countertrade is exchanging goods or services that are paid for, in whole or part, with other goods or services.
Controlling	A management function that involves determining whether or not an organization is progressing toward its goals and objectives, and taking corrective action if it is not is called controlling.
Verification	Verification refers to the final stage of the creative process where the validity or truthfulness of the insight is determined. The feedback portion of communication in which the receiver sends a message to the source indicating receipt of the message and the degree to which he or she understood the message.
Underwriters	Investment banks that guarantee prices on securities to corporations and then sell the securities to the public are underwriters.

Go to **Cram101.com** for the Practice Tests for this Chapter.

Go to **Cram101.com** for the Practice Tests for this Chapter.
And, **NEVER** highlight a book again!

World Trade Organization	The World Trade Organization is an international, multilateral organization, which sets the rules for the global trading system and resolves disputes between its member states, all of whom are signatories to its approximately 30 agreements.
Uruguay round	The eighth and most recent round of trade negotiations under GATT is referred to as Uruguay round.
Free On Board	Free On Board is an Incoterm. It means that the seller pays for transportation of the goods to the port of shipment, plus loading costs. The buyer pays freight, insurance, unloading costs and transportation from the port of destination to his factory. The passing of risks occurs when the goods pass the ship's rail at the port of shipment.
Cost and Freight	Cost and Freight is an Incoterm. It means that the seller pays for transportation to the port of shipment, loading and freight. The buyer pays for the insurance and transportation of the goods from the port of destination to his factory. The passing of risk occurs when the goods pass the ship's rail at the port of shipment.
Incoterm	Incoterm describes a series of international sales terms that is used throughout the world, divides transaction costs and responsibilities between buyer and seller, reflects state of the art transportation practices and closely corresponds to the U.N. Convention on Contracts for the International Sale of Goods.
Invoice	The itemized bill for a transaction, stating the nature of the transaction and its cost. In international trade, the invoice price is often the preferred basis for levying an ad valorem tariff.
Credit report	Information about a person's credit history that can be secured from a credit bureau is referred to as credit report.
Legal system	Legal system refers to system of rules that regulate behavior and the processes by which the laws of a country are enforced and through which redress of grievances is obtained.
Credit risk	The risk of loss due to a counterparty defaulting on a contract, or more generally the risk of loss due to some "credit event" is called credit risk.
Contract	A contract is a "promise" or an "agreement" that is enforced or recognized by the law. In the civil law, a contract is considered to be part of the general law of obligations.
Advance payment	An advance payment is the part of a contractually due sum that is paid in advance, while the balance will only follow after receipt on the counterpart in goods or services.
Competitive disadvantage	A situation in which a firm is not implementing using strategies that are being used by competing organizations is competitive disadvantage.
Draft	A signed, written order by which one party instructs another party to pay a specified sum to a third party, at sight or at a specific date is a draft.
Compliance	A type of influence process where a receiver accepts the position advocated by a source to obtain favorable outcomes or to avoid punishment is the compliance.
Broker	In commerce, a broker is a party that mediates between a buyer and a seller. A broker who also acts as a seller or as a buyer becomes a principal party to the deal.
Bill of lading	Bill of lading refers to the receipt given by a transportation company to an exporter when the former accepts goods for transport. It includes the contract specifying what transport service will be provided and the limits of liability.
Political risk	Refers to the many different actions of people, subgroups, and whole countries that have the potential to affect the financial status of a firm is called political risk.
Consideration	Consideration in contract law, a basic requirement for an enforceable agreement under

Go to **Cram101.com** for the Practice Tests for this Chapter.

traditional contract principles, defined in this text as legal value, bargained for and given in exchange for an act or promise. In corporation law, cash or property contributed to a corporation in exchange for shares, or a promise to contribute such cash or property.

Financial institution	A financial institution acts as an agent that provides financial services for its clients. Financial institutions generally fall under financial regulation from a government authority.
Sight draft	Sight draft refers to a draft or bill that is payable on demand or upon presentation.
Discount	The difference between the face value of a bond and its selling price, when a bond is sold for less than its face value it's referred to as a discount.
Litigation	The process of bringing, maintaining, and defending a lawsuit is litigation.
Default	In finance, default occurs when a debtor has not met its legal obligations according to the debt contract, e.g. it has not made a scheduled payment, or violated a covenant (condition) of the debt contract.
International Business	International business refers to any firm that engages in international trade or investment.
Subsidiary	A company that is controlled by another company or corporation is a subsidiary.
Bill of exchange	Any negotiable or nonnegotiable document demanding payment to the drawer or to a third person is a bill of exchange.
Promissory note	Commercial paper or instrument in which the maker promises to pay a specific sum of money to another person, to his order, or to bearer is referred to as a promissory note.
Factoring	In mathematics, factorization or factoring is the decomposition of an object into a product of other objects, or factors, which when multiplied together give the original.
Accounts receivable	Accounts receivable is one of a series of accounting transactions dealing with the billing of customers which owe money to a person, company or organization for goods and services that have been provided to the customer. This is typically done in a one person organization by writing an invoice and mailing or delivering it to each customer.
Principal	In agency law, one under whose direction an agent acts and for whose benefit that agent acts is a principal.
Preparation	Preparation refers to usually the first stage in the creative process. It includes education and formal training.
Financial transaction	A financial transaction involves a change in the status of the finances of two or more businesses or individuals.
Specialist	A specialist is a trader who makes a market in one or several stocks and holds the limit order book for those stocks.
Brand	A name, symbol, or design that identifies the goods or services of one seller or group of sellers and distinguishes them from the goods and services of competitors is a brand.
Customs procedure	Customs procedure refers to the practices used by customs officers to clear goods into a country and levy tariffs. Includes clearance procedures such as documentation and inspection, methods of determining a good's classification, and methods of assignment.
Foreign trade zone	Foreign trade zone refers to an area within a country where imported goods can be stored or processed without being subject to import duty. Also called a 'free zone,' 'free port,' or 'bonded warehouse.'
Free trade zone	A free trade zone is one or more areas of a country where tariffs and quotas are eliminated and bureaucratic requirements are lowered in order to attract companies by raising the

Go to **Cram101.com** for the Practice Tests for this Chapter.

incentives for doing business there.

Free trade	Free trade refers to a situation in which there are no artificial barriers to trade, such as tariffs and quotas. Usually used, often only implicitly, with frictionless trade, so that it implies that there are no barriers to trade of any kind.
Host country	The country in which the parent-country organization seeks to locate or has already located a facility is a host country.
Manufacturing	Production of goods primarily by the application of labor and capital to raw materials and other intermediate inputs, in contrast to agriculture, mining, forestry, fishing, and services a manufacturing.
Allowance	Reduction in the selling price of goods extended to the buyer because the goods are defective or of lower quality than the buyer ordered and to encourage a buyer to keep merchandise that would otherwise be returned is the allowance.
Operation	A standardized method or technique that is performed repetitively, often on different materials resulting in different finished goods is called an operation.
Labor	People's physical and mental talents and efforts that are used to help produce goods and services are called labor.
Performance requirement	Performance requirement refers to a requirement that an importer or exporter achieve some level of performance, in terms of exporting, domestic content, etc., in order to obtain an import or export license.
Maquiladora	A maquiladora is a factory that imports materials and equipment on a duty-free and tariff-free basis for assembly or manufacturing and then re-exports the assembled product usually back to the originating country.
Investment	Investment refers to spending for the production and accumulation of capital and additions to inventories. In a financial sense, buying an asset with the expectation of making a return.
Wage	The payment for the service of a unit of labor, per unit time. In trade theory, it is the only payment to labor, usually unskilled labor. In empirical work, wage data may exclude other compenzation, which must be added to get the total cost of employment.
Logistics	Those activities that focus on getting the right amount of the right products to the right place at the right time at the lowest possible cost is referred to as logistics.
Profit	Profit refers to the return to the resource entrepreneurial ability; total revenue minus total cost.
Margin	A deposit by a buyer in stocks with a seller or a stockbroker, as security to cover fluctuations in the market in reference to stocks that the buyer has purchased but for which he has not paid is a margin. Commodities are also traded on margin.
International firm	International firm refers to those firms who have responded to stiff competition domestically by expanding their sales abroad. They may start a production facility overseas and send some of their managers, who report to a global division, to that country.
Inventory	Tangible property held for sale in the normal course of business or used in producing goods or services for sale is an inventory.
Interdependence	The extent to which departments depend on each other for resources or materials to accomplish their tasks is referred to as interdependence.
Carrying costs	Carrying costs refers to costs that arise while holding an inventory of goods for sale.
Carrying cost	The cost to hold an asset, usually inventory is called a carrying cost. For inventory, a carrying cost includes such items as interest, warehousing costs, insurance, and material-

Go to Cram101.com for the Practice Tests for this Chapter.

	handling expenses.
In transit	A state in which goods are in the possession of a bailee or carrier and not in the hands of the buyer, seller, lessee, or lessor is referred to as in transit.
Distribution center	Designed to facilitate the timely movement of goods and represent a very important part of a supply chain is a distribution center.
Points	Loan origination fees that may be deductible as interest by a buyer of property. A seller of property who pays points reduces the selling price by the amount of the points paid for the buyer.
Customer service	The ability of logistics management to satisfy users in terms of time, dependability, communication, and convenience is called the customer service.
Cost of capital	Cost of capital refers to the percentage cost of funds used for acquiring resources for an organization, typically a weighted average of the firms cost of equity and cost of debt.
Capital	Capital generally refers to financial wealth, especially that used to start or maintain a business. In classical economics, capital is one of four factors of production, the others being land and labor and entrepreneurship.
Competitive Strategy	An outline of how a business intends to compete with other firms in the same industry is called competitive strategy.
Warehouse	Warehouse refers to a location, often decentralized, that a firm uses to store, consolidate, age, or mix stock; house product-recall programs; or ease tax burdens.
Optimum	Optimum refers to the best. Usually refers to a most preferred choice by consumers subject to a budget constraint or a profit maximizing choice by firms or industry subject to a technological constraint.
Variable	A variable is something measured by a number; it is used to analyze what happens to other things when the size of that number changes.
Scope	Scope of a project is the sum total of all projects products and their requirements or features.
Total logistics cost	Total logistics cost refers to expenses associated with transportation, materials handling and warehousing, inventory, stockouts, order processing, and return goods handling.
Stock	In financial terminology, stock is the capital raized by a corporation, through the issuance and sale of shares.
Cost advantage	Possession of a lower cost of production or operation than a competing firm or country is cost advantage.
Working capital	The dollar difference between total current assets and total current liabilities is called working capital.
Management	Management characterizes the process of leading and directing all or part of an organization, often a business, through the deployment and manipulation of resources. Early twentieth-century management writer Mary Parker Follett defined management as "the art of getting things done through people."
Total cost	The sum of fixed cost and variable cost is referred to as total cost.
Innovation	Innovation refers to the first commercially successful introduction of a new product, the use of a new method of production, or the creation of a new form of business organization.
Continuous improvement	The constant effort to eliminate waste, reduce response time, simplify the design of both products and processes, and improve quality and customer service is referred to as continuous

Go to **Cram101.com** for the Practice Tests for this Chapter.

	improvement.
Deregulation	The lessening or complete removal of government regulations on an industry, especially concerning the price that firms are allowed to charge and leaving price to be determined by market forces a deregulation.
Union	A worker association that bargains with employers over wages and working conditions is called a union.
United parcel service	United Parcel Service is the world's largest package delivery company, delivering more than 14 million packages a day to more than 200 countries around the world. It has recently expanded its operations to include logistics and other transportation-related areas.
Federal Express	The company officially began operations on April 17, 1973, utilizing a network of 14 Dassault Falcon 20s which connected 25 U.S. cities. FedEx, the first cargo airline to use jet aircraft for its services, expanded greatly after the deregulation of the cargo airlines sector. Federal Express use of the hub-spoke distribution paradigm in air freight enabled it to become a world leader in its field.
Logistics Management	Logistics management refers to the practice of organizing the cost-effective flow of raw materials, in-process inventory, finished goods, and related information from point of origin to point of consumption to satisfy customer requirements.
Globalization	The increasing world-wide integration of markets for goods, services and capital that attracted special attention in the late 1990s is called globalization.
Holding	The holding is a court's determination of a matter of law based on the issue presented in the particular case. In other words: under this law, with these facts, this result.
Customer value	Customer value refers to the unique combination of benefits received by targeted buyers that includes quality, price, convenience, on-time delivery, and both before-sale and after-sale service.
Common carrier	One who undertakes, for hire or reward, to transport the goods of such of the public as choose to employ him is a common carrier.
Customs officer	The government official who monitors goods moving across a national border and levies tariffs is called a customs officer.
Supply chain	Supply chain refers to the flow of goods, services, and information from the initial sources of materials and services to the delivery of products to consumers.
Gatekeeper	Gatekeeper refers to an individual who has a strategic position in the network that allows him or her to control information moving in either direction through a channel.
Core	A core is the set of feasible allocations in an economy that cannot be improved upon by subset of the set of the economy's consumers (a coalition). In construction, when the force in an element is within a certain center section, the core, the element will only be under compression.
Complexity	The technical sophistication of the product and hence the amount of understanding required to use it is referred to as complexity. It is the opposite of simplicity.
Browser	A program that allows a user to connect to the World Wide Web by simply typing in a URL is a browser.
Total revenue	Total revenue refers to the total number of dollars received by a firm from the sale of a product; equal to the total expenditures for the product produced by the firm; equal to the quantity sold multiplied by the price at which it is sold.
Cisco Systems	While Cisco Systems was not the first company to develop and sell a router (a device that

Go to **Cram101.com** for the Practice Tests for this Chapter.

forwards computer traffic from one network to another), it did create the first commercially successful multi-protocol router to allow previously incompatible computers to communicate using different network protocols.

Analyst	Analyst refers to a person or tool with a primary function of information analysis, generally with a more limited, practical and short term set of goals than a researcher.
Enabling	Enabling refers to giving workers the education and tools they need to assume their new decision-making powers.
Inventory management	The planning, coordinating, and controlling activities related to the flow of inventory into, through, and out of an organization is referred to as inventory management.
Product cost	Product cost refers to sum of the costs assigned to a product for a specific purpose. A concept used in applying the cost plus approach to product pricing in which only the costs of manufacturing the product are included in the cost amount to which the markup is added.
Unit cost	Unit cost refers to cost computed by dividing some amount of total costs by the related number of units. Also called average cost.
Remainder	A remainder in property law is a future interest created in a transferee that is capable of becoming possessory upon the natural termination of a prior estate created by the same instrument.

General manager	A manager who is responsible for several departments that perform different functions is called general manager.
Operation	A standardized method or technique that is performed repetitively, often on different materials resulting in different finished goods is called an operation.
Industry	A group of firms that produce identical or similar products is an industry. It is also used specifically to refer to an area of economic production focused on manufacturing which involves large amounts of capital investment before any profit can be realized, also called "heavy industry".
Hasbro	Hasbro originated with the Mr. Potato Head toy. Mr. Potato Head was the invention of George Lerner in the late 1940s. The idea was originally sold to a breakfast cereal manufacturer so that the separate parts could be distributed as cereal package premiums.
Marketing	Promoting and selling products or services to customers, or prospective customers, is referred to as marketing.
Channel	Channel, in communications (sometimes called communications channel), refers to the medium used to convey information from a sender (or transmitter) to a receiver.
Retailing	All activities involved in selling, renting, and providing goods and services to ultimate consumers for personal, family, or household use is referred to as retailing.
Option	A contract that gives the purchaser the option to buy or sell the underlying financial instrument at a specified price, called the exercise price or strike price, within a specific period of time.
Promotion	Promotion refers to all the techniques sellers use to motivate people to buy products or services. An attempt by marketers to inform people about products and to persuade them to participate in an exchange.
Market	A market is, as defined in economics, a social arrangement that allows buyers and sellers to discover information and carry out a voluntary exchange of goods or services.
Disney	Disney is one of the largest media and entertainment corporations in the world. Founded on October 16, 1923 by brothers Walt and Roy Disney as a small animation studio, today it is one of the largest Hollywood studios and also owns nine theme parks and several television networks, including the American Broadcasting Company (ABC).
Promotional mix	Promotional mix refers to the combination of one or more of the promotional elements a firm uses to communicate with consumers. The promotional elements include: advertising, personal selling, sales promotion, public relations, and direct marketing.
Service	Service refers to a "non tangible product" that is not embodied in a physical good and that typically effects some change in another product, person, or institution. Contrasts with good.
Communication channel	The pathways through which messages are communicated are called a communication channel.
Target market	One or more specific groups of potential consumers toward which an organization directs its marketing program are a target market.
Public relations	Public relations refers to the management function that evaluates public attitudes, changes policies and procedures in response to the public's requests, and executes a program of action and information to earn public understanding and acceptance.
Sales promotion	Sales promotion refers to the promotional tool that stimulates consumer purchasing and dealer interest by means of short-term activities.

Go to **Cram101.com** for the Practice Tests for this Chapter.

Go to **Cram101.com** for the Practice Tests for this Chapter.
And, **NEVER** highlight a book again!

361

Advertising	Advertising refers to paid, nonpersonal communication through various media by organizations and individuals who are in some way identified in the advertising message.
Synergy	Corporate synergy occurs when corporations interact congruently. A corporate synergy refers to a financial benefit that a corporation expects to realize when it merges with or acquires another corporation.
Personal selling	Personal selling is interpersonal communication, often face to face, between a sales representative and an individual or group, usually with the objective of making a sale.
Sponsorship	When the advertiser assumes responsibility for the production and usually the content of a television program as well as the advertising that appears within it, we have sponsorship.
Sweepstakes	Sales promotions consisting of a game of chance requiring no analytical or creative effort by the consumer is a sweepstakes.
Sweepstake	A sweepstake is technically a lottery in which the prize is financed through the tickets sold. In the United States the word has become associated with promotions where prizes are given away for free.
Coupon	In finance, a coupon is "attached" to a bond, either physically (as with old bonds) or electronically. Each coupon represents a predetermined payment promized to the bond-holder in return for his or her loan of money to the bond-issuer. .
Trial	An examination before a competent tribunal, according to the law of the land, of the facts or law put in issue in a cause, for the purpose of determining such issue is a trial. When the court hears and determines any issue of fact or law for the purpose of determining the rights of the parties, it may be considered a trial.
Stock	In financial terminology, stock is the capital raized by a corporation, through the issuance and sale of shares.
Distribution	Distribution in economics, the manner in which total output and income is distributed among individuals or factors.
Discount	The difference between the face value of a bond and its selling price, when a bond is sold for less than its face value it's referred to as a discount.
Brand	A name, symbol, or design that identifies the goods or services of one seller or group of sellers and distinguishes them from the goods and services of competitors is a brand.
Brand awareness	How quickly or easily a given brand name comes to mind when a product category is mentioned is brand awareness.
Premium	Premium refers to the fee charged by an insurance company for an insurance policy. The rate of losses must be relatively predictable: In order to set the premium (prices) insurers must be able to estimate them accurately.
Budget	Budget refers to an account, usually for a year, of the planned expenditures and the expected receipts of an entity. For a government, the receipts are tax revenues.
Product concept	The verbal and perhaps pictorial description of the benefits and features of a proposed product; also the early stage of the product development process in which only the product concept exists.
Market share	That fraction of an industry's output accounted for by an individual firm or group of firms is called market share.
Gerber	Gerber is perhaps the most well-known purveyor of baby food and baby products in the world. The company was founded in 1927 in Fremont, Michigan by Daniel Frank Gerber, owner of the Fremont Canning Company.

Go to **Cram101.com** for the Practice Tests for this Chapter.

Nestle	Nestle is the world's biggest food and beverage company. In the 1860s, a pharmacist, developed a food for babies who were unable to be breastfed. His first success was a premature infant who could not tolerate his own mother's milk nor any of the usual substitutes. The value of the new product was quickly recognized when his new formula saved the child's life.
Gain	In finance, gain is a profit or an increase in value of an investment such as a stock or bond. Gain is calculated by fair market value or the proceeds from the sale of the investment minus the sum of the purchase price and all costs associated with it.
Goodwill	Goodwill is an important accounting concept that describes the value of a business entity not directly attributable to its tangible assets and liabilities.
Competitor	Other organizations in the same industry or type of business that provide a good or service to the same set of customers is referred to as a competitor.
Global marketing	A strategy of using a common marketing plan and program for all countries in which a company operates, thus selling the product or services the same way everywhere in the world is called global marketing.
Sweatshop	A sweatshop is a factory or workshop that has attributes in common with the workplaces of the pejoratively-named sweating system of the 1840s. Sweatshops arose at a time when workers did not have the protections afforded by trade unions or labor laws, and sweatshops are synonymous with working conditions that violate human rights sensibilities and sometimes public policies. .
Journal	Book of original entry, in which transactions are recorded in a general ledger system, is referred to as a journal.
Labor	People's physical and mental talents and efforts that are used to help produce goods and services are called labor.
Nike	Because Nike creates goods for a wide range of sports, they have competition from every sports and sports fashion brand there is. Nike has no direct competitors because there is no single brand which can compete directly with their range of sports and non-sports oriented gear, except for Reebok.
Market research	Market research is the process of systematic gathering, recording and analyzing of data about customers, competitors and the market. Market research can help create a business plan, launch a new product or service, fine tune existing products and services, expand into new markets etc. It can be used to determine which portion of the population will purchase the product/service, based on variables like age, gender, location and income level. It can be found out what market characteristics your target market has.
Marketing strategy	Marketing strategy refers to the means by which a marketing goal is to be achieved, usually characterized by a specified target market and a marketing program to reach it.
Social Security	Social security primarily refers to a field of social welfare concerned with social protection, or protection against socially recognized conditions, including poverty, old age, disability, unemployment, families with children and others.
Security	Security refers to a claim on the borrower future income that is sold by the borrower to the lender. A security is a type of transferable interest representing financial value.
Global marketing strategy	The practice of standardizing marketing activities when there are cultural similarities and adapting them when cultures differ is referred to as global marketing strategy.
Business opportunity	A business opportunity involves the sale or lease of any product, service, equipment, etc. that will enable the purchaser-licensee to begin a business

World Trade Organization	The World Trade Organization is an international, multilateral organization, which sets the rules for the global trading system and resolves disputes between its member states, all of whom are signatories to its approximately 30 agreements.
Firm	An organization that employs resources to produce a good or service for profit and owns and operates one or more plants is referred to as a firm.
Personnel	A collective term for all of the employees of an organization. Personnel is also commonly used to refer to the personnel management function or the organizational unit responsible for administering personnel programs.
Price war	Price war refers to successive and continued decreases in the prices charged by firms in an oligopolistic industry. Each firm lowers its price below rivals' prices, hoping to increase its sales and revenues at its rivals' expense.
Public relations firm	An organization that develops and implements programs to manage a company's publicity, image, and affairs with consumers and other relevant publics is referred to as a public relations firm.
Regulation	Regulation refers to restrictions state and federal laws place on business with regard to the conduct of its activities.
Subsidiary	A company that is controlled by another company or corporation is a subsidiary.
Hearing	A hearing is a proceeding before a court or other decision-making body or officer. A hearing is generally distinguished from a trial in that it is usually shorter and often less formal.
Firestone Tire	The Firestone Tire and Rubber Company was founded to supply pneumatic tires for wagons, buggies, and other forms of wheeled transportation common in the era. They soon saw the huge potential for marketing tires for automobiles and befriended Henry Ford, the first industrialist to produce them using the techniques of mass production. This relationship was used to become the original equipment supplier of Ford Motor Company automobiles, and was also active in the replacement market.
Big Business	Big business is usually used as a pejorative reference to the significant economic and political power which large and powerful corporations (especially multinational corporations), are capable of wielding.
Emerging markets	The term emerging markets is commonly used to describe business and market activity in industrializing or emerging regions of the world. It is sometimes loosely used as a replacement for emerging economies, but really signifies a business phenomenon that is not fully described by or constrained to geography or economic strength; such countries are considered to be in a transitional phase between developing and developed status.
Emerging market	The term emerging market is commonly used to describe business and market activity in industrializing or emerging regions of the world.
Business Week	Business Week is a business magazine published by McGraw-Hill. It was first published in 1929 under the direction of Malcolm Muir, who was serving as president of the McGraw-Hill Publishing company at the time. It is considered to be the standard both in industry and among students.
Merger	Merger refers to the combination of two firms into a single firm.
Event sponsorship	A type of promotion whereby a company develops sponsorship relations with a particular event such as a concert, sporting event, or other activity is referred to as event sponsorship.
Advertising regulation	Advertising regulation refers to the laws and rules defining the ways in which products can be advertized in a particular region. Rules can define a wide number of different aspects, such as placement, timing, and content. In the United States, false advertising and health-

366

Go to **Cram101.com** for the Practice Tests for this Chapter.

related ads are regulated the most. Many communities have their own rules, particularly for outdoor advertising.

Grant	Grant refers to an intergovernmental transfer of funds . Since the New Deal, state and local governments have become increasingly dependent upon federal grants for an almost infinite variety of programs.
Targeting	In advertizing, targeting is to select a demographic or other group of people to advertise to, and create advertisements appropriately.
Global advertising	Global advertising refers to the use of the same basic advertising message in all international markets.
Economy	The income, expenditures, and resources that affect the cost of running a business and household are called an economy.
Mass media	Mass media refers to non-personal channels of communication that allow a message to be sent to many individuals at one time.
Economic development	Increase in the economic standard of living of a country's population, normally accomplished by increasing its stocks of physical and human capital and improving its technology is an economic development.
Marketing mix	The marketing mix approach to marketing is a model of crafting and implementing marketing strategies. It stresses the "mixing" or blending of various factors in such a way that both organizational and consumer (target markets) objectives are attained.
Value system	A value system refers to how an individual or a group of individuals organize their ethical or ideological values. A well-defined value system is a moral code.
Emotional appeals	Advertising messages that appeal to consumers' feelings and emotions are referred to as emotional appeals.
Advertisement	Advertisement is the promotion of goods, services, companies and ideas, usually by an identified sponsor. Marketers see advertising as part of an overall promotional strategy.
Appeal	Appeal refers to the act of asking an appellate court to overturn a decision after the trial court's final judgment has been entered.
Advertising Age	Advertising Age is the world's leading source of news, analysis, information and data on advertising, marketing and media. The magazine was started as a broadsheet newspaper in Chicago in 1930.
Toyota	Toyota is a Japanese multinational corporation that manufactures automobiles, trucks and buses. Toyota is the world's second largest automaker by sales. Toyota also provides financial services through its subsidiary, Toyota Financial Services, and participates in other lines of business.
Advertising campaign	A comprehensive advertising plan that consists of a series of messages in a variety of media that center on a single theme or idea is referred to as an advertising campaign.
Marketing research	Marketing research refers to the analysis of markets to determine opportunities and challenges, and to find the information needed to make good decisions.
Market segments	Market segments refer to the groups that result from the process of market segmentation; these groups ideally have common needs and will respond similarly to a marketing action.
Advertising agency	A firm that specializes in the creation, production, and placement of advertising messages and may provide other services that facilitate the marketing communications process is an advertising agency.
Appropriation	A privacy tort that consists of using a person's name or likeness for commercial gain without

Go to **Cram101.com** for the Practice Tests for this Chapter.

the person's permission is an appropriation.

Authority	Authority in agency law, refers to an agent's ability to affect his principal's legal relations with third parties. Also used to refer to an actor's legal power or ability to do something. In addition, sometimes used to refer to a statute, case, or other legal source that justifies a particular result.
Domestic	From or in one's own country. A domestic producer is one that produces inside the home country. A domestic price is the price inside the home country. Opposite of 'foreign' or 'world.'.
Standardization	Standardization, in the context related to technologies and industries, is the process of establishing a technical standard among competing entities in a market, where this will bring benefits without hurting competition.
Balance	In banking and accountancy, the outstanding balance is the amount of money owned, (or due), that remains in a deposit account (or a loan account) at a given date, after all past remittances, payments and withdrawal have been accounted for. It can be positive (then, in the balance sheet of a firm, it is an asset) or negative (a liability).
Gillette	On October 1, 2005, Gillette finalized its purchase by Procter & Gamble. As a result of this merger, the Gillette Company no longer exists. Its last day of market trading - symbol G on the New York Stock Exchange - was September 30, 2005. The merger created the world's largest personal care and household products company.
Standardized product	Standardized product refers to a product whose buyers are indifferent to the seller from whom they purchase it, as long as the price charged by all sellers is the same; a product all units of which are identical and thus are perfect substitutes.
Ford	Ford is an American company that manufactures and sells automobiles worldwide. Ford introduced methods for large-scale manufacturing of cars, and large-scale management of an industrial workforce, especially elaborately engineered manufacturing sequences typified by the moving assembly lines.
International Business	International business refers to any firm that engages in international trade or investment.
Localization	As an element of wireless marketing strategy, transmitting messages that are relevant to the user's current geographical location are referred to as localization.
Wall Street Journal	Dow Jones & Company was founded in 1882 by reporters Charles Dow, Edward Jones and Charles Bergstresser. Jones converted the small Customers' Afternoon Letter into The Wall Street Journal, first published in 1889, and began delivery of the Dow Jones News Service via telegraph. The Journal featured the Jones 'Average', the first of several indexes of stock and bond prices on the New York Stock Exchange.
Household	An economic unit that provides the economy with resources and uses the income received to purchase goods and services that satisfy economic wants is called household.
Utility	Utility refers to the want-satisfying power of a good or service; the satisfaction or pleasure a consumer obtains from the consumption of a good or service.
Pleading	In the law, a pleading is one of the papers filed with a court in a civil action, such as a complaint, a demurrer, or an answer.
Publicity	Publicity refers to any information about an individual, product, or organization that's distributed to the public through the media and that's not paid for or controlled by the seller.
Logo	Logo refers to device or other brand name that cannot be spoken.

Commodity	Could refer to any good, but in trade a commodity is usually a raw material or primary product that enters into international trade, such as metals or basic agricultural products.
Management	Management characterizes the process of leading and directing all or part of an organization, often a business, through the deployment and manipulation of resources. Early twentieth-century management writer Mary Parker Follett defined management as "the art of getting things done through people."
Lucent Technologies	Lucent Technologies is a company composed of what was formerly AT&T Technologies, which included Western Electric and Bell Labs. It was spun-off from AT&T on September 30, 1996. On April 2, 2006, they announced a merger with its French competitor, Alcatel. The combined company has revenues of approximately $25 billion U.S. based on 2005 calendar results.
Technology	The body of knowledge and techniques that can be used to combine economic resources to produce goods and services is called technology.
Microsoft	Microsoft is a multinational computer technology corporation with 2004 global annual sales of US$39.79 billion and 71,553 employees in 102 countries and regions as of July 2006. It develops, manufactures, licenses, and supports a wide range of software products for computing devices.
DuPont	DuPont was the inventor of CFCs (along with General Motors) and the largest producer of these ozone depleting chemicals (used primarily in aerosol sprays and refrigerants) in the world, with a 25% market share in the late 1980s.
Futures	Futures refer to contracts for the sale and future delivery of stocks or commodities, wherein either party may waive delivery, and receive or pay, as the case may be, the difference in market price at the time set for delivery.
Layout	Layout refers to the physical arrangement of the various parts of an advertisement including the headline, subheads, illustrations, body copy, and any identifying marks.
Core	A core is the set of feasible allocations in an economy that cannot be improved upon by subset of the set of the economy's consumers (a coalition). In construction, when the force in an element is within a certain center section, the core, the element will only be under compression.
Reuters	Reuters is best known as a news service that provides reports from around the world to newspapers and broadcasters. Its main focus is on supplying the financial markets with information and trading products.
Corporation	A legal entity chartered by a state or the Federal government that is distinct and separate from the individuals who own it is a corporation. This separation gives the corporation unique powers which other legal entities lack.
Context	The effect of the background under which a message often takes on more and richer meaning is a context. Context is especially important in cross-cultural interactions because some cultures are said to be high context or low context.
Receiver	A person that is appointed as a custodian of other people's property by a court of law or a creditor of the owner, pending a lawsuit or reorganization is called a receiver.
Evaluation	The consumer's appraisal of the product or brand on important attributes is called evaluation.
Effective communication	When the intended meaning equals the perceived meaning it is called effective communication.
Mistake	In contract law a mistake is incorrect understanding by one or more parties to a contract and may be used as grounds to invalidate the agreement. Common law has identified three different

types of mistake in contract: unilateral mistake, mutual mistake, and common mistake.

Preference	The act of a debtor in paying or securing one or more of his creditors in a manner more favorable to them than to other creditors or to the exclusion of such other creditors is a preference. In the absence of statute, a preference is perfectly good, but to be legal it must be bona fide, and not a mere subterfuge of the debtor to secure a future benefit to himself or to prevent the application of his property to his debts.
DIRECTV	DirecTV was launched in 1994 by General Motors subsidiary Hughes Electronics. It was the first high-powered direct broadcast satellite service in the world. Digital Equipment Corporation provided the customer-care out of their existing technical support center in Colorado Springs, Colorado.
Standing	Standing refers to the legal requirement that anyone seeking to challenge a particular action in court must demonstrate that such action substantially affects his legitimate interests before he will be entitled to bring suit.
Contract	A contract is a "promise" or an "agreement" that is enforced or recognized by the law. In the civil law, a contract is considered to be part of the general law of obligations.
Complexity	The technical sophistication of the product and hence the amount of understanding required to use it is referred to as complexity. It is the opposite of simplicity.
Consideration	Consideration in contract law, a basic requirement for an enforceable agreement under traditional contract principles, defined in this text as legal value, bargained for and given in exchange for an act or promise. In corporation law, cash or property contributed to a corporation in exchange for shares, or a promise to contribute such cash or property.
Production	The creation of finished goods and services using the factors of production: land, labor, capital, entrepreneurship, and knowledge.
Comparative advertising	The practice of either directly or indirectly naming one or more competitors in an advertising message and usually making a comparison on one or more specific attributes or characteristics is referred to as comparative advertising.
Jurisdiction	The power of a court to hear and decide a case is called jurisdiction. It is the practical authority granted to a formally constituted body or to a person to deal with and make pronouncements on legal matters and, by implication, to administer justice within a defined area of responsibility.
Mitsubishi	In a statement, the Mitsubishi says that forced labor is inconsistent with the company's values, and that the various lawsuits targeting Mitsubishi are misdirected. Instead, a spokesman says the Mitsubishi of World War II is not the same Mitsubishi of today. The conglomerate also rejected a Chinese slave labor lawsuit demand by saying it bore no responsibility since it was national policy to employ Chinese laborers."
Broadcast media	Media that use the airwaves to transmit their signal and programming is broadcast media, such as radio and television.
Infomercial	An infomercials is a television commercial that runs as long as a typical television program. Also known as paid programming (or teleshopping in Europe), they are normally shown outside of peak hours, such as late at night or early in the morning.
Objection	In the trial of a case the formal remonstrance made by counsel to something that has been said or done, in order to obtain the court's ruling thereon is an objection.
Assimilation	Assimilation refers to the process through which a minority group learns the ways of the dominant group. In organizations, this means that when people of different types and backgrounds are hired, the organization attempts to mold them to fit the existing organizational culture.

Go to **Cram101.com** for the Practice Tests for this Chapter.

Sensation	Sensation refers to the immediate and direct response of the senses to a stimulus such as an advertisement, package, brand name, or point-of-purchase display.
American Marketing Association	The American Marketing Association is a professional association for marketers. It has approximately 38,000 members. It was formed in 1937 from the merger of two predecessor organizations.
Cost ratio	An equality, the cost ratio shows the number of units of two products that can be produced with the same resources..
Chrysler	The Chrysler Corporation was an American automobile manufacturer that existed independently from 1925–1998. The company was formed by Walter Percy Chrysler on June 6, 1925, with the remaining assets of Maxwell Motor Company.
Buyer	A buyer refers to a role in the buying center with formal authority and responsibility to select the supplier and negotiate the terms of the contract.
Abstraction	Abstraction is a model building simplification process that refers to retaining only the essential facts, and the elimination of irrelevant and non-economic facts, to obtain an economic principle.
Negotiable instrument	A negotiable instrument is a specialized type of contract which obligates a party to pay a certain sum of money on specified terms.
Instrument	Instrument refers to an economic variable that is controlled by policy makers and can be used to influence other variables, called targets. Examples are monetary and fiscal policies used to achieve external and internal balance.
Negotiable	A negotiable instrument is one that can be bought and sold after being issued - in other words, it is a tradable instrument.
Marketing communication	The communication components of marketing, which include public relations, advertising, personal selling, and sales promotion is a marketing communication.
Euro	The common currency of a subset of the countries of the EU, adopted January 1, 1999 is called euro.
Empathy	Empathy refers to dimension of service quality-caring individualized attention provided to customers.
General Mills	In 2001, the General Mills purchased Pillsbury, although it was officially described as a "merger." While many of the Pillsbury-branded products are still manufactured by General Mills, some products had to be sold off to allow the merger since the new company would have held a very strong monopoly position.
Preparation	Preparation refers to usually the first stage in the creative process. It includes education and formal training.
Subculture	A subgroups within the larger, or national, culture with unique values, ideas, and attitudes is a subculture.
Starbucks	Although it has endured much criticism for its purported monopoly on the global coffee-bean market, Starbucks purchases only 3% of the coffee beans grown worldwide. In 2000 the company introduced a line of fair trade products and now offers three options for socially conscious coffee drinkers. According to Starbucks, they purchased 4.8 million pounds of Certified Fair Trade coffee in fiscal year 2004 and 11.5 million pounds in 2005.
Creative strategy	A determination of what an advertising message will say or communicate to a target audience is called creative strategy.
Regulatory	Regulatory agency refers to an agency, commission, or board established by the Federal

agency	government or a state government to regulates businesses in the public interest.
Billboard	The most common form of outdoor advertising is called a billboard.
Warrant	A warrant is a security that entitles the holder to buy or sell a certain additional quantity of an underlying security at an agreed-upon price, at the holder's discretion.
Edict	Edict refers to a command or prohibition promulgated by a sovereign and having the effect of
Negotiation	Negotiation is the process whereby interested parties resolve disputes, agree upon courses of action, bargain for individual or collective advantage, and/or attempt to craft outcomes which serve their mutual interests.
Agent	A person who makes economic decisions for another economic actor. A hired manager operates as an agent for a firm's owner.
Points	Loan origination fees that may be deductible as interest by a buyer of property. A seller of property who pays points reduces the selling price by the amount of the points paid for the buyer.
Consumer good	Products and services that are ultimately consumed rather than used in the production of another good are a consumer good.
Siemens	Siemens is the world's largest conglomerate company. Worldwide, Siemens and its subsidiaries employs 461,000 people (2005) in 190 countries and reported global sales of €75.4 billion in fiscal year 2005.
Cabinet	The heads of the executive departments of a jurisdiction who report to and advise its chief executive; examples would include the president's cabinet, the governor's cabinet, and the mayor's cabinet.
Verification	Verification refers to the final stage of the creative process where the validity or truthfulness of the insight is determined. The feedback portion of communication in which the receiver sends a message to the source indicating receipt of the message and the degree to which he or she understood the message.
Audit	An examination of the financial reports to ensure that they represent what they claim and conform with generally accepted accounting principles is referred to as audit.
Market penetration	A strategy of increasing sales of present products in their existing markets is called market penetration.
Composition	An out-of-court settlement in which creditors agree to accept a fractional settlement on their original claim is referred to as composition.
Scope	Scope of a project is the sum total of all projects products and their requirements or features.
Revenue	Revenue is a U.S. business term for the amount of money that a company receives from its activities, mostly from sales of products and/or services to customers.
Export	In economics, an export is any good or commodity, shipped or otherwise transported out of a country, province, town to another part of the world in a legitimate fashion, typically for use in trade or sale.
Monopoly	A monopoly is defined as a persistent market situation where there is only one provider of a kind of product or service.
Spot advertising	Commercials shown on local television stations, with the negotiation and purchase of time being made directly from the individual stations is spot advertising.
Policy	Similar to a script in that a policy can be a less than completely rational decision-making

	method. Involves the use of a pre-existing set of decision steps for any problem that presents itself.
Partnership	In the common law, a partnership is a type of business entity in which partners share with each other the profits or losses of the business undertaking in which they have all invested.
Consultant	A professional that provides expert advice in a particular field or area in which customers occassionaly require this type of knowledge is a consultant.
Gap	In December of 1995, Gap became the first major North American retailer to accept independent monitoring of the working conditions in a contract factory producing its garments. Gap is the largest specialty retailer in the United States.
Consumption	In Keynesian economics consumption refers to personal consumption expenditure, i.e., the purchase of currently produced goods and services out of income, out of savings (net worth), or from borrowed funds. It refers to that part of disposable income that does not go to saving.
Per capita	Per capita refers to per person. Usually used to indicate the average per person of any given statistic, commonly income.
Television network	Television network refers to the provider of news and programming to a series of affiliated local television stations.
Drawback	Drawback refers to rebate of import duties when the imported good is re-exported or used as input to the production of an exported good.
Estate	An estate is the totality of the legal rights, interests, entitlements and obligations attaching to property. In the context of wills and probate, it refers to the totality of the property which the deceased owned or in which some interest was held.
Industrial goods	Components produced for use in the production of other products are called industrial goods.
Users	Users refer to people in the organization who actually use the product or service purchased by the buying center.
Dell Computer	Dell Computer, formerly PC's Limited, was founded on the principle that by selling personal computer systems directly to customers, PC's Limited could best understand their needs and provide the most effective computing solutions to meet those needs.
Nielsen	When TV viewers or entertainment professionals in the United States mention "ratings" they are generally referring to Nielsen Ratings, a system developed by Nielsen Media Research to determine the audience size and composition of television programming. Nielsen Ratings are offered in over forty countries.
Unfair competition	Antitrust or competition laws, legislate against trade practices that undermine competitiveness or are considered to be unfair competition. The term antitrust derives from the U.S. law that was originally formulated to combat business trusts - now commonly known as cartels.
Samsung	On November 30, 2005 Samsung pleaded guilty to a charge it participated in a worldwide DRAM price fixing conspiracy during 1999-2002 that damaged competition and raized PC prices.
Banner ad	A banner ad is a form of advertising on the World Wide Web. This form of online advertising entails embedding an advertisement into a web page.
Postal Service	The postal service was created in Philadelphia under Benjamin Franklin on July 26, 1775 by decree of the Second Continental Congress. Based on a clause in the United States Constitution empowering Congress "To establish Post Offices and post Roads."
Manufacturing	Production of goods primarily by the application of labor and capital to raw materials and

380

Go to **Cram101.com** for the Practice Tests for this Chapter.

other intermediate inputs, in contrast to agriculture, mining, forestry, fishing, and services a manufacturing.

Holding

The holding is a court's determination of a matter of law based on the issue presented in the particular case. In other words: under this law, with these facts, this result.

Compromise

Compromise occurs when the interaction is moderately important to meeting goals and the goals are neither completely compatible nor completely incompatible.

Interest

In finance and economics, interest is the price paid by a borrower for the use of a lender's money. In other words, interest is the amount of paid to "rent" money for a period of time.

Commission system

Commission system refers to a method of compensating advertising agencies whereby the agency receives a specified commission from the media on any advertising time or space it purchases.

Developing country

Developing country refers to a country whose per capita income is low by world standards. Same as LDC. As usually used, it does not necessarily connote that the country's income is rising.

Credit

Credit refers to a recording as positive in the balance of payments, any transaction that gives rise to a payment into the country, such as an export, the sale of an asset, or borrowing from abroad.

Union

A worker association that bargains with employers over wages and working conditions is called a union.

Deception

According to the Federal Trade Commission, a misrepresentation, omission, or practice that is likely to mislead the consumer acting reasonably in the circumstances to the consumer's detriment is referred to as deception.

Trend

Trend refers to the long-term movement of an economic variable, such as its average rate of increase or decrease over enough years to encompass several business cycles.

Controlling

A management function that involves determining whether or not an organization is progressing toward its goals and objectives, and taking corrective action if it is not is called controlling.

Aid

Assistance provided by countries and by international institutions such as the World Bank to developing countries in the form of monetary grants, loans at low interest rates, in kind, or a combination of these is called aid. Aid can also refer to assistance of any type rendered to benefit some group or individual.

Bottom line

The bottom line is net income on the last line of a income statement.

Assault

An intentional tort that prohibits any attempt or offer to cause harmful or offensive contact with another if it results in a well-grounded apprehension of imminent battery in the mind of the threatened person is called assault.

World Health Organization

The World Health Organization is a specialized agency of the United Nations, acting as a coordinating authority on international public health, headquartered in Geneva, Switzerland. It's constitution states that its mission "is the attainment by all peoples of the highest possible level of health". Its major task is to combat disease, especially key infectious diseases, and to promote the general health of the peoples of the world.

Product placement

Using a brand-name product in a movie, television show, video, or a commercial for another product is a product placement.

Complaint

The pleading in a civil case in which the plaintiff states his claim and requests relief is called complaint. In the common law, it is a formal legal document that sets out the basic facts and legal reasons that the filing party (the plaintiffs) believes are sufficient to support a claim against another person, persons, entity or entities (the defendants) that

382

Go to **Cram101.com** for the Practice Tests for this Chapter.

	entitles the plaintiff(s) to a remedy (either money damages or injunctive relief).
Credibility	The extent to which a source is perceived as having knowledge, skill, or experience relevant to a communication topic and can be trusted to give an unbiased opinion or present objective information on the issue is called credibility.
Consumerism	Consumerism is a term used to describe the effects of equating personal happiness with purchasing material possessions and consumption.
Legal system	Legal system refers to system of rules that regulate behavior and the processes by which the laws of a country are enforced and through which redress of grievances is obtained.
Homogeneous	In the context of procurement/purchasing, homogeneous is used to describe goods that do not vary in their essential characteristic irrespective of the source of supply.

Service	Service refers to a "non tangible product" that is not embodied in a physical good and that typically effects some change in another product, person, or institution. Contrasts with good.
Restructuring	Restructuring is the corporate management term for the act of partially dismantling and reorganizing a company for the purpose of making it more efficient and therefore more profitable.
Wholesale	According to the United Nations Statistics Division Wholesale is the resale of new and used goods to retailers, to industrial, commercial, institutional or professional users, or to other wholesalers, or involves acting as an agent or broker in buying merchandise for, or selling merchandise, to such persons or companies.
Resource management	Resource management is the efficient and effective deployment of an organization's resources when they are needed. Such resources may include financial resources, inventory, human skills, production resources, or information technology.
Management	Management characterizes the process of leading and directing all or part of an organization, often a business, through the deployment and manipulation of resources. Early twentieth-century management writer Mary Parker Follett defined management as "the art of getting things done through people."
Journal	Book of original entry, in which transactions are recorded in a general ledger system, is referred to as a journal.
Marketing strategy	Marketing strategy refers to the means by which a marketing goal is to be achieved, usually characterized by a specified target market and a marketing program to reach it.
Global marketing	A strategy of using a common marketing plan and program for all countries in which a company operates, thus selling the product or services the same way everywhere in the world is called global marketing.
Marketing	Promoting and selling products or services to customers, or prospective customers, is referred to as marketing.
Global marketing strategy	The practice of standardizing marketing activities when there are cultural similarities and adapting them when cultures differ is referred to as global marketing strategy.
Global competition	Global competition exists when competitive conditions across national markets are linked strongly enough to form a true international market and when leading competitors compete head to head in many different countries.
Relationship marketing	Marketing whose goal is to keep individual customers over time by offering them products that exactly meet their requirements is called relationship marketing.
Effective communication	When the intended meaning equals the perceived meaning it is called effective communication.
Buyer	A buyer refers to a role in the buying center with formal authority and responsibility to select the supplier and negotiate the terms of the contract.
Customer relationship management	Learning as much as possible about customers and doing everything you can to satisfy them or even delight them with goods and services over time is customer relationship management.
International Business	International business refers to any firm that engages in international trade or investment.
Information technology	Information technology refers to technology that helps companies change business by allowing them to use new methods.

Marketing research	Marketing research refers to the analysis of markets to determine opportunities and challenges, and to find the information needed to make good decisions.
Sales management	Planning the selling program and implementing and controlling the personal selling effort of the firm is called sales management.
Personal selling	Personal selling is interpersonal communication, often face to face, between a sales representative and an individual or group, usually with the objective of making a sale.
Advertising	Advertising refers to paid, nonpersonal communication through various media by organizations and individuals who are in some way identified in the advertising message.
Technology	The body of knowledge and techniques that can be used to combine economic resources to produce goods and services is called technology.
Relationship management	A method for developing long-term associations with customers is referred to as relationship management.
Distribution	Distribution in economics, the manner in which total output and income is distributed among individuals or factors.
Respondent	Respondent refers to a term often used to describe the party charged in an administrative proceeding. The party adverse to the appellant in a case appealed to a higher court.
Operation	A standardized method or technique that is performed repetitively, often on different materials resulting in different finished goods is called an operation.
Assignment	A transfer of property or some right or interest is referred to as assignment.
Personnel	A collective term for all of the employees of an organization. Personnel is also commonly used to refer to the personnel management function or the organizational unit responsible for administering personnel programs.
Firm	An organization that employs resources to produce a good or service for profit and owns and operates one or more plants is referred to as a firm.
Market	A market is, as defined in economics, a social arrangement that allows buyers and sellers to discover information and carry out a voluntary exchange of goods or services.
Information system	An information system is a system whether automated or manual, that comprises people, machines, and/or methods organized to collect, process, transmit, and disseminate data that represent user information.
Customer retention	Customer retention refers to the percentage of customers who return to a service provider or continue to purchase a manufactured product.
Private exchange	A marketplace that is sponsored by a single enterprise for the benefit of its suppliers or customers or both is the private exchange.
Exchange	The trade of things of value between buyer and seller so that each is better off after the trade is called the exchange.
Marketing management	Marketing management refers to the process of planning and executing the conception, pricing, promotion, and distribution of ideas, goods, and services to create mutually beneficial exchanges.
Consumer good	Products and services that are ultimately consumed rather than used in the production of another good are a consumer good.
Industry	A group of firms that produce identical or similar products is an industry. It is also used specifically to refer to an area of economic production focused on manufacturing which involves large amounts of capital investment before any profit can be realized, also called

388

Go to **Cram101.com** for the Practice Tests for this Chapter.

Go to **Cram101.com** for the Practice Tests for this Chapter.
And, **NEVER** highlight a book again!

"heavy industry".

PepsiCo
In many ways, PepsiCo differs from its main competitor, having three times as many employees, larger revenues, but a smaller net profit.

Channel
Channel, in communications (sometimes called communications channel), refers to the medium used to convey information from a sender (or transmitter) to a receiver.

Downturn
A decline in a stock market or economic cycle is a downturn.

Ford Motor Company
Ford Motor Company introduced methods for large-scale manufacturing of cars, and large-scale management of an industrial workforce, especially elaborately engineered manufacturing sequences typified by the moving assembly lines. Henry Ford's combination of highly efficient factories, highly paid workers, and low prices revolutionized manufacturing and came to be known around the world as Fordism by 1914.

Ford
Ford is an American company that manufactures and sells automobiles worldwide. Ford introduced methods for large-scale manufacturing of cars, and large-scale management of an industrial workforce, especially elaborately engineered manufacturing sequences typified by the moving assembly lines.

Incentive
An incentive is any factor (financial or non-financial) that provides a motive for a particular course of action, or counts as a reason for preferring one choice to the alternatives.

Direct sale
A direct sale is a sale to customers through distributors or self-employed sales people rather than through shops. Includes both personal contact with consumers in their homes (and other nonstore locations such as offices) and phone solicitations initiated by a retailer.

Expatriate
Employee sent by his or her company to live and manage operations in a different country is called an expatriate.

Corporation
A legal entity chartered by a state or the Federal government that is distinct and separate from the individuals who own it is a corporation. This separation gives the corporation unique powers which other legal entities lack.

Operations research
Operations research is the use of mathematical models, statistics and algorithms to aid in decision-making. It is most often used to analyze complex real-world systems, typically with the goal of improving or optimizing performance.

Inputs
The inputs used by a firm or an economy are the labor, raw materials, electricity and other resources it uses to produce its outputs.

Resource allocation
Resource allocation refers to the manner in which an economy distributes its resources among the potential uses so as to produce a particular set of final goods.

Staffing
Staffing refers to a management function that includes hiring, motivating, and retaining the best people available to accomplish the company's objectives.

Product line
A group of products that are physically similar or are intended for a similar market are called the product line.

Senior executive
Senior executive means a chief executive officer, chief operating officer, chief financial officer and anyone in charge of a principal business unit or function.

Parent company
Parent company refers to the entity that has a controlling influence over another company. It may have its own operations, or it may have been set up solely for the purpose of owning the Subject Company.

Asset
An item of property, such as land, capital, money, a share in ownership, or a claim on others for future payment, such as a bond or a bank deposit is an asset.

Go to **Cram101.com** for the Practice Tests for this Chapter.

Commerce	Commerce is the exchange of something of value between two entities. It is the central mechanism from which capitalism is derived.
Management system	A management system is the framework of processes and procedures used to ensure that an organization can fulfill all tasks required to achieve its objectives.
Total cost	The sum of fixed cost and variable cost is referred to as total cost.
Expense	In accounting, an expense represents an event in which an asset is used up or a liability is incurred. In terms of the accounting equation, expenses reduce owners' equity.
Consideration	Consideration in contract law, a basic requirement for an enforceable agreement under traditional contract principles, defined in this text as legal value, bargained for and given in exchange for an act or promise. In corporation law, cash or property contributed to a corporation in exchange for shares, or a promise to contribute such cash or property.
Holiday Inn	The original Holiday Inn chain of hotels was founded in 1952 in Memphis, Tennessee by homebuilder Kemmons Wilson to provide inexpensive family accommodation for travellers within the USA. The first Holiday Inn was built by Wilson on Sumner Avenue in Memphis on the main road to and from Nashville.
Policy	Similar to a script in that a policy can be a less than completely rational decision-making method. Involves the use of a pre-existing set of decision steps for any problem that presents itself.
Complaint	The pleading in a civil case in which the plaintiff states his claim and requests relief is called complaint. In the common law, it is a formal legal document that sets out the basic facts and legal reasons that the filing party (the plaintiffs) believes are sufficient to support a claim against another person, persons, entity or entities (the defendants) that entitles the plaintiff(s) to a remedy (either money damages or injunctive relief).
Business Week	Business Week is a business magazine published by McGraw-Hill. It was first published in 1929 under the direction of Malcolm Muir, who was serving as president of the McGraw-Hill Publishing company at the time. It is considered to be the standard both in industry and among students.
Economics	The social science dealing with the use of scarce resources to obtain the maximum satisfaction of society's virtually unlimited economic wants is an economics.
Avon	Avon is an American cosmetics, perfume and toy seller with markets in over 135 countries across the world and a sales of $7.74 billion worldwide.
Barter	Barter is a type of trade where goods or services are exchanged for a certain amount of other goods or services; no money is involved in the transaction.
Direct selling	The direct personal presentation, demonstration, and sale of products and services to consumers usually in their homes or at their jobs is referred to as direct selling.
Authority	Authority in agency law, refers to an agent's ability to affect his principal's legal relations with third parties. Also used to refer to an actor's legal power or ability to do something. In addition, sometimes used to refer to a statute, case, or other legal source that justifies a particular result.
Wall Street Journal	Dow Jones & Company was founded in 1882 by reporters Charles Dow, Edward Jones and Charles Bergstresser. Jones converted the small Customers' Afternoon Letter into The Wall Street Journal, first published in 1889, and began delivery of the Dow Jones News Service via telegraph. The Journal featured the Jones 'Average', the first of several indexes of stock and bond prices on the New York Stock Exchange.
Internationa-	Internationalization refers to another term for fragmentation. Used by Grossman and Helpman.

ization	
General manager	A manager who is responsible for several departments that perform different functions is called general manager.
Subsidiary	A company that is controlled by another company or corporation is a subsidiary.
Burroughs	Burroughs developed three highly innovative architectures, based on the design philosophy of "language directed design". Their machine instruction sets favored one or many high level programming languages, such as ALGOL, COBOL or FORTRAN. All three architectures were considered "main-frame" class machines.
Double taxation	The taxation of both corporate net income and the dividends paid from this net income when they become the personal income of households a double taxation.
Compensation package	The total array of money, incentives, benefits, perquisites, and awards provided by the organization to an employee is the compensation package.
Property	Assets defined in the broadest legal sense. Property includes the unrealized receivables of a cash basis taxpayer, but not services rendered.
Gain	In finance, gain is a profit or an increase in value of an investment such as a stock or bond. Gain is calculated by fair market value or the proceeds from the sale of the investment minus the sum of the purchase price and all costs associated with it.
Immigration	Immigration refers to the migration of people into a country.
Aid	Assistance provided by countries and by international institutions such as the World Bank to developing countries in the form of monetary grants, loans at low interest rates, in kind, or a combination of these is called aid. Aid can also refer to assistance of any type rendered to benefit some group or individual.
Transnational	Transnational focuses on the heightened interconnectivity between people all around the world and the loosening of boundaries between countries.
Maturity	Maturity refers to the final payment date of a loan or other financial instrument, after which point no further interest or principal need be paid.
Domestic	From or in one's own country. A domestic producer is one that produces inside the home country. A domestic price is the price inside the home country. Opposite of 'foreign' or 'world.'.
Customs	Customs is an authority or agency in a country responsible for collecting customs duties and for controlling the flow of people, animals and goods (including personal effects and hazardous items) in and out of the country.
Empathy	Empathy refers to dimension of service quality-caring individualized attention provided to customers.
Closing	The finalization of a real estate sales transaction that passes title to the property from the seller to the buyer is referred to as a closing. Closing is a sales term which refers to the process of making a sale. It refers to reaching the final step, which may be an exchange of money or acquiring a signature.
Brief	Brief refers to a statement of a party's case or legal arguments, usually prepared by an attorney. Also used to make legal arguments before appellate courts.
Developing country	Developing country refers to a country whose per capita income is low by world standards. Same as LDC. As usually used, it does not necessarily connote that the country's income is rising.
Recruitment	Recruitment refers to the set of activities used to obtain a sufficient number of the right

Go to **Cram101.com** for the Practice Tests for this Chapter.

people at the right time; its purpose is to select those who best meet the needs of the organization.

Promotion	Promotion refers to all the techniques sellers use to motivate people to buy products or services. An attempt by marketers to inform people about products and to persuade them to participate in an exchange.
Job satisfaction	Job satisfaction describes how content an individual is with his or her job. It is a relatively recent term since in previous centuries the jobs available to a particular person were often predetermined by the occupation of that person's parent.
Negotiation	Negotiation is the process whereby interested parties resolve disputes, agree upon courses of action, bargain for individual or collective advantage, and/or attempt to craft outcomes which serve their mutual interests.
Contract	A contract is a "promise" or an "agreement" that is enforced or recognized by the law. In the civil law, a contract is considered to be part of the general law of obligations.
Hierarchy	A system of grouping people in an organization according to rank from the top down in which all subordinate managers must report to one person is called a hierarchy.
Bond	Bond refers to a debt instrument, issued by a borrower and promising a specified stream of payments to the purchaser, usually regular interest payments plus a final repayment of principal.
Assessment	Collecting information and providing feedback to employees about their behavior, communication style, or skills is an assessment.
Users	Users refer to people in the organization who actually use the product or service purchased by the buying center.
Sun Microsystems	Sun Microsystems is most well known for its Unix systems, which have a reputation for system stability and a consistent design philosophy.
Foreign Corrupt Practices Act	The Foreign Corrupt Practices Act of 1977 is a United States federal law requiring any company that has publicly-traded stock to maintain records that accurately and fairly represent the company's transactions; additionally, requires any publicly-traded company to have an adequate system of internal accounting controls.
Corporate policy	Dimension of social responsibility that refers to the position a firm takes on social and political issues is referred to as corporate policy.
Corporate culture	The whole collection of beliefs, values, and behaviors of a firm that send messages to those within and outside the company about how business is done is the corporate culture.
Commission system	Commission system refers to a method of compensating advertising agencies whereby the agency receives a specified commission from the media on any advertising time or space it purchases.
Organizational commitment	A person's identification with and attachment to an organization is called organizational commitment.
Guest worker	Guest worker refers to a foreign worker who is permitted to enter a country temporarily in order to take a job for which there is shortage of domestic labor.
Evaluation	The consumer's appraisal of the product or brand on important attributes is called evaluation.
Extension	Extension refers to an out-of-court settlement in which creditors agree to allow the firm more time to meet its financial obligations. A new repayment schedule will be developed, subject to the acceptance of creditors.
Trust	An arrangement in which shareholders of independent firms agree to give up their stock in

exchange for trust certificates that entitle them to a share of the trust's common profits.

Context | The effect of the background under which a message often takes on more and richer meaning is a context. Context is especially important in cross-cultural interactions because some cultures are said to be high context or low context.

Balance | In banking and accountancy, the outstanding balance is the amount of money owned, (or due), that remains in a deposit account (or a loan account) at a given date, after all past remittances, payments and withdrawal have been accounted for. It can be positive (then, in the balance sheet of a firm, it is an asset) or negative (a liability).

Productivity | Productivity refers to the total output of goods and services in a given period of time divided by work hours.

Fringe benefits | The rewards other than wages that employees receive from their employers and that include pensions, medical and dental insurance, paid vacations, and sick leaves are referred to as fringe benefits.

Fringe benefit | Benefits such as sick-leave pay, vacation pay, pension plans, and health plans that represent additional compenzation to employees beyond base wages is a fringe benefit.

Standard of living | Standard of living refers to the level of consumption that people enjoy, on the average, and is measured by average income per person.

Cost of living | The amount of money it takes to buy the goods and services that a typical family consumes is the cost of living.

Conglomerate | A conglomerate is a large company that consists of divisions of often seemingly unrelated businesses.

Allowance | Reduction in the selling price of goods extended to the buyer because the goods are defective or of lower quality than the buyer ordered and to encourage a buyer to keep merchandise that would otherwise be returned is the allowance.

Contribution | In business organization law, the cash or property contributed to a business by its owners is referred to as contribution.

Consultant | A professional that provides expert advice in a particular field or area in which customers occassionaly require this type of knowledge is a consultant.

Frequency | Frequency refers to the speed of the up and down movements of a fluctuating economic variable; that is, the number of times per unit of time that the variable completes a cycle of up and down movement.

Disparity | Disparity refers to the regional and economic differences in a country, province, state, or continent

Performance management | The means through which managers ensure that employees' activities and outputs are congruent with the organization's goals is referred to as performance management.

Controlling | A management function that involves determining whether or not an organization is progressing toward its goals and objectives, and taking corrective action if it is not is called controlling.

Revenue | Revenue is a U.S. business term for the amount of money that a company receives from its activities, mostly from sales of products and/or services to customers.

Quota | A government-imposed restriction on quantity, or sometimes on total value, used to restrict the import of something to a specific quantity is called a quota.

Supervisor | A Supervisor is an employee of an organization with some of the powers and responsibilities of management, occupying a role between true manager and a regular employee. A Supervisor

Go to Cram101.com for the Practice Tests for this Chapter.

position is typically the first step towards being promoted into a management role.

Incentive system	An incentive system refers to plans in which employees can earn additional compenzation in return for certain types of performance.
Failure rate	Failure rate is the frequency with an engineered system or component fails, expressed for example in failures per hour. Failure rate is usually time dependent. In the special case when the likelihood of failure remains constant as time passes, failure rate is simply the inverse of the mean time to failure, expressed for example in hours per failure.
Attrition	The practice of not hiring new employees to replace older employees who either quit or retire is referred to as attrition.
Consumption	In Keynesian economics consumption refers to personal consumption expenditure, i.e., the purchase of currently produced goods and services out of income, out of savings (net worth), or from borrowed funds. It refers to that part of disposable income that does not go to saving.
Assimilation	Assimilation refers to the process through which a minority group learns the ways of the dominant group. In organizations, this means that when people of different types and backgrounds are hired, the organization attempts to mold them to fit the existing organizational culture.
Ombudsman	An ombudsman is an official, usually appointed by the government or by parliament, who is charged with representing the interests of the public by investigating and addressing complaints reported by individual citizens. An ombudsman need not be appointed by government; they may work for a corporation, a newspaper, an NGO, or even for the general public.
Culture shock	Feelings of confusion, disorientation, and anxiety that result from being immersed in a foreign culture are referred to as culture shock.
Incidence	The ultimate economic effect of a tax on the real incomes of producers or consumers. Thus a sales tax may be paid by a retailer, but it is likely that the incidence falls upon the consumer.
Conference Board	The Conference Board is the world's preeminent business membership and research organization, best known for the Consumer Confidence Index and the index of leading indicators. For 90 years, The Conference Board has equipped the world's leading corporations with practical knowledge through issues-oriented research and senior executive peer-to-peer meetings.
Comprehensive	A comprehensive refers to a layout accurate in size, color, scheme, and other necessary details to show how a final ad will look. For presentation only, never for reproduction.
Inflation	An increase in the overall price level of an economy, usually as measured by the CPI or by the implicit price deflator is called inflation.
Fixture	Fixture refers to a thing that was originally personal property and that has been actually or constructively affixed to the soil itself or to some structure legally a part of the land.
Career planning	Process in which individuals evaluate their abilities and interests, consider alternative career opportunities, establish career goals, and plan practical development activities is referred to as career planning.
Liaison	An individual who serves as a bridge between groups, tying groups together and facilitating the communication flow needed to integrate group activities is a liaison.
Mentor	An experienced employee who supervises, coaches, and guides lower-level employees by introducing them to the right people and generally being their organizational sponsor is a mentor.
Preparation	Preparation refers to usually the first stage in the creative process. It includes education

	and formal training.
Expatriate failure	The premature return of an expatriate manager to the home country is referred to as an expatriate failure.
Interest	In finance and economics, interest is the price paid by a borrower for the use of a lender's money. In other words, interest is the amount of paid to "rent" money for a period of time.
Manufacturing	Production of goods primarily by the application of labor and capital to raw materials and other intermediate inputs, in contrast to agriculture, mining, forestry, fishing, and services a manufacturing.
Globalization	The increasing world-wide integration of markets for goods, services and capital that attracted special attention in the late 1990s is called globalization.
Demographic	A demographic is a term used in marketing and broadcasting, to describe a demographic grouping or a market segment.
Speculation	The purchase or sale of an asset in hopes that its price will rise or fall respectively, in order to make a profit is called speculation.
Airbus	In 2003, for the first time in its 33-year history, Airbus delivered more jet-powered airliners than Boeing. Boeing states that the Boeing 777 has outsold its Airbus counterparts, which include the A340 family as well as the A330-300. The smaller A330-200 competes with the 767, outselling its Boeing counterpart.
Boeing	Boeing is the world's largest aircraft manufacturer by revenue. Headquartered in Chicago, Illinois, Boeing is the second-largest defense contractor in the world. In 2005, the company was the world's largest civil aircraft manufacturer in terms of value.
Leadership	Management merely consists of leadership applied to business situations; or in other words: management forms a sub-set of the broader process of leadership.
Applicant	In many tribunal and administrative law suits, the person who initiates the claim is called the applicant.
Product management	Product management is a function within a company dealing with the day-to-day management and welfare of a product or family of products at all stages of the product lifecycle. The product management function is responsible for defining the products in the marketing mix.
Foreign subsidiary	A company owned in a foreign country by another company is referred to as foreign subsidiary.
Graduation	Termination of a country's eligibility for GSP tariff preferences on the grounds that it has progressed sufficiently, in terms of per capita income or another measure, that it is no longer in need to special and differential treatment is graduation.
Total revenue	Total revenue refers to the total number of dollars received by a firm from the sale of a product; equal to the total expenditures for the product produced by the firm; equal to the quantity sold multiplied by the price at which it is sold.
Human resources	Human resources refers to the individuals within the firm, and to the portion of the firm's organization that deals with hiring, firing, training, and other personnel issues.
Gillette	On October 1, 2005, Gillette finalized its purchase by Procter & Gamble. As a result of this merger, the Gillette Company no longer exists. Its last day of market trading - symbol G on the New York Stock Exchange - was September 30, 2005. The merger created the world's largest personal care and household products company.
Supply	Supply is the aggregate amount of any material good that can be called into being at a certain price point; it comprises one half of the equation of supply and demand. In classical

Go to **Cram101.com** for the Practice Tests for this Chapter.

economic theory, a curve representing supply is one of the factors that produce price.

Management team | A management team is directly responsible for managing the day-to-day operations (and profitability) of a company.

Chicago School | An approach to antitrust policy that is based solely on the goal of economic efficiency, or the maximization of consumer welfare is referred to as Chicago School.

Composition | An out-of-court settlement in which creditors agree to accept a fractional settlement on their original claim is referred to as composition.

404

Go to **Cram101.com** for the Practice Tests for this Chapter.

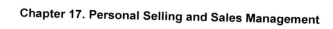
Go to **Cram101.com** for the Practice Tests for this Chapter.
And, **NEVER** highlight a book again!

405

Market	A market is, as defined in economics, a social arrangement that allows buyers and sellers to discover information and carry out a voluntary exchange of goods or services.
Economics	The social science dealing with the use of scarce resources to obtain the maximum satisfaction of society's virtually unlimited economic wants is an economics.
Distribution	Distribution in economics, the manner in which total output and income is distributed among individuals or factors.
Interest	In finance and economics, interest is the price paid by a borrower for the use of a lender's money. In other words, interest is the amount of paid to "rent" money for a period of time.
Absorption	Total demand for goods and services by all residents of a country is absorption. The term was introduced as part of the Absorption Approach.
Production	The creation of finished goods and services using the factors of production: land, labor, capital, entrepreneurship, and knowledge.
Brand	A name, symbol, or design that identifies the goods or services of one seller or group of sellers and distinguishes them from the goods and services of competitors is a brand.
Gain	In finance, gain is a profit or an increase in value of an investment such as a stock or bond. Gain is calculated by fair market value or the proceeds from the sale of the investment minus the sum of the purchase price and all costs associated with it.
Annual report	An annual report is prepared by corporate management that presents financial information including financial statements, footnotes, and the management discussion and analysis.
Market share	That fraction of an industry's output accounted for by an individual firm or group of firms is called market share.
Operation	A standardized method or technique that is performed repetitively, often on different materials resulting in different finished goods is called an operation.
Matching	Matching refers to an accounting concept that establishes when expenses are recognized. Expenses are matched with the revenues they helped to generate and are recognized when those revenues are recognized.
Direct marketing	Promotional element that uses direct communication with consumers to generate a response in the form of an order, a request for further information, or a visit to a retail outlet is direct marketing.
Advertising	Advertising refers to paid, nonpersonal communication through various media by organizations and individuals who are in some way identified in the advertising message.
Marketing	Promoting and selling products or services to customers, or prospective customers, is referred to as marketing.
Marketing strategy	Marketing strategy refers to the means by which a marketing goal is to be achieved, usually characterized by a specified target market and a marketing program to reach it.
Global marketing	A strategy of using a common marketing plan and program for all countries in which a company operates, thus selling the product or services the same way everywhere in the world is called global marketing.
Global marketing strategy	The practice of standardizing marketing activities when there are cultural similarities and adapting them when cultures differ is referred to as global marketing strategy.
Analyst	Analyst refers to a person or tool with a primary function of information analysis, generally with a more limited, practical and short term set of goals than a researcher.

Go to **Cram101.com** for the Practice Tests for this Chapter.

Channel	Channel, in communications (sometimes called communications channel), refers to the medium used to convey information from a sender (or transmitter) to a receiver.
Channel of distribution	A whole set of marketing intermediaries, such as wholesalers and retailers, who join together to transport and store goods in their path from producers to consumers is referred to as channel of distribution.
Domestic	From or in one's own country. A domestic producer is one that produces inside the home country. A domestic price is the price inside the home country. Opposite of 'foreign' or 'world.'.
Balance	In banking and accountancy, the outstanding balance is the amount of money owned, (or due), that remains in a deposit account (or a loan account) at a given date, after all past remittances, payments and withdrawal have been accounted for. It can be positive (then, in the balance sheet of a firm, it is an asset) or negative (a liability).
Buyer	A buyer refers to a role in the buying center with formal authority and responsibility to select the supplier and negotiate the terms of the contract.
Globalization	The increasing world-wide integration of markets for goods, services and capital that attracted special attention in the late 1990s is called globalization.
Price competition	Price competition is where a company tries to distinguish its product or service from competing products on the basis of low price.
Exporting	Selling products to another country is called exporting.
Variable	A variable is something measured by a number; it is used to analyze what happens to other things when the size of that number changes.
Tariff	A tax imposed by a nation on an imported good is called a tariff.
Countertrade	Countertrade is exchanging goods or services that are paid for, in whole or part, with other goods or services.
Escalation	Regarding the structure of tariffs. In the context of a trade war, escalation refers to the increase in tariffs that occurs as countries retaliate again and again.
Policy	Similar to a script in that a policy can be a less than completely rational decision-making method. Involves the use of a pre-existing set of decision steps for any problem that presents itself.
Firm	An organization that employs resources to produce a good or service for profit and owns and operates one or more plants is referred to as a firm.
Pricing objective	An expectation that specifies the role of prices in an organization's marketing and strategic plan is referred to as a pricing objective.
Instrument	Instrument refers to an economic variable that is controlled by policy makers and can be used to influence other variables, called targets. Examples are monetary and fiscal policies used to achieve external and internal balance.
Profit	Profit refers to the return to the resource entrepreneurial ability; total revenue minus total cost.
Return on investment	Return on investment refers to the return a businessperson gets on the money he and other owners invest in the firm; for example, a business that earned $100 on a $1,000 investment would have a ROI of 10 percent: 100 divided by 1000.
Investment	Investment refers to spending for the production and accumulation of capital and additions to inventories. In a financial sense, buying an asset with the expectation of making a return.

Go to **Cram101.com** for the Practice Tests for this Chapter.
And, **NEVER** highlight a book again!

Liquidity	Liquidity refers to the capacity to turn assets into cash, or the amount of assets in a portfolio that have that capacity.
Product line	A group of products that are physically similar or are intended for a similar market are called the product line.
Controlling	A management function that involves determining whether or not an organization is progressing toward its goals and objectives, and taking corrective action if it is not is called controlling.
Subsidiary	A company that is controlled by another company or corporation is a subsidiary.
End user	End user refers to the ultimate user of a product or service.
Parallel import	Trade that is made possible when the owner of intellectual property causes the same product to be sold in different countries for different prices. If someone else imports the low-price good into the high-price country, it is a parallel import.
Import quota	Import quota refers to a limit imposed by a nation on the quantity of a good that may be imported during some period of time.
Quota	A government-imposed restriction on quantity, or sometimes on total value, used to restrict the import of something to a specific quantity is called a quota.
Union	A worker association that bargains with employers over wages and working conditions is called a union.
Wall Street Journal	Dow Jones & Company was founded in 1882 by reporters Charles Dow, Edward Jones and Charles Bergstresser. Jones converted the small Customers' Afternoon Letter into The Wall Street Journal, first published in 1889, and began delivery of the Dow Jones News Service via telegraph. The Journal featured the Jones 'Average', the first of several indexes of stock and bond prices on the New York Stock Exchange.
Inventory	Tangible property held for sale in the normal course of business or used in producing goods or services for sale is an inventory.
Journal	Book of original entry, in which transactions are recorded in a general ledger system, is referred to as a journal.
Export	In economics, an export is any good or commodity, shipped or otherwise transported out of a country, province, town to another part of the world in a legitimate fashion, typically for use in trade or sale.
Discount	The difference between the face value of a bond and its selling price, when a bond is sold for less than its face value it's referred to as a discount.
Margin	A deposit by a buyer in stocks with a seller or a stockbroker, as security to cover fluctuations in the market in reference to stocks that the buyer has purchased but for which he has not paid is a margin. Commodities are also traded on margin.
Distribution channel	A distribution channel is a chain of intermediaries, each passing a product down the chain to the next organization, before it finally reaches the consumer or end-user.
Costco	Costco focuses on selling products at low prices, often at very high volume. These goods are usually bulk-packaged and marketed primarily to large families and small businesses. As a warehouse club, Costco is only open to members and their guests, except for purchases of liquor, gasoline and prescription drugs in some U.S. states due to state law and liquor license restrictions.
Commerce	Commerce is the exchange of something of value between two entities. It is the central mechanism from which capitalism is derived.

Go to **Cram101.com** for the Practice Tests for this Chapter.

Supply	Supply is the aggregate amount of any material good that can be called into being at a certain price point; it comprises one half of the equation of supply and demand. In classical economic theory, a curve representing supply is one of the factors that produce price.
Gucci	Gucci, or the House of Gucci, is an Italian fashion and leather goods label. It was founded by Guccio Gucci (1881-1953) in Florence in 1921. In the late 1980s made Gucci one of the world's most influential fashion houses and a highly profitable business operation. In October of 1995 Gucci decided to go public and had its first initial public offering on the AEX and NYSE for $22 per share..
Profit margin	Profit margin is a measure of profitability. It is calculated using a formula and written as a percentage or a number. Profit margin = Net income before tax and interest / Revenue.
Wholesale	According to the United Nations Statistics Division Wholesale is the resale of new and used goods to retailers, to industrial, commercial, institutional or professional users, or to other wholesalers, or involves acting as an agent or broker in buying merchandise for, or selling merchandise, to such persons or companies.
Industry	A group of firms that produce identical or similar products is an industry. It is also used specifically to refer to an area of economic production focused on manufacturing which involves large amounts of capital investment before any profit can be realized, also called "heavy industry".
Adidas	Adidas is a German sports apparel manufacturer, part of the Adidas Group. The company was named after its founder, Adolf Dassler, who started producing shoes in the 1920s in Herzogenaurach near Nuremberg with the help of his brother Rudolf Dassler who later formed rival shoe company PUMA AG.
Nike	Because Nike creates goods for a wide range of sports, they have competition from every sports and sports fashion brand there is. Nike has no direct competitors because there is no single brand which can compete directly with their range of sports and non-sports oriented gear, except for Reebok.
Trademark	A distinctive word, name, symbol, device, or combination thereof, which enables consumers to identify favored products or services and which may find protection under state or federal law is a trademark.
Licensee	A person lawfully on land in possession of another for purposes unconnected with the business interests of the possessor is referred to as the licensee.
Exporter	A firm that sells its product in another country is an exporter.
Retail sale	The sale of goods and services to consumers for their own use is a retail sale.
Freight forwarder	An organization that puts many small shipments together to create a single large shipment that can be transported cost-effectively to the final destination is called freight forwarder.
Possession	Possession refers to respecting real property, exclusive dominion and control such as owners of like property usually exercise over it. Manual control of personal property either as owner or as one having a qualified right in it.
Bill of lading	Bill of lading refers to the receipt given by a transportation company to an exporter when the former accepts goods for transport. It includes the contract specifying what transport service will be provided and the limits of liability.
Warranty	An obligation of a company to replace defective goods or correct any deficiencies in performance or quality of a product is called a warranty.
Service	Service refers to a "non tangible product" that is not embodied in a physical good and that

Go to Cram101.com for the Practice Tests for this Chapter.

	typically effects some change in another product, person, or institution. Contrasts with good.
Dealer	People who link buyers with sellers by buying and selling securities at stated prices are referred to as a dealer.
Purchasing	Purchasing refers to the function in a firm that searches for quality material resources, finds the best suppliers, and negotiates the best price for goods and services.
Euro	The common currency of a subset of the countries of the EU, adopted January 1, 1999 is called euro.
Harmonization	Harmonization refers to the changing of government regulations and practices, as a result of an international agreement, to make those of different countries the same or more compatible.
Consideration	Consideration in contract law, a basic requirement for an enforceable agreement under traditional contract principles, defined in this text as legal value, bargained for and given in exchange for an act or promise. In corporation law, cash or property contributed to a corporation in exchange for shares, or a promise to contribute such cash or property.
Industrial goods	Components produced for use in the production of other products are called industrial goods.
Incremental cost	Additional total cost incurred for an activity is called incremental cost. A form of costing that classifies costs into their fixed and variable elements in order to calculate the extra cost of making and selling an additional batch of units.
Competitive advantage	A business is said to have a competitive advantage when its unique strengths, often based on cost, quality, time, and innovation, offer consumers a greater percieved value and there by differtiating it from its competitors.
Total cost	The sum of fixed cost and variable cost is referred to as total cost.
Penetration pricing	Setting a low initial price for a new product in order to penetrate the market deeply and gain a large and broad market share is referred to as penetration pricing.
Premium	Premium refers to the fee charged by an insurance company for an insurance policy. The rate of losses must be relatively predictable: In order to set the premium (prices) insurers must be able to estimate them accurately.
Revenue	Revenue is a U.S. business term for the amount of money that a company receives from its activities, mostly from sales of products and/or services to customers.
Market segments	Market segments refer to the groups that result from the process of market segmentation; these groups ideally have common needs and will respond similarly to a marketing action.
Disparity	Disparity refers to the regional and economic differences in a country, province, state, or continent
Target market	One or more specific groups of potential consumers toward which an organization directs its marketing program are a target market.
Emerging markets	The term emerging markets is commonly used to describe business and market activity in industrializing or emerging regions of the world. It is sometimes loosely used as a replacement for emerging economies, but really signifies a business phenomenon that is not fully described by or constrained to geography or economic strength; such countries are considered to be in a transitional phase between developing and developed status.
Research report	A research report is a business report produced by business research firms by their financial analysts. They are designed to dig out the important pieces of companies operational and financial reporting to paint a picture of the future of companies to assist debt and equity investing.

Emerging market	The term emerging market is commonly used to describe business and market activity in industrializing or emerging regions of the world.
Complexity	The technical sophistication of the product and hence the amount of understanding required to use it is referred to as complexity. It is the opposite of simplicity.
Preference	The act of a debtor in paying or securing one or more of his creditors in a manner more favorable to them than to other creditors or to the exclusion of such other creditors is a preference. In the absence of statute, a preference is perfectly good, but to be legal it must be bona fide, and not a mere subterfuge of the debtor to secure a future benefit to himself or to prevent the application of his property to his debts.
Complaint	The pleading in a civil case in which the plaintiff states his claim and requests relief is called complaint. In the common law, it is a formal legal document that sets out the basic facts and legal reasons that the filing party (the plaintiffs) believes are sufficient to support a claim against another person, persons, entity or entities (the defendants) that entitles the plaintiff(s) to a remedy (either money damages or injunctive relief).
Reuters	Reuters is best known as a news service that provides reports from around the world to newspapers and broadcasters. Its main focus is on supplying the financial markets with information and trading products.
Price level	The overall level of prices in a country, as usually measured empirically by a price index, but often captured in theoretical models by a single variable is a price level.
Economy	The income, expenditures, and resources that affect the cost of running a business and household are called an economy.
Competitor	Other organizations in the same industry or type of business that provide a good or service to the same set of customers is referred to as a competitor.
Sony	Sony is a multinational corporation and one of the world's largest media conglomerates founded in Tokyo, Japan. One of its divisions Sony Electronics is one of the leading manufacturers of electronics, video, communications, and information technology products for the consumer and professional markets.
Global strategy	Global strategy refers to strategy focusing on increasing profitability by reaping cost reductions from experience curve and location economies.
Turnover	Turnover in a financial context refers to the rate at which a provider of goods cycles through its average inventory. Turnover in a human resources context refers to the characteristic of a given company or industry, relative to rate at which an employer gains and loses staff.
Brand extension	The practice of using a current brand name to enter a completely different product class is referred to as brand extension.
Extension	Extension refers to an out-of-court settlement in which creditors agree to allow the firm more time to meet its financial obligations. A new repayment schedule will be developed, subject to the acceptance of creditors.
Single market	A single market is a customs union with common policies on product regulation, and freedom of movement of all the four factors of production (goods, services, capital and labor).
Pricing strategy	The process in which the price of a product can be determined and is decided upon is a pricing strategy.
Markup	Markup is a term used in marketing to indicate how much the price of a product is above the cost of producing and distributing the product.
Inflation	An increase in the overall price level of an economy, usually as measured by the CPI or by

416

Go to **Cram101.com** for the Practice Tests for this Chapter.

the implicit price deflator is called inflation.

Trade barrier
An artificial disincentive to export and/or import, such as a tariff, quota, or other NTB is called a trade barrier.

Excess profit
Profit of a firm over and above what provides its owners with a normal return to capital is called excess profit.

Administrative cost
An administrative cost is all executive, organizational, and clerical costs associated with the general management of an organization rather than with manufacturing, marketing, or selling

License
A license in the sphere of Intellectual Property Rights (IPR) is a document, contract or agreement giving permission or the 'right' to a legally-definable entity to do something (such as manufacture a product or to use a service), or to apply something (such as a trademark), with the objective of achieving commercial gain.

Cost of goods sold
In accounting, the cost of goods sold describes the direct expenses incurred in producing a particular good for sale, including the actual cost of materials that comprise the good, and direct labor expense in putting the good in salable condition.

Replacement cost
The current purchase price of replacing a property damaged or lost with similar property is the replacement cost.

Exchange
The trade of things of value between buyer and seller so that each is better off after the trade is called the exchange.

Contract
A contract is a "promise" or an "agreement" that is enforced or recognized by the law. In the civil law, a contract is considered to be part of the general law of obligations.

Consignment
Consignment refers to a bailment for sale. The consignee does not undertake the absolute obligation to sell or pay for the goods.

Developing country
Developing country refers to a country whose per capita income is low by world standards. Same as LDC. As usually used, it does not necessarily connote that the country's income is rising.

Deflation
Deflation is an increase in the market value of money which is equivalent to a decrease in the general price level, over a period of time. The term is also used to refer to a decrease in the size of the money supply

Business Week
Business Week is a business magazine published by McGraw-Hill. It was first published in 1929 under the direction of Malcolm Muir, who was serving as president of the McGraw-Hill Publishing company at the time. It is considered to be the standard both in industry and among students.

Trust
An arrangement in which shareholders of independent firms agree to give up their stock in exchange for trust certificates that entitle them to a share of the trust's common profits.

Exchange rate
Exchange rate refers to the price at which one country's currency trades for another, typically on the exchange market.

Future value
Future value measures what money is worth at a specified time in the future assuming a certain interest rate. This is used in time value of money calculations.

Hedging
A technique for avoiding a risk by making a counteracting transaction is referred to as hedging.

Vendor
A person who sells property to a vendee is a vendor. The words vendor and vendee are more commonly applied to the seller and purchaser of real estate, and the words seller and buyer are more commonly applied to the seller and purchaser of personal property.

Stock market	An organized marketplace in which common stocks are traded. In the United States, the largest stock market is the New York Stock Exchange, on which are traded the stocks of the largest U.S. companies.
Leadership	Management merely consists of leadership applied to business situations; or in other words: management forms a sub-set of the broader process of leadership.
Stock	In financial terminology, stock is the capital raized by a corporation, through the issuance and sale of shares.
Central Bank	Central bank refers to the institution in a country that is normally responsible for managing the supply of the country's money and the value of its currency on the foreign exchange market.
Corporation	A legal entity chartered by a state or the Federal government that is distinct and separate from the individuals who own it is a corporation. This separation gives the corporation unique powers which other legal entities lack.
Option	A contract that gives the purchaser the option to buy or sell the underlying financial instrument at a specified price, called the exercise price or strike price, within a specific period of time.
Currency exchange rate	The rate between two currencies that specifies how much one country's currency is worth expressed in terms of the other country's currency is the currency exchange rate.
Proactive	To be proactive is to act before a situation becomes a source of confrontation or crisis. It is the opposite of "retroactive," which refers to actions taken after an event.
Entrepreneur	The owner/operator. The person who organizes, manages, and assumes the risks of a firm, taking a new idea or a new product and turning it into a successful business is an entrepreneur.
Channel length	The number of intermediaries that a product has to go through before it reaches the final consumer is called channel length.
Expense	In accounting, an expense represents an event in which an asset is used up or a liability is incurred. In terms of the accounting equation, expenses reduce owners' equity.
Raw material	Raw material refers to a good that has not been transformed by production; a primary product.
Downturn	A decline in a stock market or economic cycle is a downturn.
Goodwill	Goodwill is an important accounting concept that describes the value of a business entity not directly attributable to its tangible assets and liabilities.
Marketing research	Marketing research refers to the analysis of markets to determine opportunities and challenges, and to find the information needed to make good decisions.
Cadillac	Cadillac was formed from the remnants of the Henry Ford Company when Henry Ford departed along with several of his key partners. With the intent of liquidating the firm's assets, Ford's financial backers, William Murphy and Lemuel Bowen called in engineer Henry M. Leland to appraise the plant and equipment prior to selling them. Instead, Leland persuaded them to continue in the automobile business.
Purchasing power	The amount of goods that money will buy, usually measured by the CPI is referred to as purchasing power.
Insurance	Insurance refers to a system by which individuals can reduce their exposure to risk of large losses by spreading the risks among a large number of persons.
Manufacturing costs	Costs incurred in a manufacturing process, which consist of direct material, direct labor, and manufacturing overhead are referred to as manufacturing costs.

Go to Cram101.com for the Practice Tests for this Chapter.

Manufacturing	Production of goods primarily by the application of labor and capital to raw materials and other intermediate inputs, in contrast to agriculture, mining, forestry, fishing, and services a manufacturing.
General Electric	In 1876, Thomas Alva Edison opened a new laboratory in Menlo Park, New Jersey. Out of the laboratory was to come perhaps the most famous invention of all—a successful development of the incandescent electric lamp. By 1890, Edison had organized his various businesses into the Edison General Electric Company.
Samsung	On November 30, 2005 Samsung pleaded guilty to a charge it participated in a worldwide DRAM price fixing conspiracy during 1999-2002 that damaged competition and raized PC prices.
Labor	People's physical and mental talents and efforts that are used to help produce goods and services are called labor.
Labor force	In economics the labor force is the group of people who have a potential for being employed.
Capital	Capital generally refers to financial wealth, especially that used to start or maintain a business. In classical economics, capital is one of four factors of production, the others being land and labor and entrepreneurship.
Quality control	The measurement of products and services against set standards is referred to as quality control.
Price war	Price war refers to successive and continued decreases in the prices charged by firms in an oligopolistic industry. Each firm lowers its price below rivals' prices, hoping to increase its sales and revenues at its rivals' expense.
Customs	Customs is an authority or agency in a country responsible for collecting customs duties and for controlling the flow of people, animals and goods (including personal effects and hazardous items) in and out of the country.
Customs classification	The category defining the tariff to be applied to an imported good is referred to as customs classification. The act of determining this category, which may be subject to various rules and/or to the discretion of the customs officer.
Competitiveness	Competitiveness usually refers to characteristics that permit a firm to compete effectively with other firms due to low cost or superior technology, perhaps internationally.
Agent	A person who makes economic decisions for another economic actor. A hired manager operates as an agent for a firm's owner.
Broker	In commerce, a broker is a party that mediates between a buyer and a seller. A broker who also acts as a seller or as a buyer becomes a principal party to the deal.
International trade	The export of goods and services from a country and the import of goods and services into a country is referred to as the international trade.
Enterprise	Enterprise refers to another name for a business organization. Other similar terms are business firm, sometimes simply business, sometimes simply firm, as well as company, and entity.
Argument	The discussion by counsel for the respective parties of their contentions on the law and the facts of the case being tried in order to aid the jury in arriving at a correct and just conclusion is called argument.
Brief	Brief refers to a statement of a party's case or legal arguments, usually prepared by an attorney. Also used to make legal arguments before appellate courts.
Differential rate	A difference in wage rate paid for the same work performed under differing conditions is a differential rate.

Go to **Cram101.com** for the Practice Tests for this Chapter.

Go to **Cram101.com** for the Practice Tests for this Chapter.
And, **NEVER** highlight a book again!

423

Nissan	Nissan is Japan's second largest car company after Toyota. Nissan is among the top three Asian rivals of the "big three" in the US.
Foreign trade zone	Foreign trade zone refers to an area within a country where imported goods can be stored or processed without being subject to import duty. Also called a 'free zone,' 'free port,' or 'bonded warehouse.'
Levy	Levy refers to imposing and collecting a tax or tariff.
Incentive	An incentive is any factor (financial or non-financial) that provides a motive for a particular course of action, or counts as a reason for preferring one choice to the alternatives.
Free trade zone	A free trade zone is one or more areas of a country where tariffs and quotas are eliminated and bureaucratic requirements are lowered in order to attract companies by raising the incentives for doing business there.
Free trade	Free trade refers to a situation in which there are no artificial barriers to trade, such as tariffs and quotas. Usually used, often only implicitly, with frictionless trade, so that it implies that there are no barriers to trade of any kind.
Distribution center	Designed to facilitate the timely movement of goods and represent a very important part of a supply chain is a distribution center.
Regulation	Regulation refers to restrictions state and federal laws place on business with regard to the conduct of its activities.
Host country	The country in which the parent-country organization seeks to locate or has already located a facility is a host country.
Overhead cost	An expenses of operating a business over and above the direct costs of producing a product is an overhead cost. They can include utilities (eg, electricity, telephone), advertizing and marketing, and any other costs not billed directly to the client or included in the price of the product.
Product cost	Product cost refers to sum of the costs assigned to a product for a specific purpose. A concept used in applying the cost plus approach to product pricing in which only the costs of manufacturing the product are included in the cost amount to which the markup is added.
Cabinet	The heads of the executive departments of a jurisdiction who report to and advise its chief executive; examples would include the president's cabinet, the governor's cabinet, and the mayor's cabinet.
International Business	International business refers to any firm that engages in international trade or investment.
Dumping	Dumping refers to a practice of charging a very low price in a foreign market for such economic purposes as putting rival suppliers out of business.
Cost of sales	Cost of sales refers to the total costs of goods made or purchased and sold.
World Trade Organization	The World Trade Organization is an international, multilateral organization, which sets the rules for the global trading system and resolves disputes between its member states, all of whom are signatories to its approximately 30 agreements.
Countervailing duty	A tariff levied against imports that are subsidized by the exporting country's government, designed to offset the effect of the subsidy, is referred to as countervailing duty.
Subsidy	Subsidy refers to government financial assistance to a domestic producer.
Commodity	Could refer to any good, but in trade a commodity is usually a raw material or primary product that enters into international trade, such as metals or basic agricultural products.

Go to **Cram101.com** for the Practice Tests for this Chapter.

Go to **Cram101.com** for the Practice Tests for this Chapter.
And, **NEVER** highlight a book again!

Countervailing duties	countervailing duties are tariffs imposed by a country on imported goods in cases where imports have been unfairly subsidized by a foreign government and hurt domestic producers. Antidumping duties are referred to as countervailing duties.
Authority	Authority in agency law, refers to an agent's ability to affect his principal's legal relations with third parties. Also used to refer to an actor's legal power or ability to do something. In addition, sometimes used to refer to a statute, case, or other legal source that justifies a particular result.
Users	Users refer to people in the organization who actually use the product or service purchased by the buying center.
Selling technique	Selling technique is the body of methods used in the profession of sales. All techniques borrow a bit from experience and mix in a bit of guesswork on the psychology of what motivates others to buy something offered to them.
Lease	A contract for the possession and use of land or other property, including goods, on one side, and a recompense of rent or other income on the other is the lease.
Direct sale	A direct sale is a sale to customers through distributors or self-employed sales people rather than through shops. Includes both personal contact with consumers in their homes (and other nonstore locations such as offices) and phone solicitations initiated by a retailer.
Political risk	Refers to the many different actions of people, subgroups, and whole countries that have the potential to affect the financial status of a firm is called political risk.
Expropriation	Expropriation is the act of removing from control the owner of an item of property. The term is used to both refer to acts by a government or by any group of people.
Devaluation	Lowering the value of a nation's currency relative to other currencies is called devaluation.
Trend	Trend refers to the long-term movement of an economic variable, such as its average rate of increase or decrease over enough years to encompass several business cycles.
PepsiCo	In many ways, PepsiCo differs from its main competitor, having three times as many employees, larger revenues, but a smaller net profit.
Barter	Barter is a type of trade where goods or services are exchanged for a certain amount of other goods or services; no money is involved in the transaction.
Protectionism	Protectionism refers to advocacy of protection. The word has a negative connotation, and few advocates of protection in particular situations will acknowledge being protectionists.
Lockheed Martin	Lockheed Martin is the world's largest defense contractor (by defense revenue). As of 2005, 95% of revenues came from the U.S. Department of Defense, other U.S. federal government agencies, and foreign military customers.
Foreign exchange	In finance, foreign exchange means currencies, such as U.S. Dollars and Euros. These are traded on foreign exchange markets.
Countertrading	The sale of goods or services that are paid for in whole or in part by the transfer of goods or services between seperate countries is called countertrading. Also referred to as bartering.
Balance of trade	Balance of trade refers to the sum of the money gained by a given economy by selling exports, minus the cost of buying imports. They form part of the balance of payments, which also includes other transactions such as the international investment position.
Nonconvertible currency	Nonconvertible currency is currency that both residents and nonresidents are prohibited from converting their holdings of that currency into another currency.
Bilateral trade	Bilateral trade refers to the trade between two countries; that is, the value or quantity of

Go to **Cram101.com** for the Practice Tests for this Chapter.
And, **NEVER** highlight a book again!

one country's exports to the other, or the sum of exports and imports between them.

Ledger	Ledger refers to a specialized accounting book in which information from accounting journals is accumulated into specific categories and posted so that managers can find all the information about one account in the same place.
Marketing channel	Individuals and firms involved in the process of making a product or service available for use or consumption by consumers or industrial users is a marketing channel.
Inflating	Inflating refers to determining real gross domestic product by increasing the dollar value of the nominal gross domestic product produced in a year in which prices are lower than those in a base year.
Creditor	A person to whom a debt or legal obligation is owed, and who has the right to enforce payment of that debt or obligation is referred to as creditor.
Foreign exchange reserves	Foreign exchange reserves are the foreign currency deposits held by national banks of different nations. These are assets of governments which are held in different reserve currencies such as the dollar, euro and yen.
Convertible currency	Convertible currency refers to a currency that can legally be exchanged for another or for gold.
General Motors	General Motors is the world's largest automaker. Founded in 1908, today it employs about 327,000 people around the world. With global headquarters in Detroit, it manufactures its cars and trucks in 33 countries.
Strike	The withholding of labor services by an organized group of workers is referred to as a strike.
Current account	Current account refers to a country's international transactions arising from current flows, as opposed to changes in stocks which are part of the capital account. Includes trade in goods and services plus inflows and outflows of transfers. A current account is a deposit account in the UK and countries with a UK banking heritage.
Deficit	The deficit is the amount by which expenditure exceed revenue.
Current Account deficit	Current account deficit occurs when a country imports more goods and services than it exports.
Remainder	A remainder in property law is a future interest created in a transferee that is capable of becoming possessory upon the natural termination of a prior estate created by the same instrument.
Credit	Credit refers to a recording as positive in the balance of payments, any transaction that gives rise to a payment into the country, such as an export, the sale of an asset, or borrowing from abroad.
Technology	The body of knowledge and techniques that can be used to combine economic resources to produce goods and services is called technology.
Negotiation	Negotiation is the process whereby interested parties resolve disputes, agree upon courses of action, bargain for individual or collective advantage, and/or attempt to craft outcomes which serve their mutual interests.
Anticipation	In finance, anticipation is where debts are paid off early, generally in order to pay less interest.
Aid	Assistance provided by countries and by international institutions such as the World Bank to developing countries in the form of monetary grants, loans at low interest rates, in kind, or a combination of these is called aid. Aid can also refer to assistance of any type rendered

Go to **Cram101.com** for the Practice Tests for this Chapter.
And, **NEVER** highlight a book again!

429

	to benefit some group or individual.
Consultant	A professional that provides expert advice in a particular field or area in which customers occassionaly require this type of knowledge is a consultant.
Citibank	In April of 2006, Citibank struck a deal with 7-Eleven to put its ATMs in over 5,500 convenience stores in the U.S. In the same month, it also announced it would sell all of its Buffalo and Rochester New York branches and accounts to M&T Bank.
Venue	A requirement distinct from jurisdiction that the court be geographically situated so that it is the most appropriate and convenient court to try the case is the venue.
Market price	Market price is an economic concept with commonplace familiarity; it is the price that a good or service is offered at, or will fetch, in the marketplace; it is of interest mainly in the study of microeconomics.
Auction	A preexisting business model that operates successfully on the Internet by announcing an item for sale and permitting multiple purchasers to bid on them under specified rules and condition is an auction.
Barter economy	Barter economy refers to an economic model of international trade in which goods are exchanged for goods without the existence of money. Most theoretical trade models take this form in order to abstract from macroeconomic and monetary considerations.
Complement	A good that is used in conjunction with another good is a complement. For example, cameras and film would complement eachother.
Affiliates	Local television stations that are associated with a major network are called affiliates. Affiliates agree to preempt time during specified hours for programming provided by the network and carry the advertising contained in the program.
Economic development	Increase in the economic standard of living of a country's population, normally accomplished by increasing its stocks of physical and human capital and improving its technology is an economic development.
Market value	Market value refers to the price of an asset agreed on between a willing buyer and a willing seller; the price an asset could demand if it is sold on the open market.
Market opportunities	Market opportunities refer to areas where a company believes there are favorable demand trends, needs, and/or wants that are not being satisfied, and where it can compete effectively.
Transfer pricing	Transfer pricing refers to the pricing of goods and services within a multi-divisional organization. Goods from the production division may be sold to the marketing division, or goods from a parent company may be sold to a foreign subsidiary.
Joint venture	Joint venture refers to an undertaking by two parties for a specific purpose and duration, taking any of several legal forms.
Transfer price	Transfer price refers to the price one subunit charges for a product or service supplied to another subunit of the same organization.
Dividend	Amount of corporate profits paid out for each share of stock is referred to as dividend.
Transaction value	The actual price of a product, paid or payable, used for customs valuation purposes is called transaction value.
Liability	A liability is a present obligation of the enterprise arizing from past events, the settlement of which is expected to result in an outflow from the enterprise of resources embodying economic benefits.
Corporate tax	Corporate tax refers to a direct tax levied by various jurisdictions on the profits made by

companies or associations. As a general principle, this varies substantially between jurisdictions.

Deductible
The dollar sum of costs that an insured individual must pay before the insurer begins to pay is called deductible.

International division
Division responsible for a firm's international activities is an international division.

Management
Management characterizes the process of leading and directing all or part of an organization, often a business, through the deployment and manipulation of resources. Early twentieth-century management writer Mary Parker Follett defined management as "the art of getting things done through people."

Accounting
A system that collects and processes financial information about an organization and reports that information to decision makers is referred to as accounting.

Audit
An examination of the financial reports to ensure that they represent what they claim and conform with generally accepted accounting principles is referred to as audit.

Pizza Hut
Pizza Hut is the world's largest pizza restaurant chain with nearly 34,000 restaurants, delivery-carry out units, and kiosks in 100 countries

Burden of proof
Used to refer both to the necessity or obligation of proving the facts needed to support a party's claim, and the persuasiveness of the evidence used to do so is a burden of proof. Regarding the second sense of the term, the usual burden of proof in a civil case is a preponderance of the evidence.

Quantity definition
Quantity definition refers to a method of defining relative factor abundance based on ratios of factor quantities.

Price fixing
Price fixing refers to the conspiring by two or more firms to set the price of their products; an illegal practice under the Sherman Act.

Administration
Administration refers to the management and direction of the affairs of governments and institutions; a collective term for all policymaking officials of a government; the execution and implementation of public policy.

Welfare
Welfare refers to the economic well being of an individual, group, or economy. For individuals, it is conceptualized by a utility function. For groups, including countries and the world, it is a tricky philosophical concept, since individuals fare differently.

Perfect competition
An idealized market structure in which there are large numbers of both buyers and sellers, all of them small, so that they act as price takers. Perfect competition also assumes homogeneous products, free entry and exit, and complete information.

Pure competition
A market structure in which a very large number of firms sells a standardized product, into which entry is very easy, in which the individual seller has no control over the product price, and in which there is no non-price competition is pure competition.

Administered price
A price for a good or service that is set and maintained by government, usually requiring accompanying restrictions on trade if the administered price differs from the world price.

Trade association
An industry trade group or trade association is generally a public relations organization founded and funded by corporations that operate in a specific industry. Its purpose is generally to promote that industry through PR activities such as advertizing, education, political donations, political pressure, publishing, and astroturfing.

Customary pricing
A method of pricing based on tradition, a standardized channel of distribution, or other competitive factors is customary pricing.

Go to **Cram101.com** for the Practice Tests for this Chapter.

Price leadership	An informal method that firms in an oligopoly may employ to set the price of their product: One firm is the first to announce a change in price, and the other firms soon announce identical or similar changes is called price leadership.
Licensing	Licensing is a form of strategic alliance which involves the sale of a right to use certain proprietary knowledge (so called intellectual property) in a defined way.
Cartel	Cartel refers to a group of firms that seeks to raise the price of a good by restricting its supply. The term is usually used for international groups, especially involving state-owned firms and/or governments.
Allocate	Allocate refers to the assignment of income for various tax purposes. A multistate corporation's nonbusiness income usually is distributed to the state where the nonbusiness assets are located; it is not apportioned with the rest of the entity's income.
Primary factor	Primary factor refers to an input that exists as a stock, providing services that contribute to production. The stock is not used up in production, although it may deteriorate with use, providing a smaller flow of services later.
Recession	A significant decline in economic activity. In the U.S., recession is approximately defined as two successive quarters of falling GDP, as judged by NBER.
Short run	Short run refers to a period of time that permits an increase or decrease in current production volume with existing capacity, but one that is too short to permit enlargement of that capacity itself (eg, the building of new plants, training of additional workers, etc.).
Monopoly	A monopoly is defined as a persistent market situation where there is only one provider of a kind of product or service.
De Beers	In 1994 De Beers was charged by the United States Justice Department with antitrust violations for conspiring to fix prices for industrial diamonds. On 14 July 2004 De Beers pleaded guilty to the charges and paid a $10 million fine. They have historically held a near-total monopoly in the diamond trade.
Market power	The ability of a single economic actor to have a substantial influence on market prices is market power.
Adverse impact	Adverse impact refers to the rejection for employment, placement, or promotion of a significantly higher percentage of a protected class, when compared with a non-protected class.
Monopsony	A market structure in which there is a single buyer is referred to as monopsony.
Grant	Grant refers to an intergovernmental transfer of funds . Since the New Deal, state and local governments have become increasingly dependent upon federal grants for an almost infinite variety of programs.
Deregulation	The lessening or complete removal of government regulations on an industry, especially concerning the price that firms are allowed to charge and leaving price to be determined by market forces a deregulation.
Exempt	Employees who are not covered by the Fair Labor Standards Act are exempt. Exempt employees are not eligible for overtime pay.
Ad valorem tariff	Ad valorem tariff refers to tariff defined as a percentage of the value of an imported good.
Specific tariff	A tariff specified as an amount of currency per unit of the good is referred to as a specific tariff.
Compound tariff	A tariff that combines both a specific and an ad valorem component is called a compound

Go to **Cram101.com** for the Practice Tests for this Chapter.
And, **NEVER** highlight a book again!

tariff.

Go to **Cram101.com** for the Practice Tests for this Chapter.

Marketing	Promoting and selling products or services to customers, or prospective customers, is referred to as marketing.
Partnership	In the common law, a partnership is a type of business entity in which partners share with each other the profits or losses of the business undertaking in which they have all invested.
Senior executive	Senior executive means a chief executive officer, chief operating officer, chief financial officer and anyone in charge of a principal business unit or function.
Marketing strategy	Marketing strategy refers to the means by which a marketing goal is to be achieved, usually characterized by a specified target market and a marketing program to reach it.
Global marketing	A strategy of using a common marketing plan and program for all countries in which a company operates, thus selling the product or services the same way everywhere in the world is called global marketing.
Global marketing strategy	The practice of standardizing marketing activities when there are cultural similarities and adapting them when cultures differ is referred to as global marketing strategy.
Standing	Standing refers to the legal requirement that anyone seeking to challenge a particular action in court must demonstrate that such action substantially affects his legitimate interests before he will be entitled to bring suit.
Negotiation	Negotiation is the process whereby interested parties resolve disputes, agree upon courses of action, bargain for individual or collective advantage, and/or attempt to craft outcomes which serve their mutual interests.
Commerce	Commerce is the exchange of something of value between two entities. It is the central mechanism from which capitalism is derived.
Marketing research	Marketing research refers to the analysis of markets to determine opportunities and challenges, and to find the information needed to make good decisions.
Promotion	Promotion refers to all the techniques sellers use to motivate people to buy products or services. An attempt by marketers to inform people about products and to persuade them to participate in an exchange.
International Business	International business refers to any firm that engages in international trade or investment.
Distribution channel	A distribution channel is a chain of intermediaries, each passing a product down the chain to the next organization, before it finally reaches the consumer or end-user.
Franchise agreement	An arrangement whereby someone with a good idea for a business sells the rights to use the business name and sell a product or service to others in a given territory is a franchise agreement.
Strategic alliance	Strategic alliance refers to a long-term partnership between two or more companies established to help each company build competitive market advantages.
Distribution	Distribution in economics, the manner in which total output and income is distributed among individuals or factors.
Advertising	Advertising refers to paid, nonpersonal communication through various media by organizations and individuals who are in some way identified in the advertising message.
Management	Management characterizes the process of leading and directing all or part of an organization, often a business, through the deployment and manipulation of resources. Early twentieth-century management writer Mary Parker Follett defined management as "the art of getting things done through people."

Go to **Cram101.com** for the Practice Tests for this Chapter.
And, **NEVER** highlight a book again!

Preference	The act of a debtor in paying or securing one or more of his creditors in a manner more favorable to them than to other creditors or to the exclusion of such other creditors is a preference. In the absence of statute, a preference is perfectly good, but to be legal it must be bona fide, and not a mere subterfuge of the debtor to secure a future benefit to himself or to prevent the application of his property to his debts.
Licensing	Licensing is a form of strategic alliance which involves the sale of a right to use certain proprietary knowledge (so called intellectual property) in a defined way.
Franchise	A contractual right to sell certain products or services, use certain trademarks, or perform activities in a geographical region is called a franchise.
Exchange	The trade of things of value between buyer and seller so that each is better off after the trade is called the exchange.
Service	Service refers to a "non tangible product" that is not embodied in a physical good and that typically effects some change in another product, person, or institution. Contrasts with good.
Channel	Channel, in communications (sometimes called communications channel), refers to the medium used to convey information from a sender (or transmitter) to a receiver.
Joint venture	Joint venture refers to an undertaking by two parties for a specific purpose and duration, taking any of several legal forms.
Vendor	A person who sells property to a vendee is a vendor. The words vendor and vendee are more commonly applied to the seller and purchaser of real estate, and the words seller and buyer are more commonly applied to the seller and purchaser of personal property.
Authority	Authority in agency law, refers to an agent's ability to affect his principal's legal relations with third parties. Also used to refer to an actor's legal power or ability to do something. In addition, sometimes used to refer to a statute, case, or other legal source that justifies a particular result.
Quorum	Quorum refers to that number of persons, shares represented, or officers who may lawfully transact the business of a meeting called for that purpose.
Journal	Book of original entry, in which transactions are recorded in a general ledger system, is referred to as a journal.
Competitiveness	Competitiveness usually refers to characteristics that permit a firm to compete effectively with other firms due to low cost or superior technology, perhaps internationally.
Loyalty	Marketers tend to define customer loyalty as making repeat purchases. Some argue that it should be defined attitudinally as a strongly positive feeling about the brand.
Harvard Business Review	Harvard Business Review is a research-based magazine written for business practitioners, it claims a high ranking business readership and enjoys the reverence of academics, executives, and management consultants. It has been the frequent publishing home for well known scholars and management thinkers.
Toyota	Toyota is a Japanese multinational corporation that manufactures automobiles, trucks and buses. Toyota is the world's second largest automaker by sales. Toyota also provides financial services through its subsidiary, Toyota Financial Services, and participates in other lines of business.
Ford Motor Company	Ford Motor Company introduced methods for large-scale manufacturing of cars, and large-scale management of an industrial workforce, especially elaborately engineered manufacturing sequences typified by the moving assembly lines. Henry Ford's combination of highly efficient factories, highly paid workers, and low prices revolutionized manufacturing and came to be

Go to **Cram101.com** for the Practice Tests for this Chapter.

known around the world as Fordism by 1914.

Corporation

A legal entity chartered by a state or the Federal government that is distinct and separate from the individuals who own it is a corporation. This separation gives the corporation unique powers which other legal entities lack.

Caterpillar

Caterpillar is a United States based corporation headquartered in Peoria, Illinois. Caterpillar is "the world's largest manufacturer of construction and mining equipment, diesel and natural gas engines, and industrial gas turbines."

Technology

The body of knowledge and techniques that can be used to combine economic resources to produce goods and services is called technology.

Innovation

Innovation refers to the first commercially successful introduction of a new product, the use of a new method of production, or the creation of a new form of business organization.

Economy

The income, expenditures, and resources that affect the cost of running a business and household are called an economy.

Fund

Independent accounting entity with a self-balancing set of accounts segregated for the purposes of carrying on specific activities is referred to as a fund.

Ford

Ford is an American company that manufactures and sells automobiles worldwide. Ford introduced methods for large-scale manufacturing of cars, and large-scale management of an industrial workforce, especially elaborately engineered manufacturing sequences typified by the moving assembly lines.

Firm

An organization that employs resources to produce a good or service for profit and owns and operates one or more plants is referred to as a firm.

Sui generis

Sui generis is a latin term used to identify a legal classification that exists independently of other categorizations because of its uniqueness or due to the specific creation of an entitlement or obligation..

Mistake

In contract law a mistake is incorrect understanding by one or more parties to a contract and may be used as grounds to invalidate the agreement. Common law has identified three different types of mistake in contract: unilateral mistake, mutual mistake, and common mistake.

Competitive advantage

A business is said to have a competitive advantage when its unique strengths, often based on cost, quality, time, and innovation, offer consumers a greater percieved value and there by differtiating it from its competitors.

Leverage

Leverage is using given resources in such a way that the potential positive or negative outcome is magnified. In finance, this generally refers to borrowing.

Sales management

Planning the selling program and implementing and controlling the personal selling effort of the firm is called sales management.

Personal selling

Personal selling is interpersonal communication, often face to face, between a sales representative and an individual or group, usually with the objective of making a sale.

Evaluation

The consumer's appraisal of the product or brand on important attributes is called evaluation.

Buyer

A buyer refers to a role in the buying center with formal authority and responsibility to select the supplier and negotiate the terms of the contract.

Business Week

Business Week is a business magazine published by McGraw-Hill. It was first published in 1929 under the direction of Malcolm Muir, who was serving as president of the McGraw-Hill Publishing company at the time. It is considered to be the standard both in industry and among students.

Go to **Cram101.com** for the Practice Tests for this Chapter.
And, **NEVER** highlight a book again!

Concession	A concession is a business operated under a contract or license associated with a degree of exclusivity in exploiting a business within a certain geographical area. For example, sports arenas or public parks may have concession stands; and public services such as water supply may be operated as concessions.
Attribution	Under certain circumstances, the tax law applies attribution rules to assign to one taxpayer the ownership interest of another taxpayer.
Brief	Brief refers to a statement of a party's case or legal arguments, usually prepared by an attorney. Also used to make legal arguments before appellate courts.
Tactic	A short-term immediate decision that, in its totality, leads to the achievement of strategic goals is called a tactic.
Appeal	Appeal refers to the act of asking an appellate court to overturn a decision after the trial court's final judgment has been entered.
Gap	In December of 1995, Gap became the first major North American retailer to accept independent monitoring of the working conditions in a contract factory producing its garments. Gap is the largest specialty retailer in the United States.
Trend	Trend refers to the long-term movement of an economic variable, such as its average rate of increase or decrease over enough years to encompass several business cycles.
Bond	Bond refers to a debt instrument, issued by a borrower and promising a specified stream of payments to the purchaser, usually regular interest payments plus a final repayment of principal.
Aid	Assistance provided by countries and by international institutions such as the World Bank to developing countries in the form of monetary grants, loans at low interest rates, in kind, or a combination of these is called aid. Aid can also refer to assistance of any type rendered to benefit some group or individual.
Wall Street Journal	Dow Jones & Company was founded in 1882 by reporters Charles Dow, Edward Jones and Charles Bergstresser. Jones converted the small Customers' Afternoon Letter into The Wall Street Journal, first published in 1889, and began delivery of the Dow Jones News Service via telegraph. The Journal featured the Jones 'Average', the first of several indexes of stock and bond prices on the New York Stock Exchange.
Organizational Behavior	The study of human behavior in organizational settings, the interface between human behavior and the organization, and the organization itself is called organizational behavior.
Bottom line	The bottom line is net income on the last line of a income statement.
Economics	The social science dealing with the use of scarce resources to obtain the maximum satisfaction of society's virtually unlimited economic wants is an economics.
Experimental economics	Experimental economics is the use of experimental methods to evaluate theoretical predictions of economic behavior. It uses controlled, scientifically-designed experiments to test economic theories under laboratory conditions.
Cooperative	A business owned and controlled by the people who use it, producers, consumers, or workers with similar needs who pool their resources for mutual gain is called cooperative.
Profit	Profit refers to the return to the resource entrepreneurial ability; total revenue minus total cost.
Collectivism	Collectivism is a term used to describe that things should be owned by the group and used for the benefit of all rather than being owned by individuals.
Black market	Black market refers to an illegal market, in which something is bought and sold outside of

	official government-sanctioned channels. Black markets tend to arise when a government tries to fix a price without providing an alternative allocation method
Market	A market is, as defined in economics, a social arrangement that allows buyers and sellers to discover information and carry out a voluntary exchange of goods or services.
Contract	A contract is a "promise" or an "agreement" that is enforced or recognized by the law. In the civil law, a contract is considered to be part of the general law of obligations.
Warranty	An obligation of a company to replace defective goods or correct any deficiencies in performance or quality of a product is called a warranty.
Context	The effect of the background under which a message often takes on more and richer meaning is a context. Context is especially important in cross-cultural interactions because some cultures are said to be high context or low context.
Personnel	A collective term for all of the employees of an organization. Personnel is also commonly used to refer to the personnel management function or the organizational unit responsible for administering personnel programs.
Maturity	Maturity refers to the final payment date of a loan or other financial instrument, after which point no further interest or principal need be paid.
Empathy	Empathy refers to dimension of service quality-caring individualized attention provided to customers.
Export	In economics, an export is any good or commodity, shipped or otherwise transported out of a country, province, town to another part of the world in a legitimate fashion, typically for use in trade or sale.
Interest	In finance and economics, interest is the price paid by a borrower for the use of a lender's money. In other words, interest is the amount of paid to "rent" money for a period of time.
Policy	Similar to a script in that a policy can be a less than completely rational decision-making method. Involves the use of a pre-existing set of decision steps for any problem that presents itself.
Nissan	Nissan is Japan's second largest car company after Toyota. Nissan is among the top three Asian rivals of the "big three" in the US.
Investment	Investment refers to spending for the production and accumulation of capital and additions to inventories. In a financial sense, buying an asset with the expectation of making a return.
Business strategy	Business strategy, which refers to the aggregated operational strategies of single business firm or that of an SBU in a diversified corporation refers to the way in which a firm competes in its chosen arenas.
Industry	A group of firms that produce identical or similar products is an industry. It is also used specifically to refer to an area of economic production focused on manufacturing which involves large amounts of capital investment before any profit can be realized, also called "heavy industry".
Globalization	The increasing world-wide integration of markets for goods, services and capital that attracted special attention in the late 1990s is called globalization.
Appreciation	Appreciation refers to a rise in the value of a country's currency on the exchange market, relative either to a particular other currency or to a weighted average of other currencies. The currency is said to appreciate. Opposite of 'depreciation.' Appreciation can also refer to the increase in value of any asset.
Preparation	Preparation refers to usually the first stage in the creative process. It includes education

Go to **Cram101.com** for the Practice Tests for this Chapter.
And, **NEVER** highlight a book again!

and formal training.

Consideration
Consideration in contract law, a basic requirement for an enforceable agreement under traditional contract principles, defined in this text as legal value, bargained for and given in exchange for an act or promise. In corporation law, cash or property contributed to a corporation in exchange for shares, or a promise to contribute such cash or property.

Jurisdiction
The power of a court to hear and decide a case is called jurisdiction. It is the practical authority granted to a formally constituted body or to a person to deal with and make pronouncements on legal matters and, by implication, to administer justice within a defined area of responsibility.

Purchasing
Purchasing refers to the function in a firm that searches for quality material resources, finds the best suppliers, and negotiates the best price for goods and services.

Trust
An arrangement in which shareholders of independent firms agree to give up their stock in exchange for trust certificates that entitle them to a share of the trust's common profits.

Time orientation
The extent to which members of a culture adopt a long term versus a short term outlook on work is time orientation.

Private exchange
A marketplace that is sponsored by a single enterprise for the benefit of its suppliers or customers or both is the private exchange.

Prentice Hall
Prentice Hall is a leading educational publisher. It is an imprint of the Pearson Education Company, based in New Jersey, USA.

Domestic
From or in one's own country. A domestic producer is one that produces inside the home country. A domestic price is the price inside the home country. Opposite of 'foreign' or 'world.'.

International firm
International firm refers to those firms who have responded to stiff competition domestically by expanding their sales abroad. They may start a production facility overseas and send some of their managers, who report to a global division, to that country.

Boeing
Boeing is the world's largest aircraft manufacturer by revenue. Headquartered in Chicago, Illinois, Boeing is the second-largest defense contractor in the world. In 2005, the company was the world's largest civil aircraft manufacturer in terms of value.

Goodwill
Goodwill is an important accounting concept that describes the value of a business entity not directly attributable to its tangible assets and liabilities.

Expense
In accounting, an expense represents an event in which an asset is used up or a liability is incurred. In terms of the accounting equation, expenses reduce owners' equity.

Jargon
Jargon is terminology, much like slang, that relates to a specific activity, profession, or group. It develops as a kind of shorthand, to express ideas that are frequently discussed between members of a group, and can also have the effect of distinguishing those belonging to a group from those who are not.

Argument
The discussion by counsel for the respective parties of their contentions on the law and the facts of the case being tried in order to aid the jury in arriving at a correct and just conclusion is called argument.

Analogy
Analogy is either the cognitive process of transferring information from a particular subject to another particular subject (the target), or a linguistic expression corresponding to such a process. In a narrower sense, analogy is an inference or an argument from a particular to another particular, as opposed to deduction, induction, and abduction, where at least one of the premises or the conclusion is general.

Legal system
Legal system refers to system of rules that regulate behavior and the processes by which the

448

Go to **Cram101.com** for the Practice Tests for this Chapter.

Go to **Cram101.com** for the Practice Tests for this Chapter.
And, **NEVER** highlight a book again!

	laws of a country are enforced and through which redress of grievances is obtained.
Objection	In the trial of a case the formal remonstrance made by counsel to something that has been said or done, in order to obtain the court's ruling thereon is an objection.
Accounts receivable	Accounts receivable is one of a series of accounting transactions dealing with the billing of customers which owe money to a person, company or organization for goods and services that have been provided to the customer. This is typically done in a one person organization by writing an invoice and mailing or delivering it to each customer.
Hedge	Hedge refers to a process of offsetting risk. In the foreign exchange market, hedgers use the forward market to cover a transaction or open position and thereby reduce exchange risk. The term applies most commonly to trade.
Estate	An estate is the totality of the legal rights, interests, entitlements and obligations attaching to property. In the context of wills and probate, it refers to the totality of the property which the deceased owned or in which some interest was held.
Discount	The difference between the face value of a bond and its selling price, when a bond is sold for less than its face value it's referred to as a discount.
Compromise	Compromise occurs when the interaction is moderately important to meeting goals and the goals are neither completely compatible nor completely incompatible.
Intermediaries	Intermediaries specialize in information either to bring together two parties to a transaction or to buy in order to sell again.
Walt Disney	As the co-founder of Walt Disney Productions, Walt became one of the most well-known motion picture producers in the world. The corporation he co-founded, now known as The Walt Disney Company, today has annual revenues of approximately US $30 billion.
Disney	Disney is one of the largest media and entertainment corporations in the world. Founded on October 16, 1923 by brothers Walt and Roy Disney as a small animation studio, today it is one of the largest Hollywood studios and also owns nine theme parks and several television networks, including the American Broadcasting Company (ABC).
Adversarial system	System of litigation in which the judge hears evidence and arguments presented by both sides in a case and then makes an objective decision based on the facts and the law as presented by each side is called adversarial system.

Go to **Cram101.com** for the Practice Tests for this Chapter.
And, **NEVER** highlight a book again!

5000937705

Printed in the United Kingdom
by Lightning Source UK Ltd.
117964UK00001B/7-14

9 781428 809925